SOUTH INDIAN HINDU FESTIVALS AND TRADITIONS

South Indian Hindu Festivals and Traditions

Maithily Jagannathan

ABHINAV PUBLICATIONS

abhinav publications
New Delhi

Cataloging in Publication Data--DK
Courtesy: D.K. Agencies (P) Ltd. <docinfo@dkagencies.com>

Jagannathan, Maithily.
South Indian Hindu festivals and traditions
/ Maithily Jagannathan.
p. cm.
ISBN 8170174155

1. Fasts and feasts--India, South--Hinduism.
2. Festivals--India, South. 3. India, South
--Religious life and customs. I. Title.

DDC 294.536 095 4 21

First published in India 2005

Publishers
Shakti Malik
Abhinav Publications
E-37, Hauz Khas
New Delhi-110016 (INDIA)
Phones: 26566387, 26562784, 26524658
Fax: 91-11-26857009
e-mail: shakti@nde.vsnl.net.in
website: http//www.abhinavexports.com

ISBN 81-7017-415-5

Lasertypeset by
S.R. Enterprises
Lajpat Nagar-IV
New Delhi-110024
Phone: 011-26236663

Printed at
D.K. Fine Art Press Pvt. Ltd.
Ashok Vihar, Delhi

CONTENTS

Recipes for Vishu, Kerala

Rice Dishes for Chitra Purnima

Recipes for Avani Avittam

Recipes for Varalakshmi Puja & Ganesh Chaturthi

Sankranti, Bogi Recipes

Traditional Recipes for Special Pujas

FOREWORD

It Gives me a deep feeling of satisfaction to introduce this book on festivals and traditions of Southern India. The book presents everyday customs and practices, social etiquette for different occasions, and describes the celebration of important festivals round the year.

The book does not propose to be a complete manual of customs, but to guide the reader on the demarcated path, for practising a way of life which nourishes our psychological and spiritual needs, and effectively offsets the mechanical drabness of a monotonous daily routine.

It is true that none of our festivals are just festivals. Very often their origin is lost in the passage of time. There has been an evolution, transformation, even the grafting of new customs on ancient ones. Without going into philosophical depths, the book shows how at every stage of life, we can derive solace, confidence and strength, from our traditions.

The spiritual nourishment derived from a fast, the magnetic pull drawing millions of pilgrims each year to shrines and temples, the celebration of festivals marking the journey of life, the significance of social etiquette like obtaining the blessing of elders, remembering and praying to ancestors, and the practical purpose of growing and worshipping the tulsi (basil) plant outside the house are discussed.

Sections on the designing and drawing of traditional rangoli, and numerous delicious festive recipes are useful additions.

New Delhi

M. Varadarajan
Former Secretary
Ministry of Culture
Government of India

INTRODUCTION

Festivals, fasts, pilgrimages, pujas are living symbols of the Hindu way of life. They open up the spiritual self, and help to fulfil our role in the family and in society. They give us guidelines at different stages in the journey of life. The ritual loses much of its positive powers if practised as a routine. By understanding both the mythological and philosophical basis of a custom we not only gain psychologically but also evolve spiritually from its practice.

This book is planned as a handbook for understanding and practising many customs, traditions, and festivals common to South Indian communities. No rigid rules are prescribed for practising rituals, but an effort has been made to answer some of the Whys and Hows which arise for each custom. Once the purpose is clear, a reader can adapt the ritual to his or her situation, and can organise puja for different occasions.

The book is divided into three sections. In the first section on the **journey of the spiritual self**, the influence of the zodiac, karmas or rituals associated with stages of life, and important family celebrations, observances, fasts, and some common beliefs are described. The linking of an individual's life to stars and planets, and the associated pujas are given, along with the social etiquette for some occasions. Charts show the Rasis with corresponding months in the Tamil lunisolar calendar, Sanskrit lunar calendar, and Gregorian or European solar calendar. Names of days of the week in Tamil with Sanskrit and English equivalents are given. There is an annual calendar of months in Tamil which is largely followed by all the great temples of South India, with corresponding Sanskrit and European calendars.

In the second section there is a **calendar of major festivals** celebrated in Andhra Pradesh, Karnataka, Kerala and Tamil Nadu. The calendar starts with New Year celebrations and concludes with the observation of Savitri vrata or Karadiyar nombu. For each festival, the astrological day and name of the month in the Tamil calendar is given. To know the actual date in the English calendar, the almanac (panchang) for the current year would have to be seen.

In the third section, **traditional recipes** are given.

At a time when the younger generation, particularly that living outside India is feeling distanced from traditional roots, it is hoped that this book will give authentic and relevant information on the traditional and spiritual aspects of life. To the extent the book fulfils this need it will have served its purpose.

Maithily Jagannathan

ACKNOWLEDGEMENTS

To Arati for giving the initial idea. To P. Kantan, Vimala Rao, Mahalakshmi Gopalakrishnan, Kamala Krishnamachari, Jayalakshmi Narasimhan, Padma mami, Padma Shankaran, R. Mangalam, Minakshi Sridhar and many other friends who helped to shape the final form and contents. To Sandipan for his creative illustrations.

This book owes its existence to my dear sister Padma Desikachari who spared no efforts in compiling all information and to my mother Indira who kept the creative spark alive through many storms.

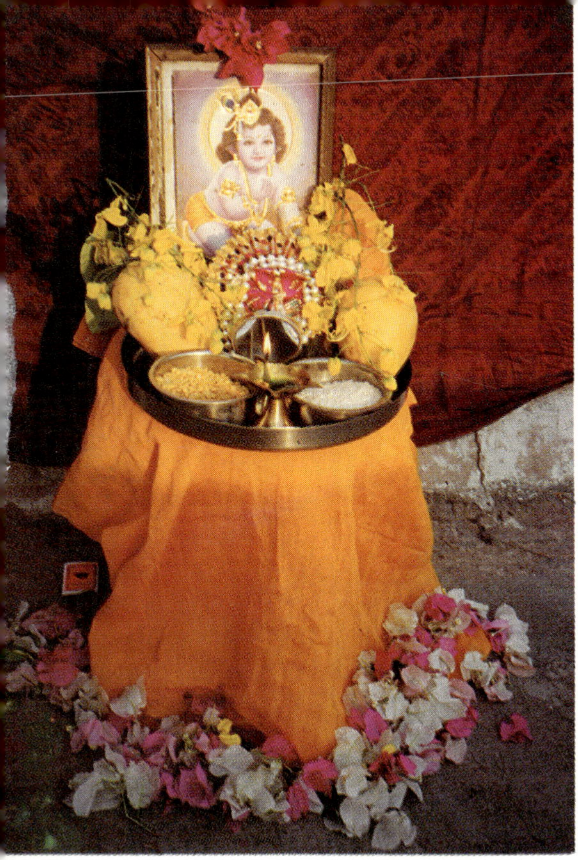

1. Vishu Kanni Kerala New Year

3. Puja to Varalakshmi

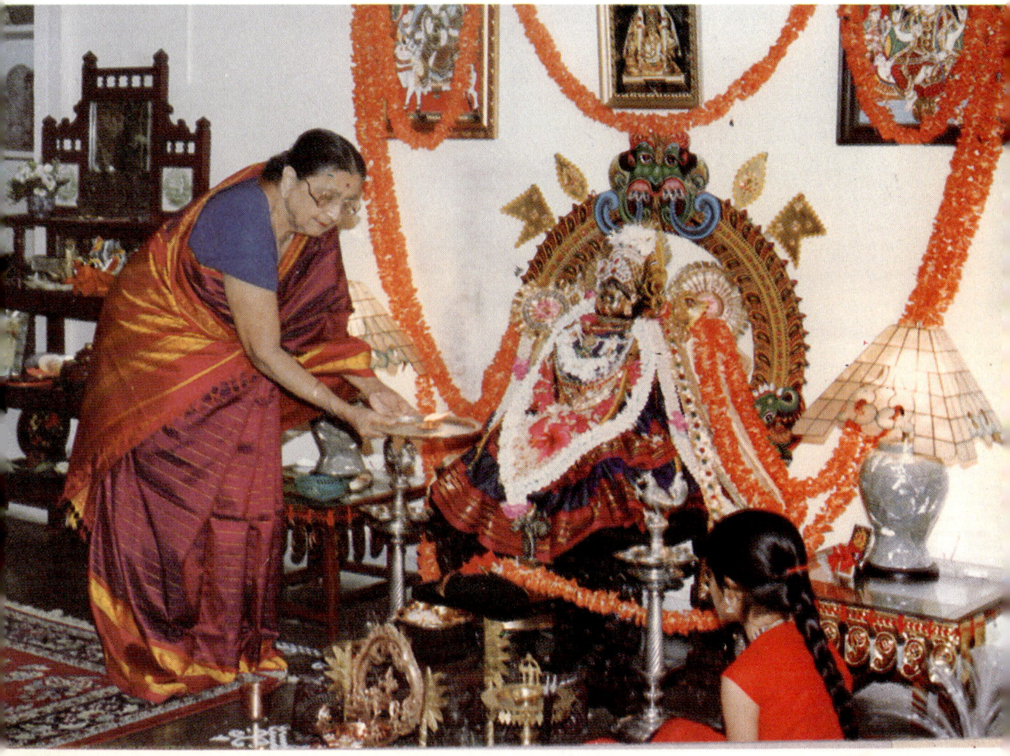

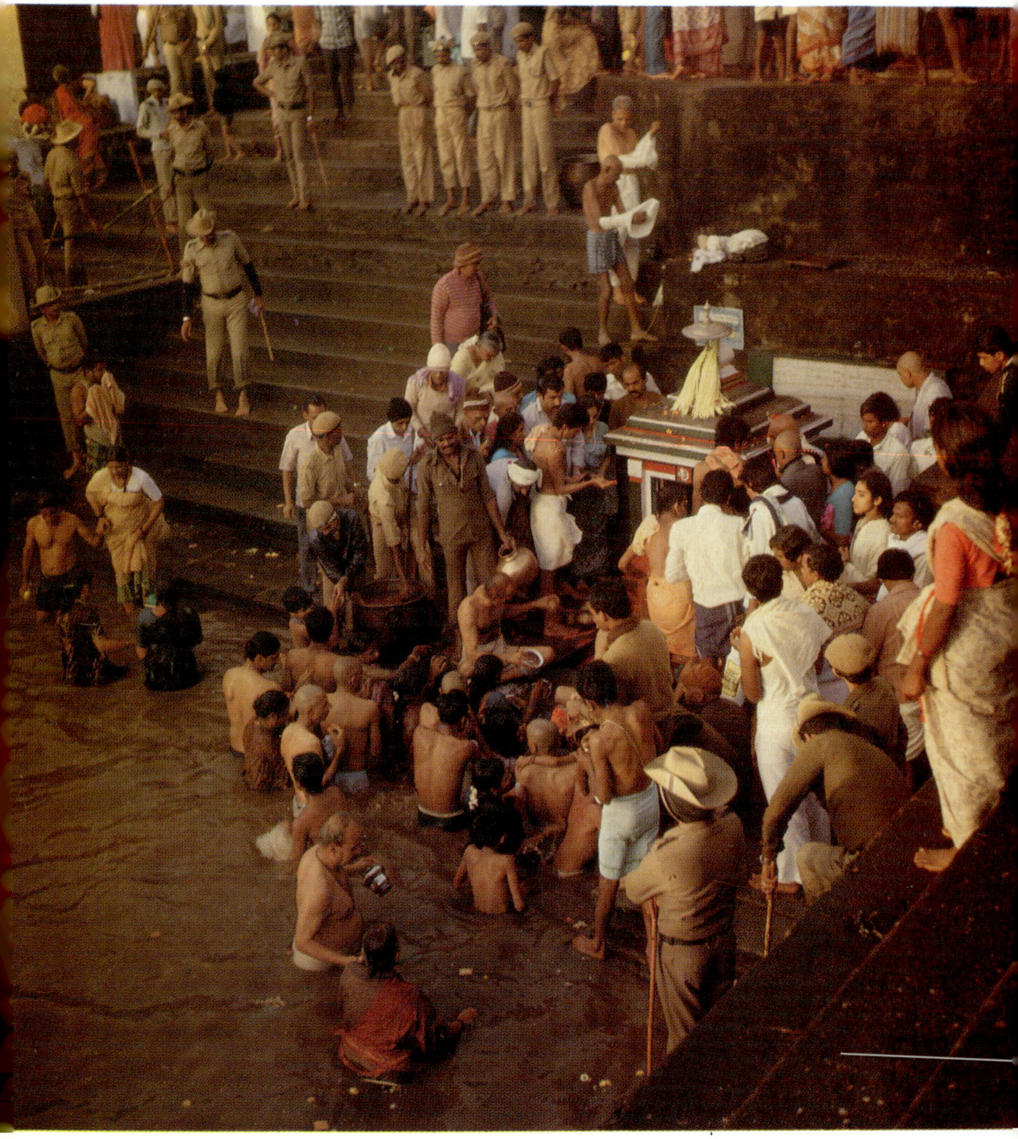

2. Kaveri Festival, Karnataka

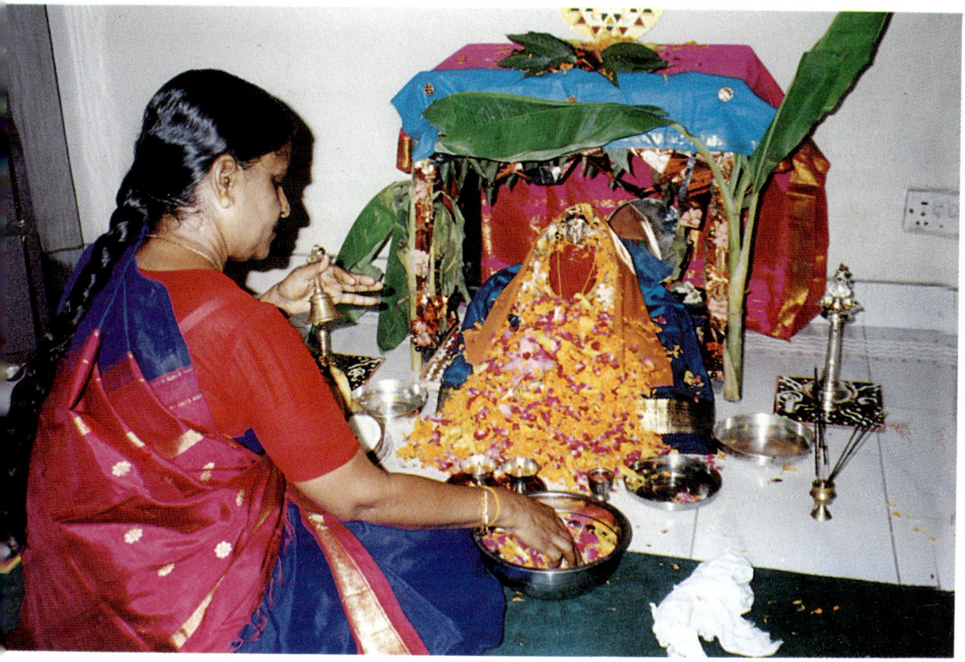

4. Puja to Varalakshmi

5. Puja to Varalakshmi

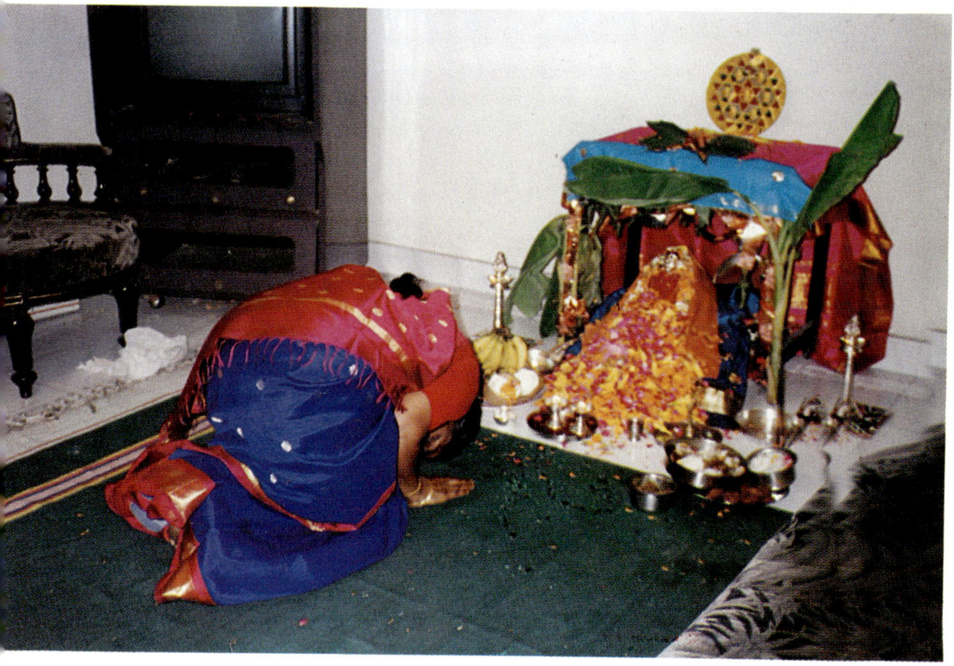

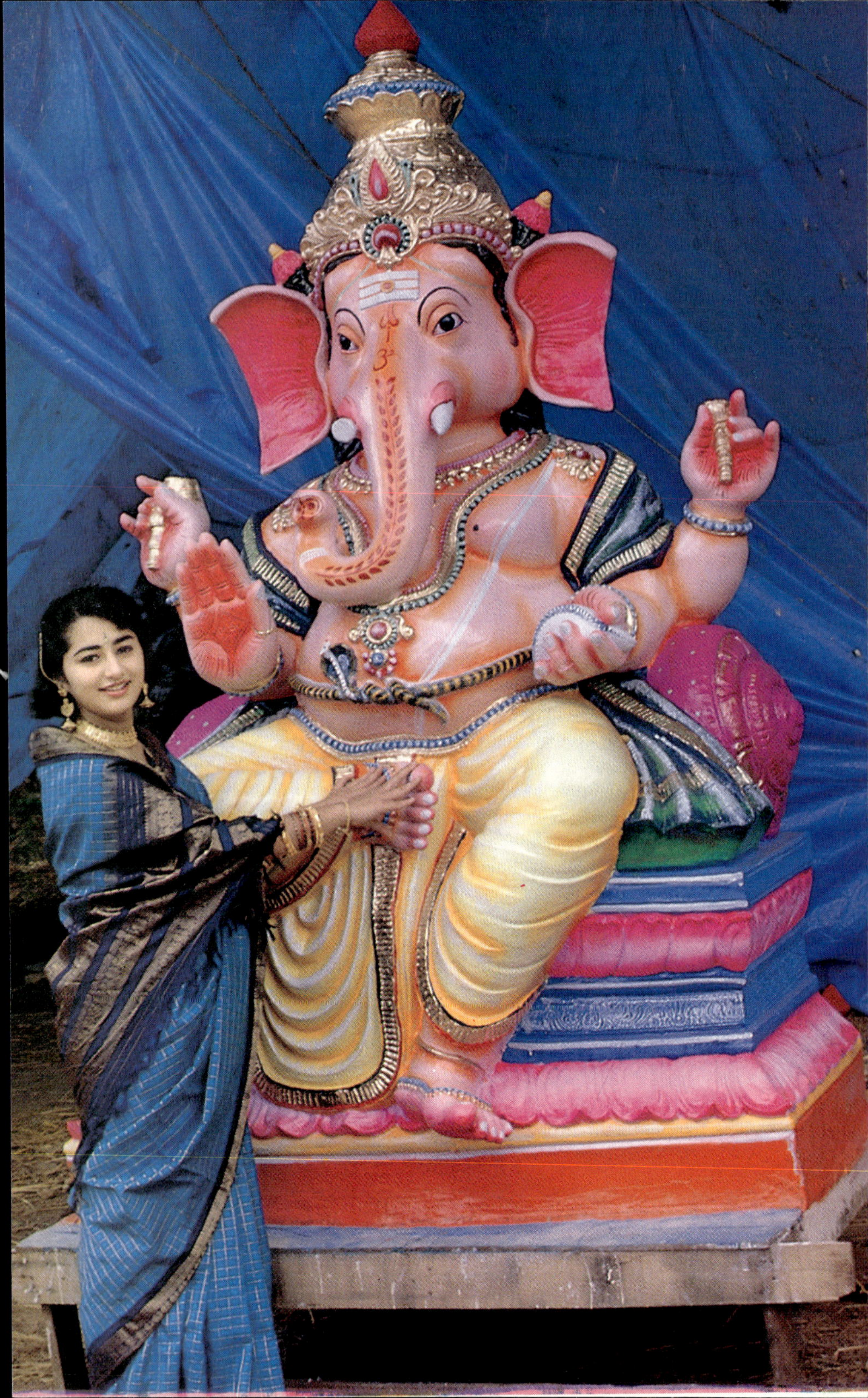

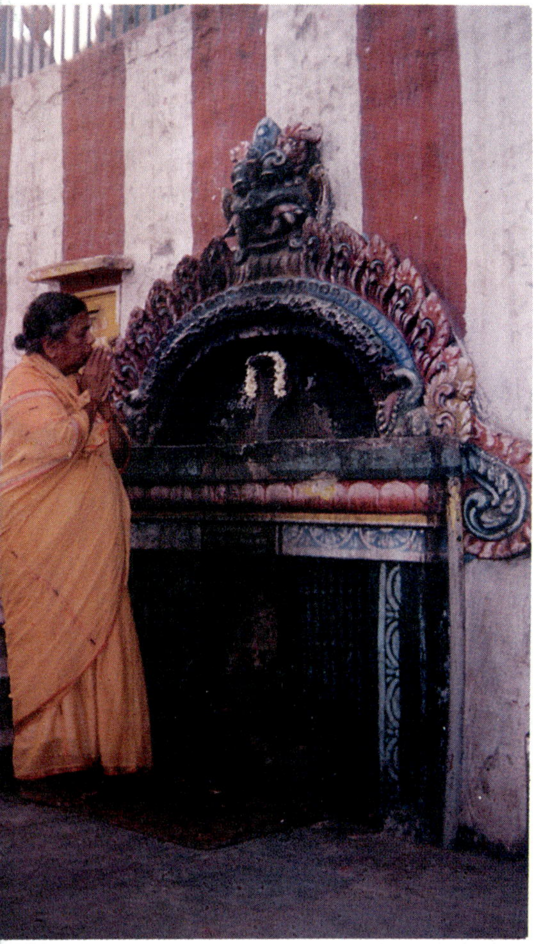

7. Nagraj Temple

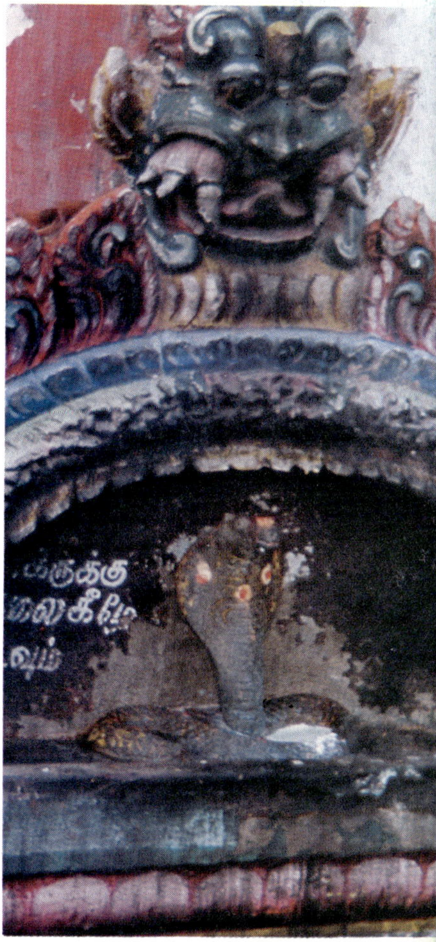

8. Nag Panchami Puja

←
6. Ganesh Puja

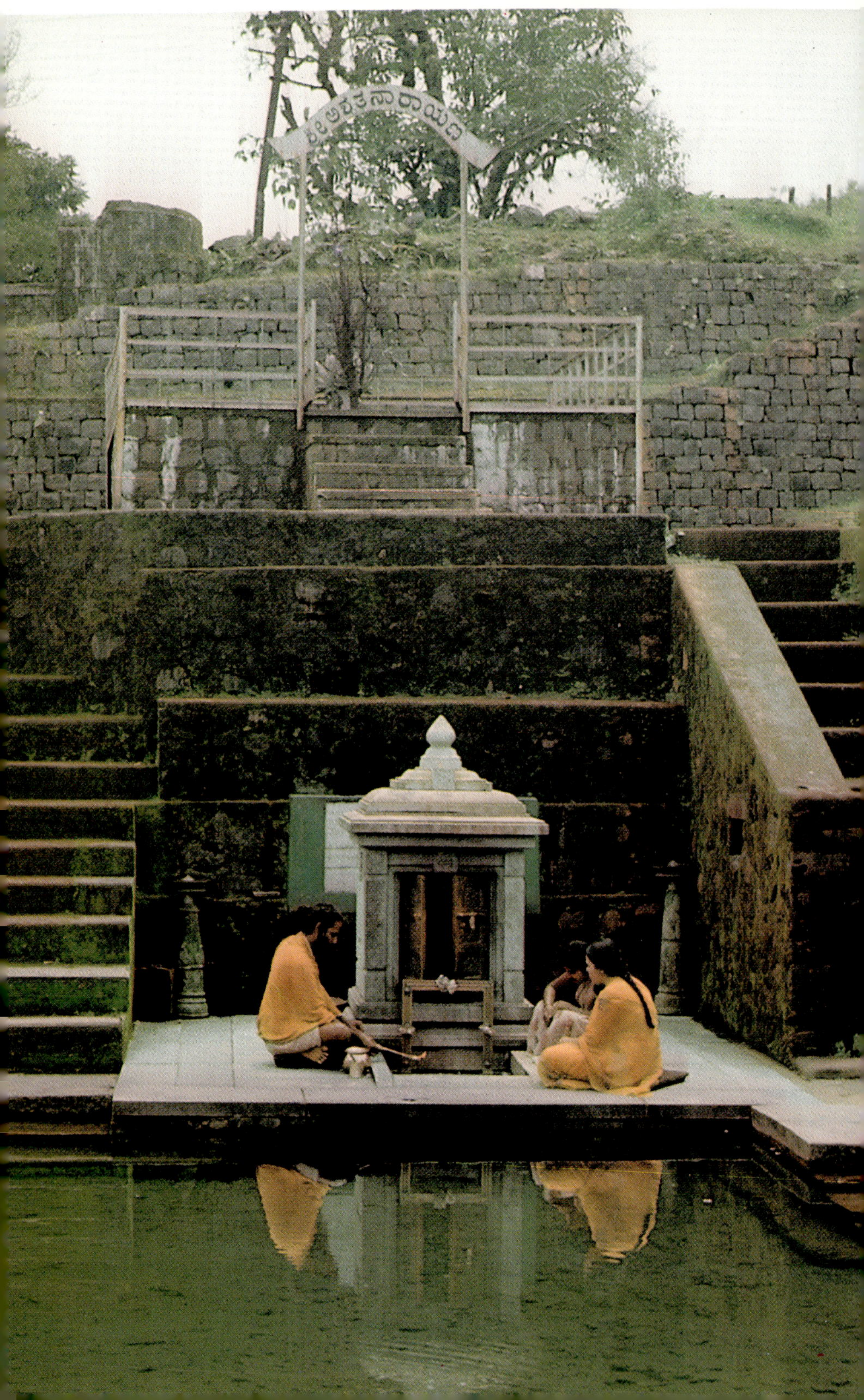

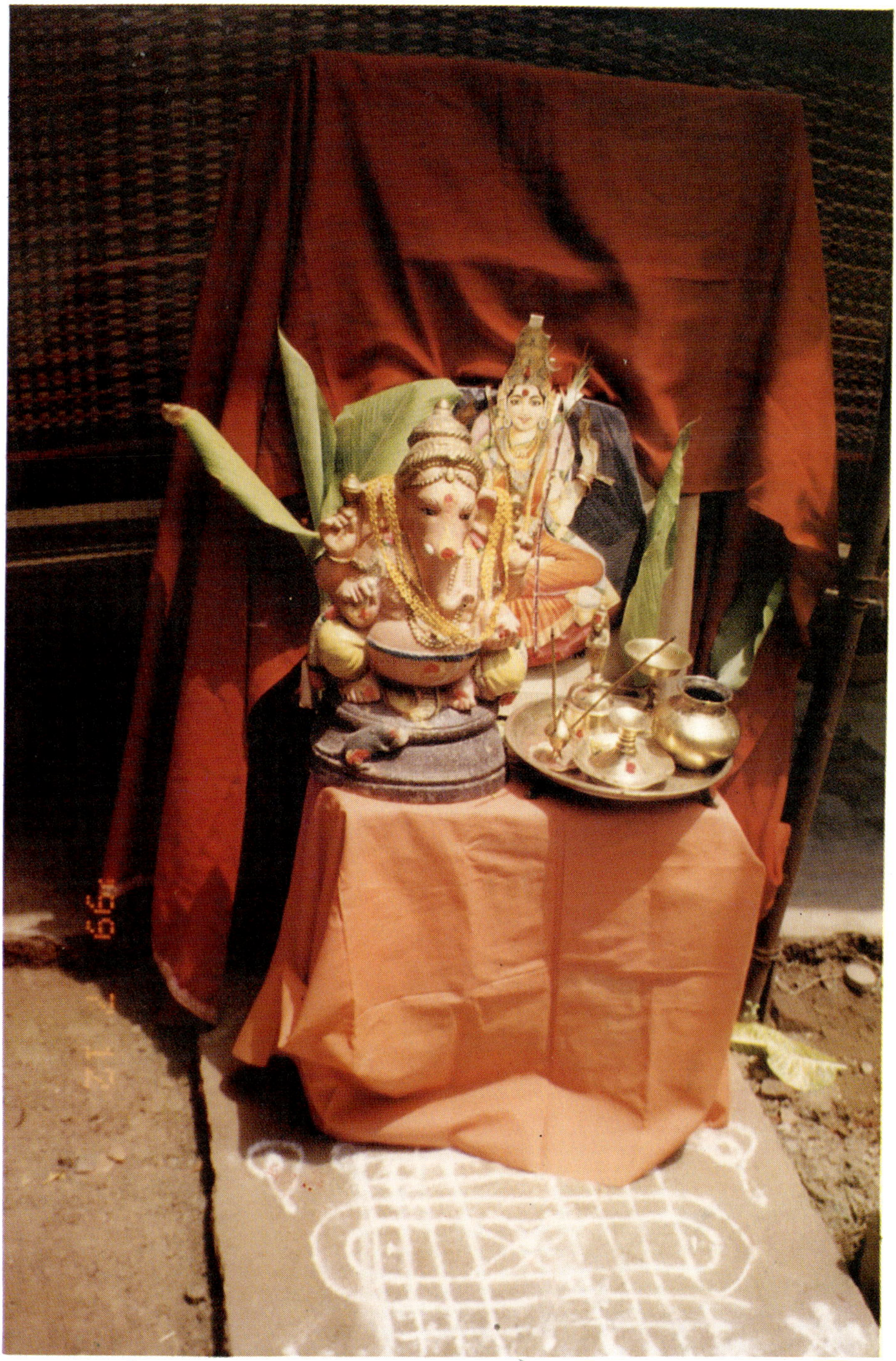

10. Puja of Gauri Ganesh

←
9. Gauri Ganesh Festival

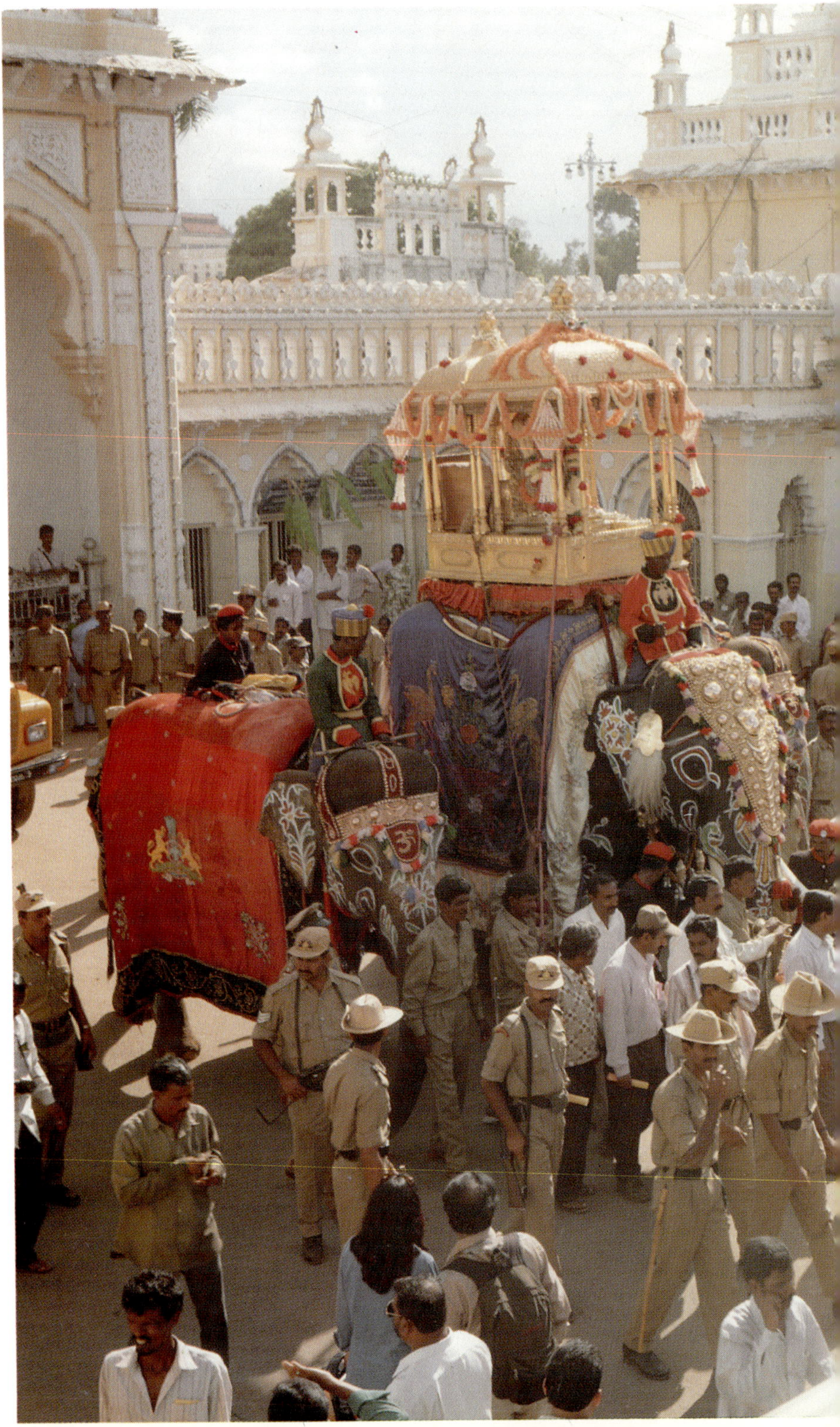

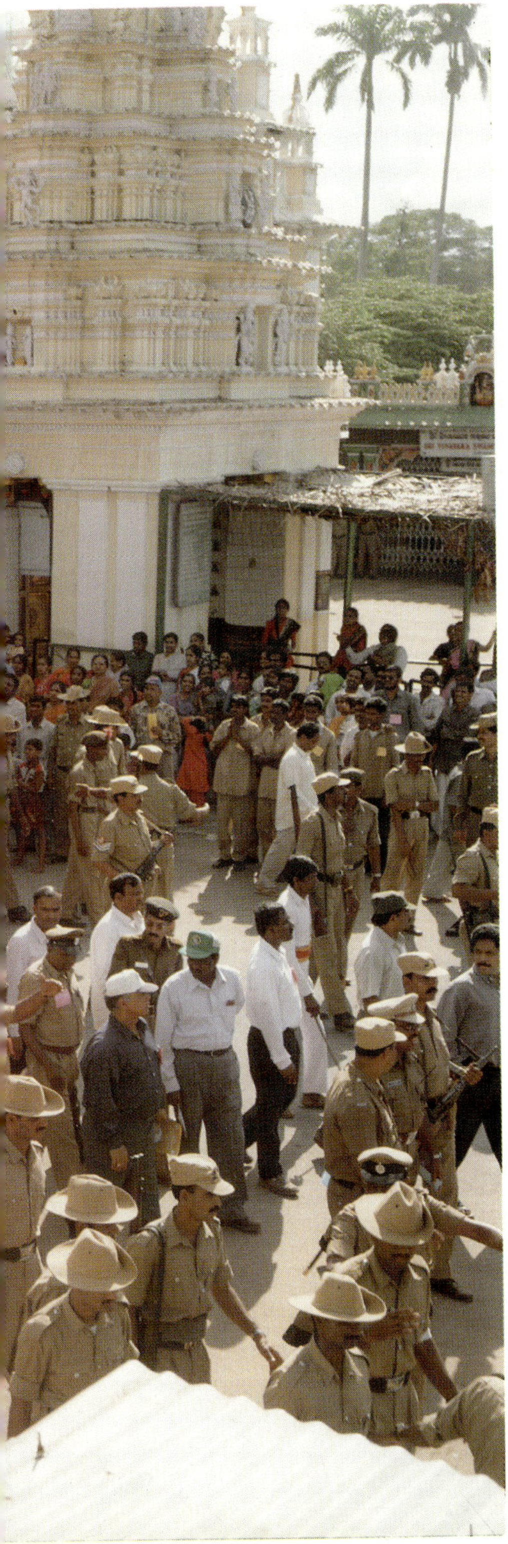

18. Mysore Dussehra

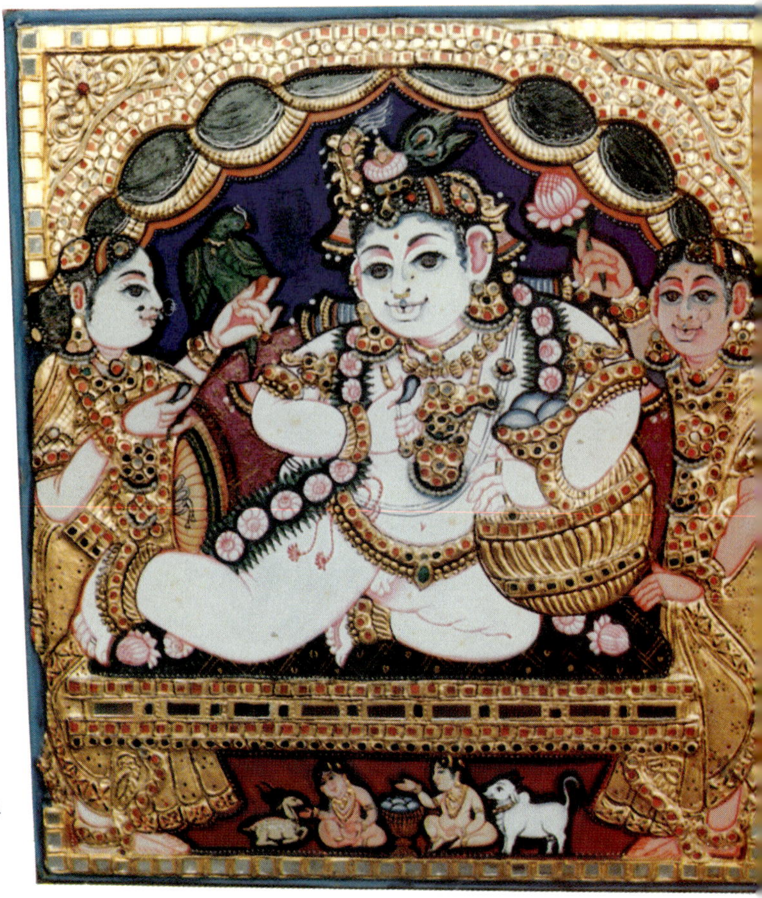

11. Baby Krishna

12. Krishna Jayanti Puja

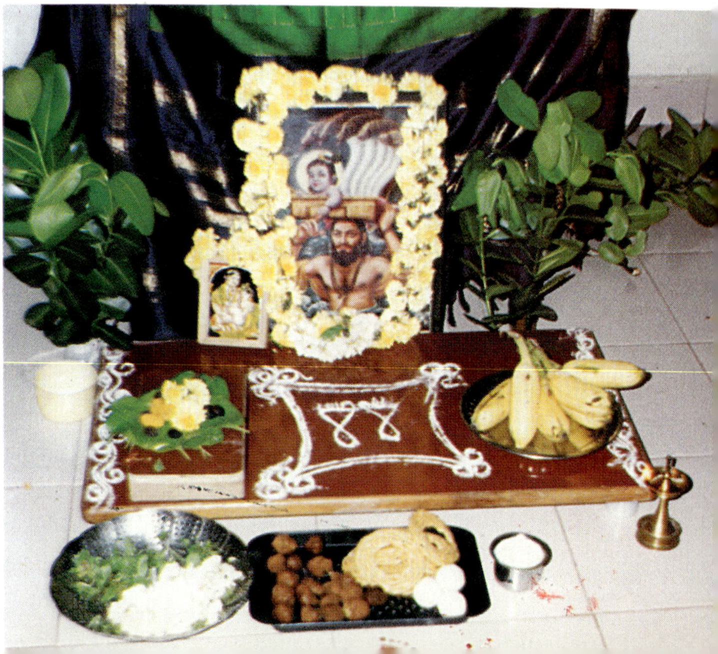

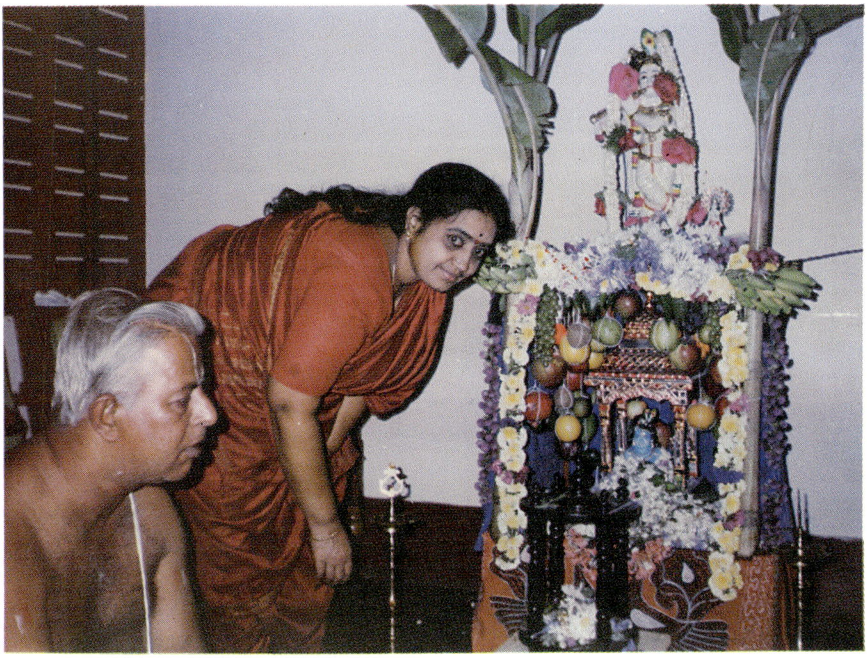

13. Krishna Jayanti Celebration at Home

14. Krishna Temple Festival, Karnataka

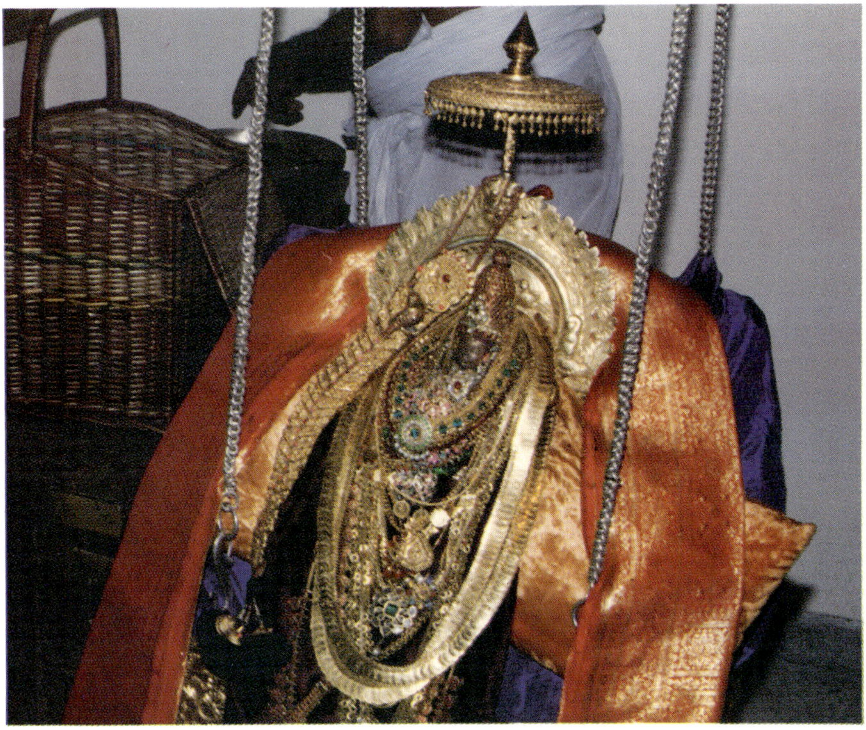

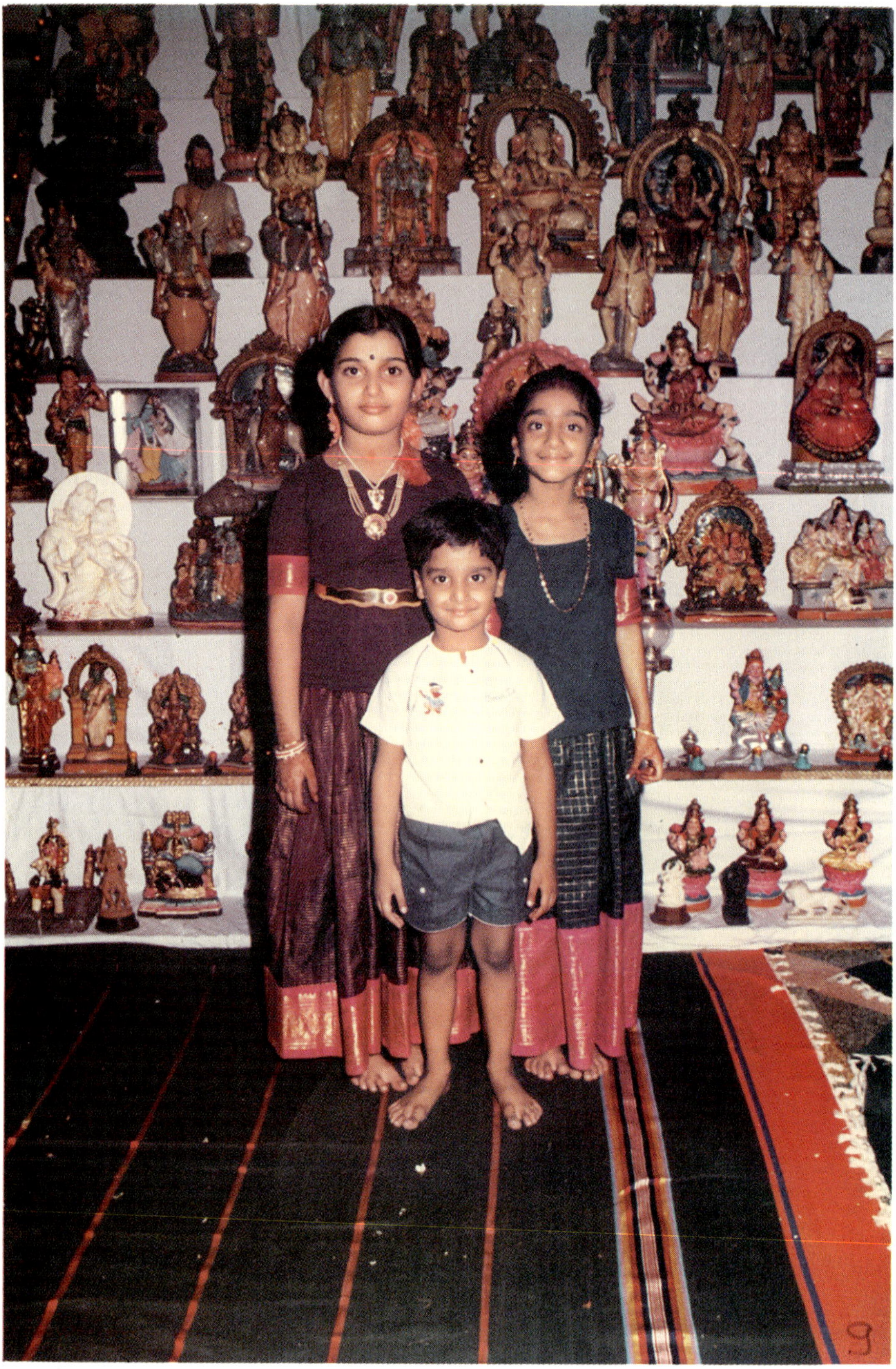

15. Devi Puja, Navratri

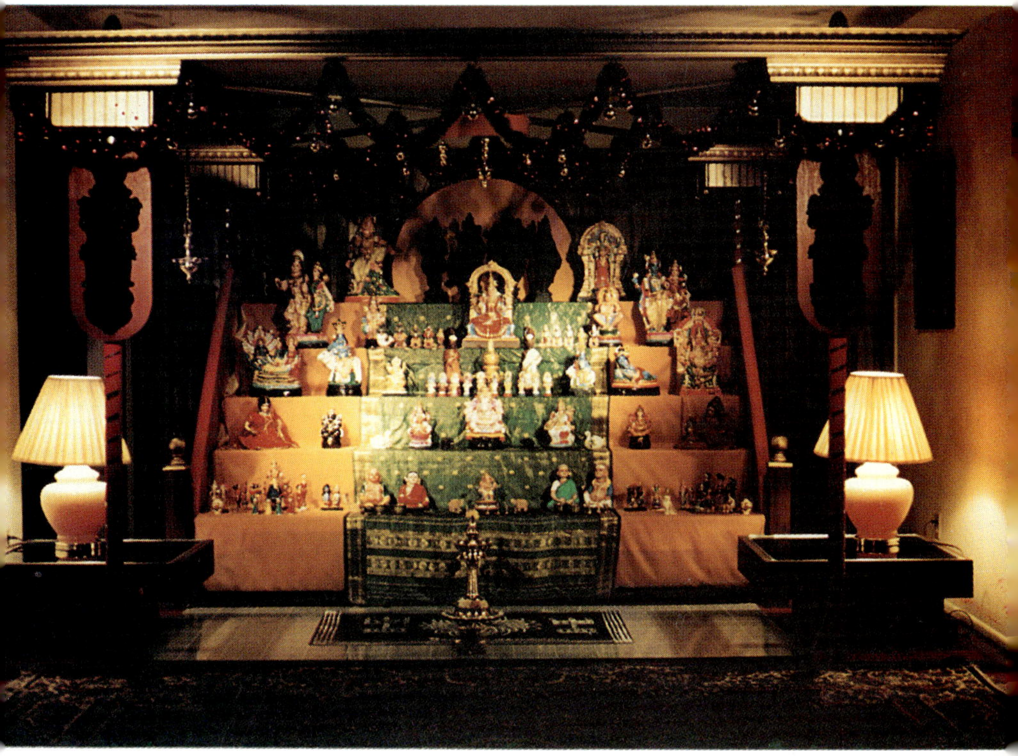

16. Dolls Arrangement at Navratri

17. Children's Section—Navratri Puja

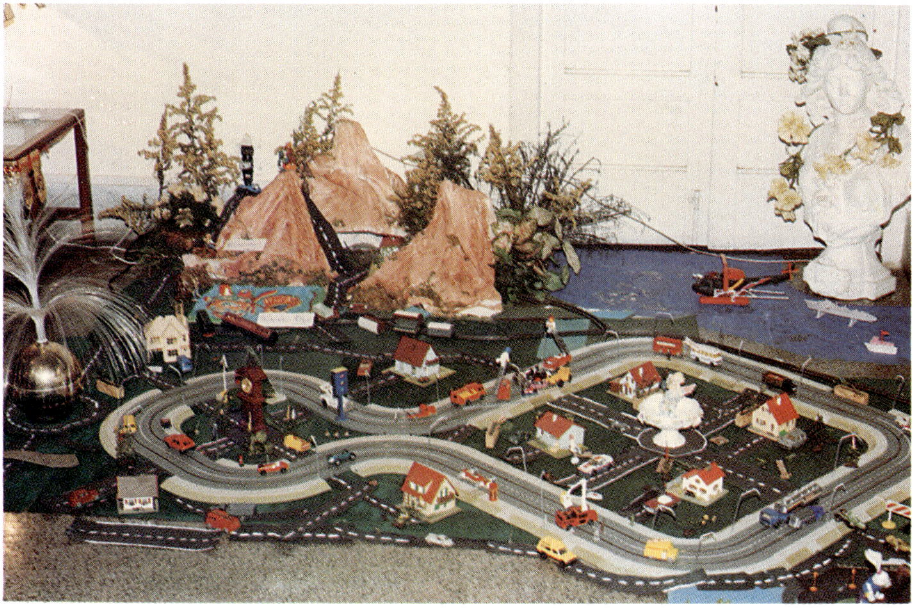

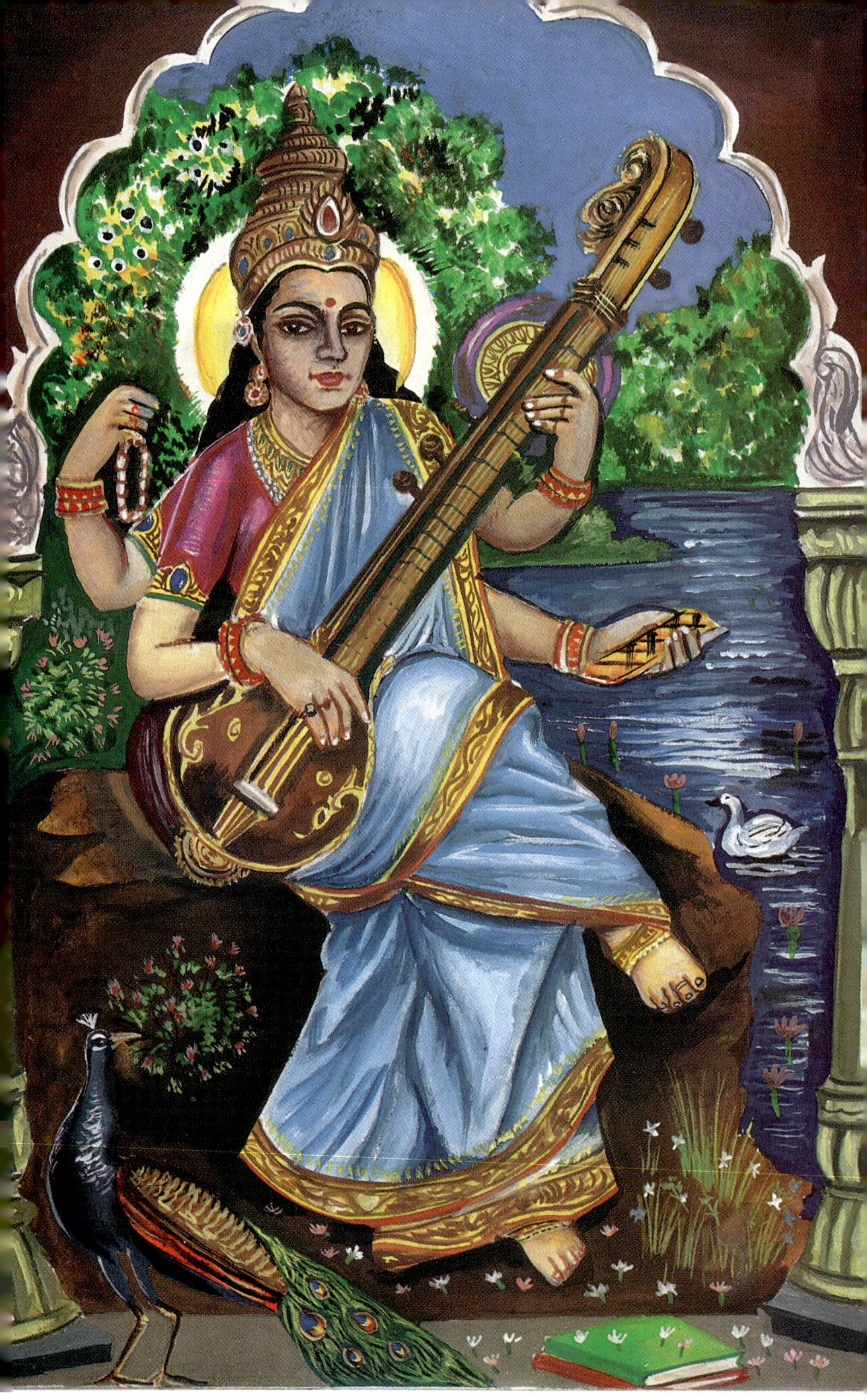

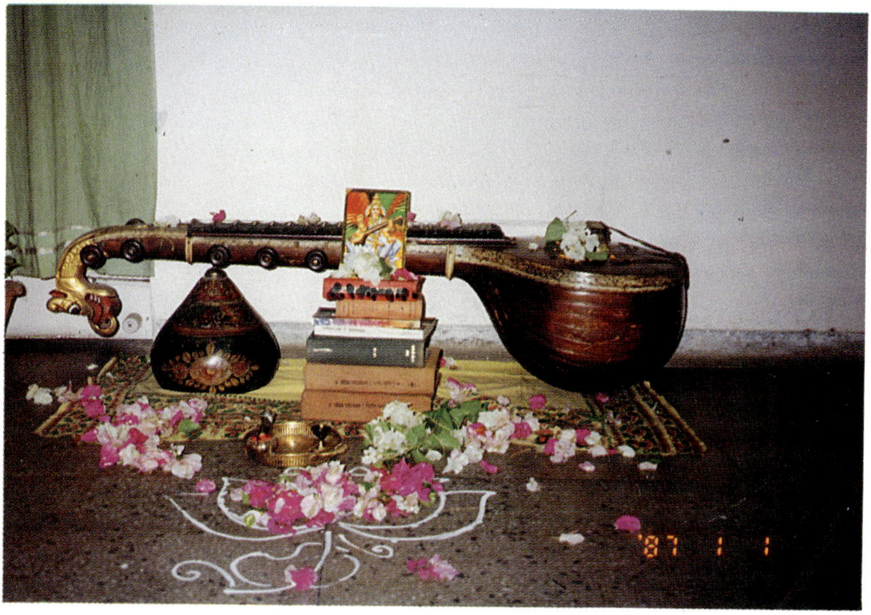

←
19. Portrait of Saraswati

20. Saraswati Puja

21. Saraswati Puja

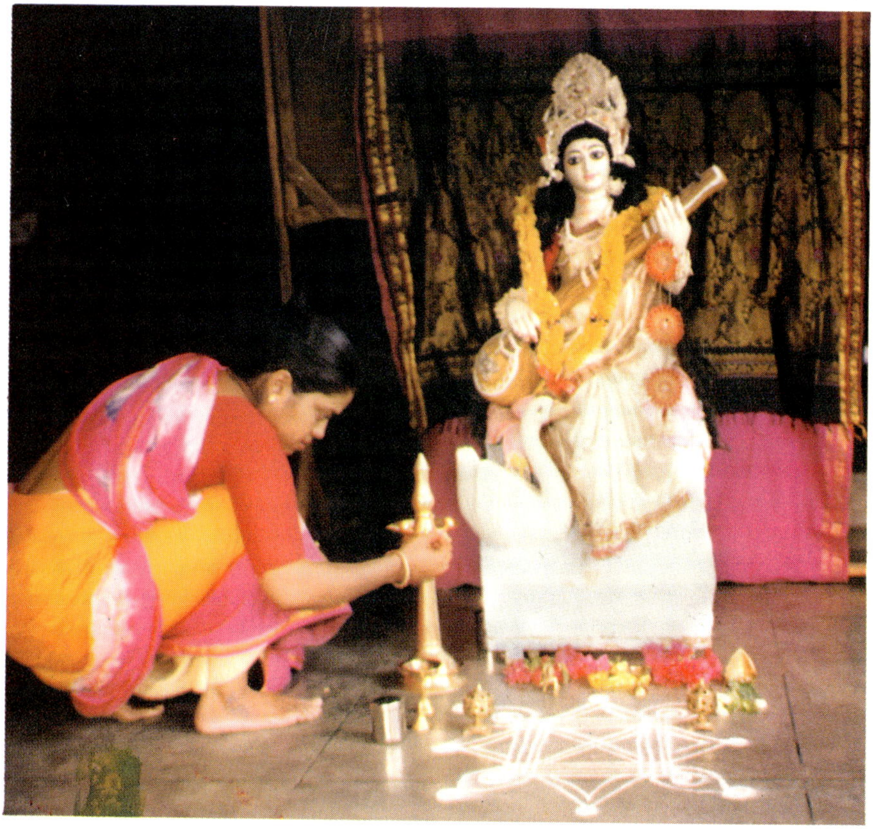

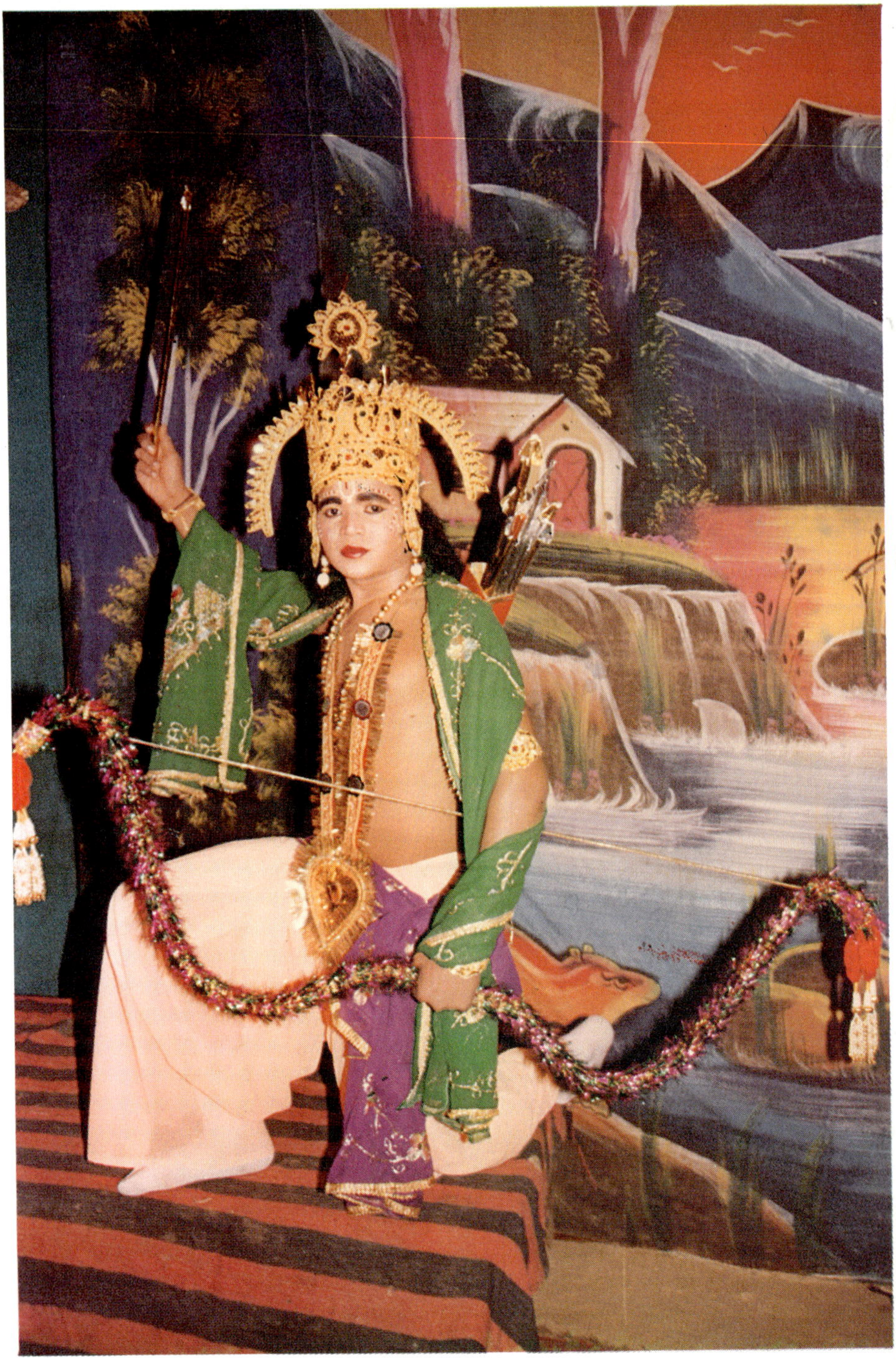

22. Ayudha Puja—Arjuna

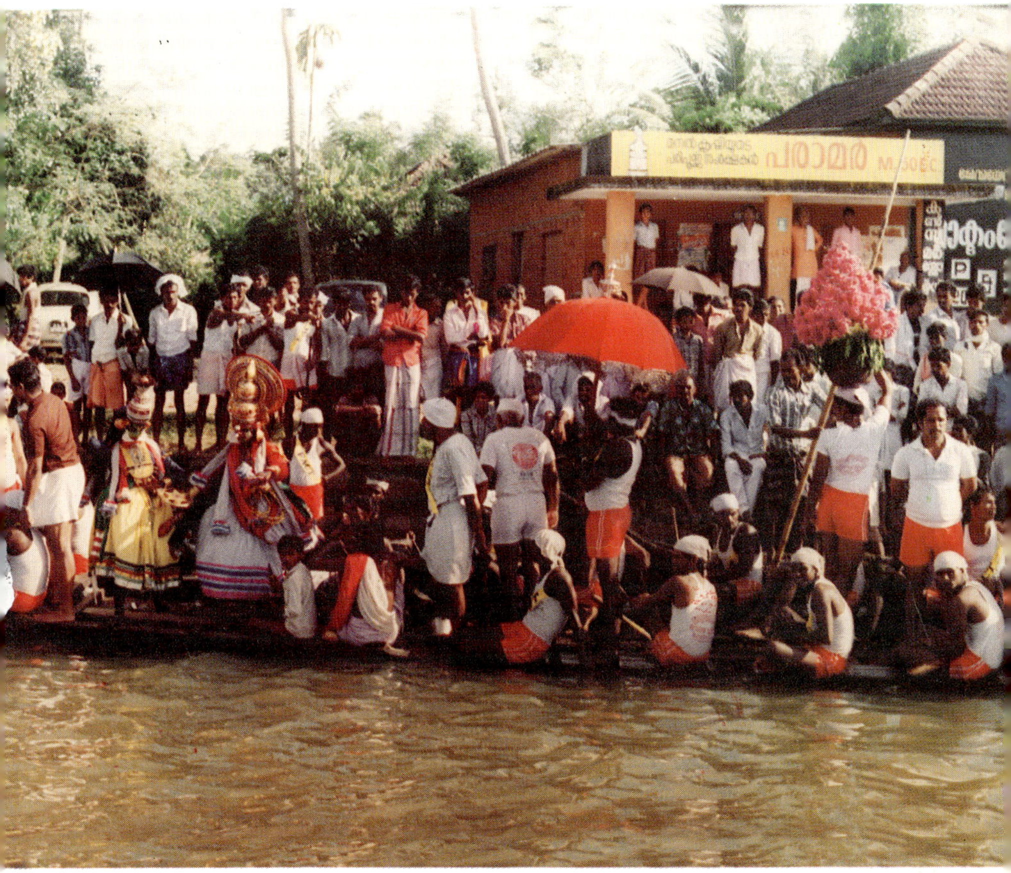

23. Onam Boat Launch

24. Onam Dance

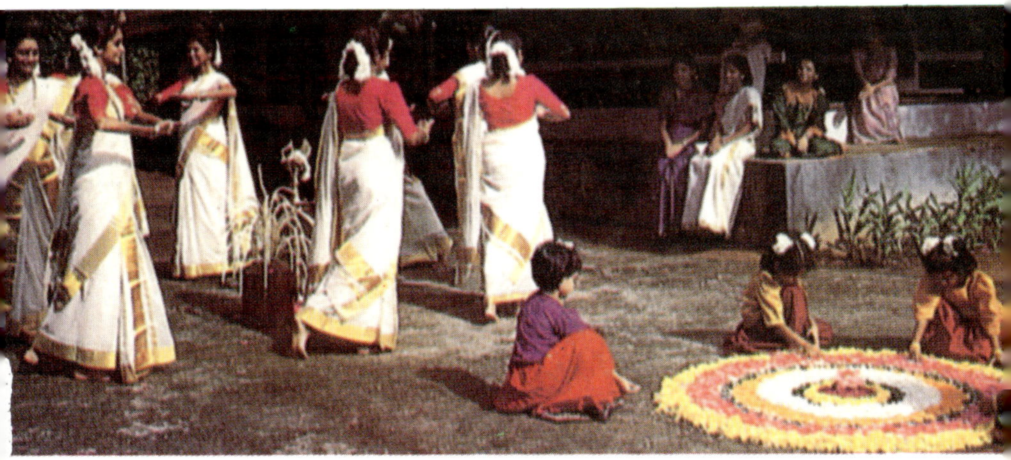

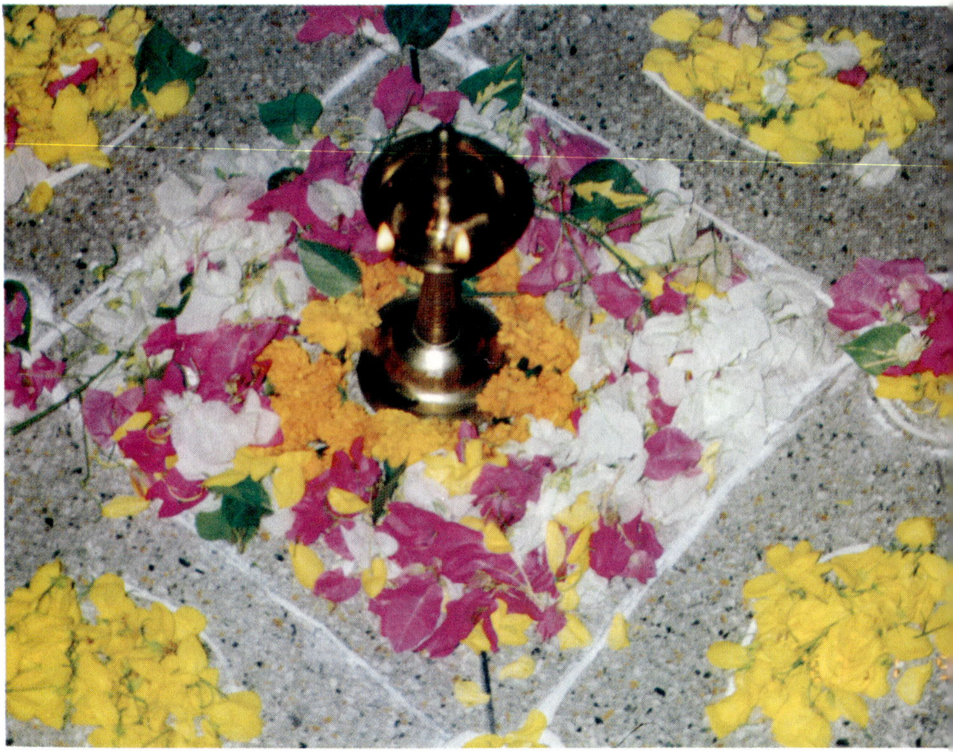

25. Onam Deepam

26. Pongal Special Rangoli

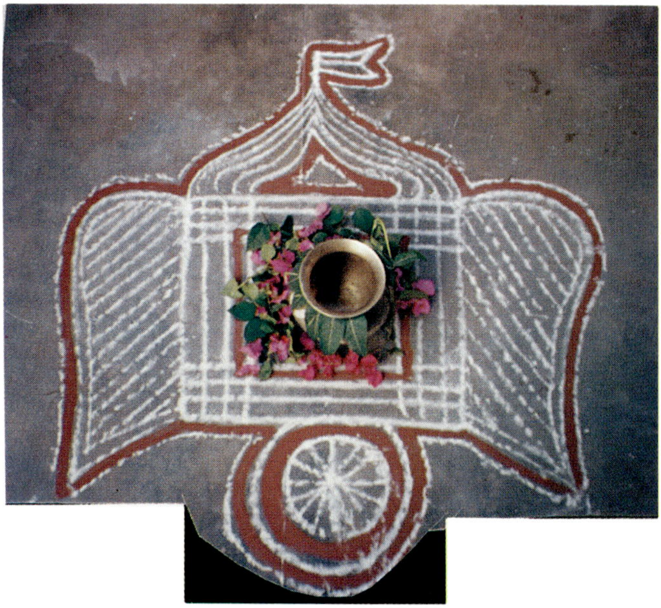

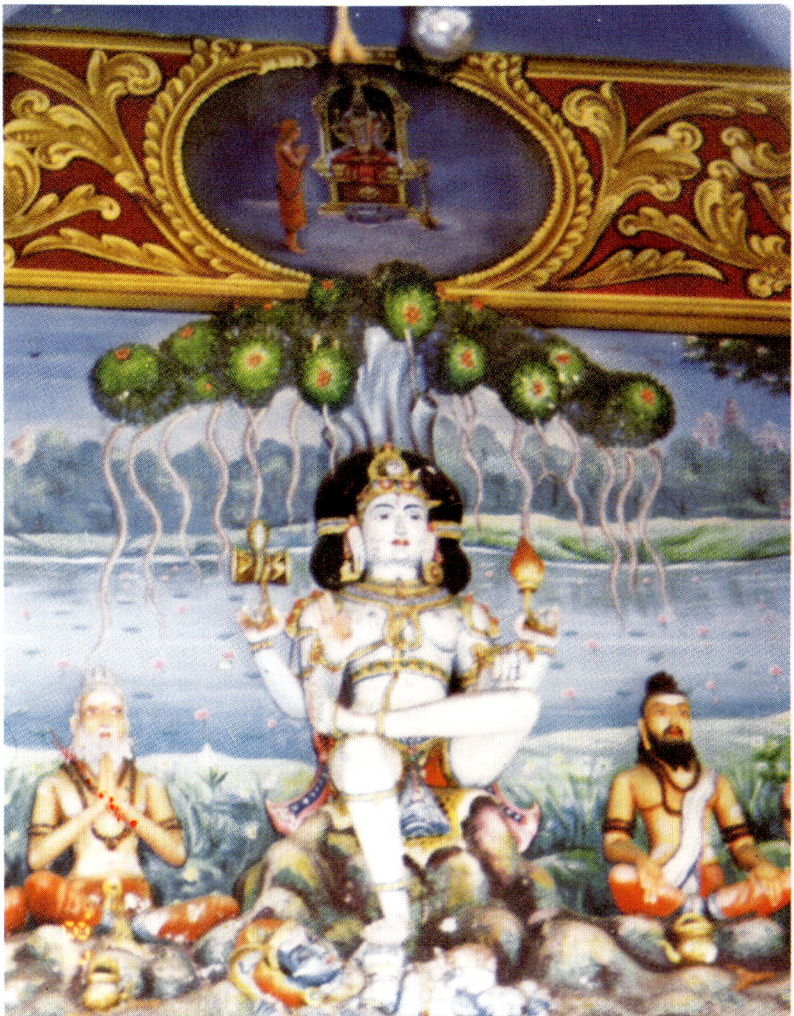

28. Yogiraj Siva

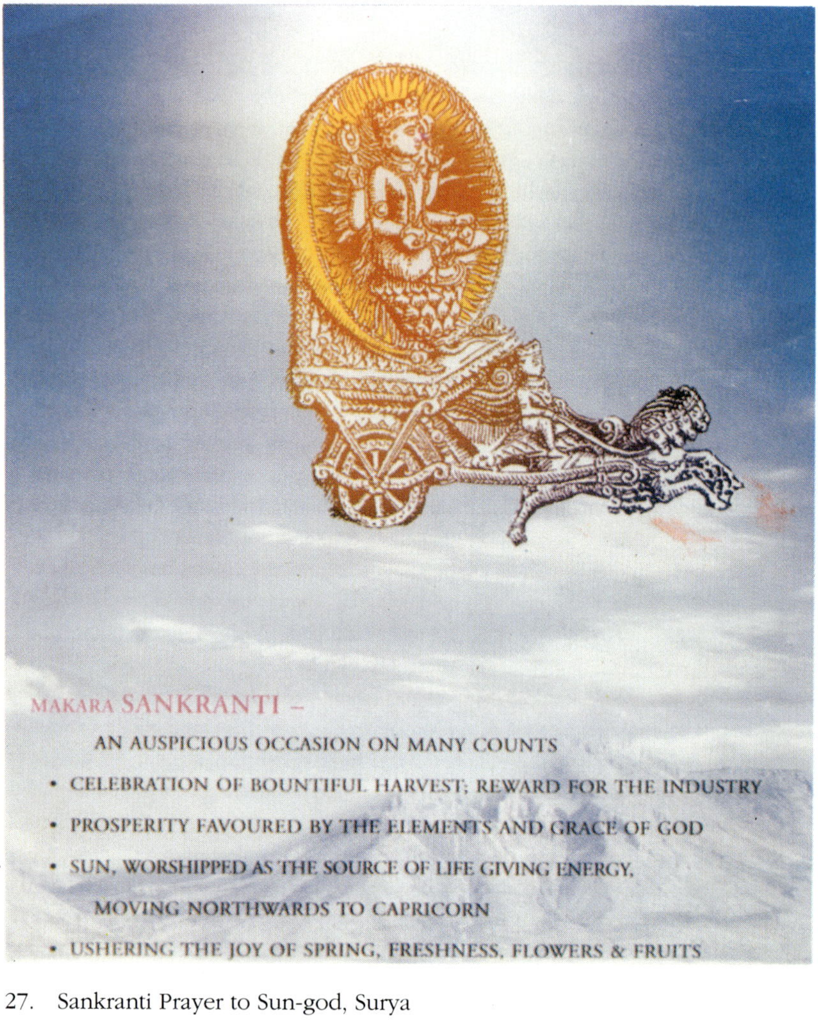

27. Sankranti Prayer to Sun-god, Surya

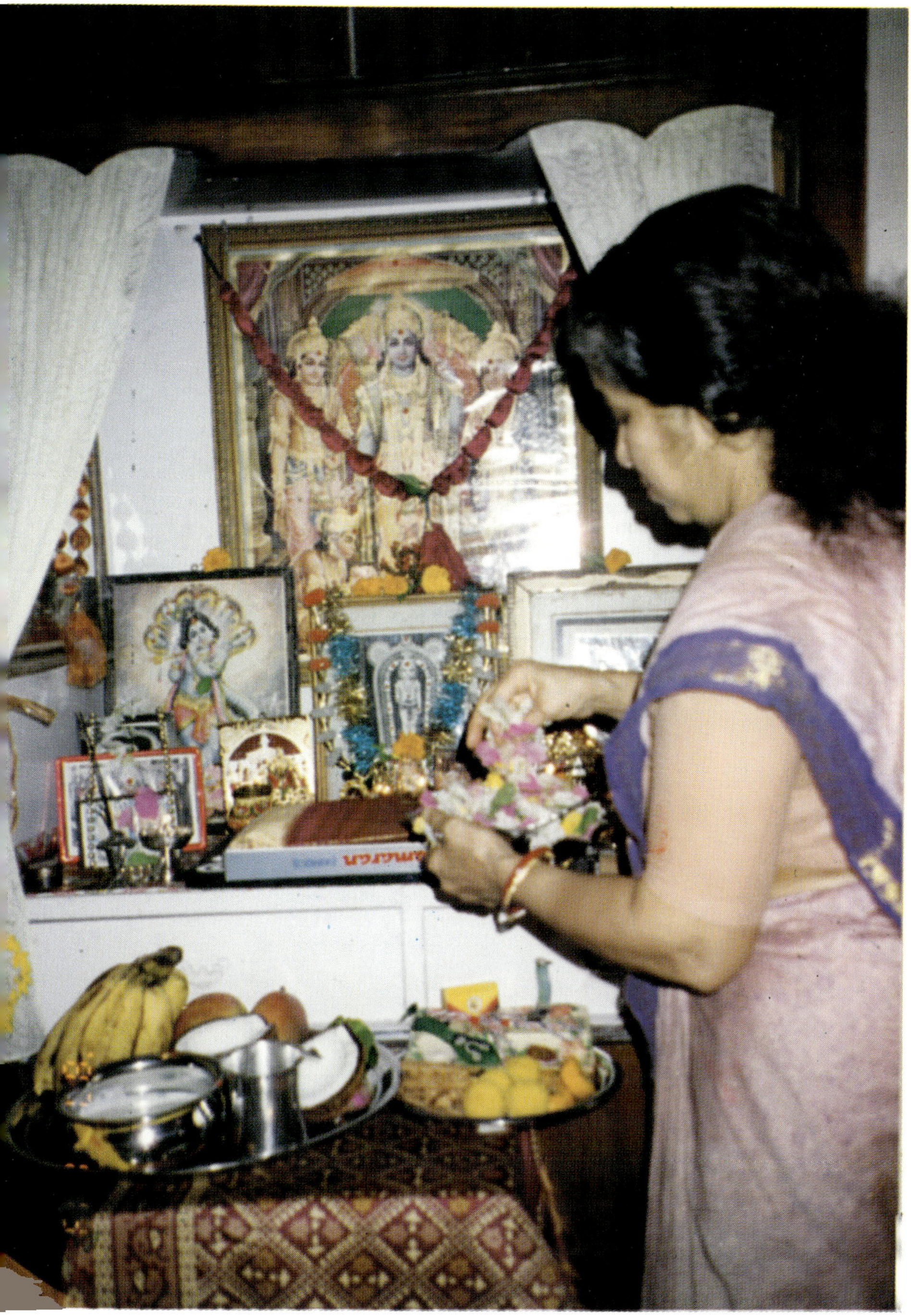

Deepawali Morning Puja

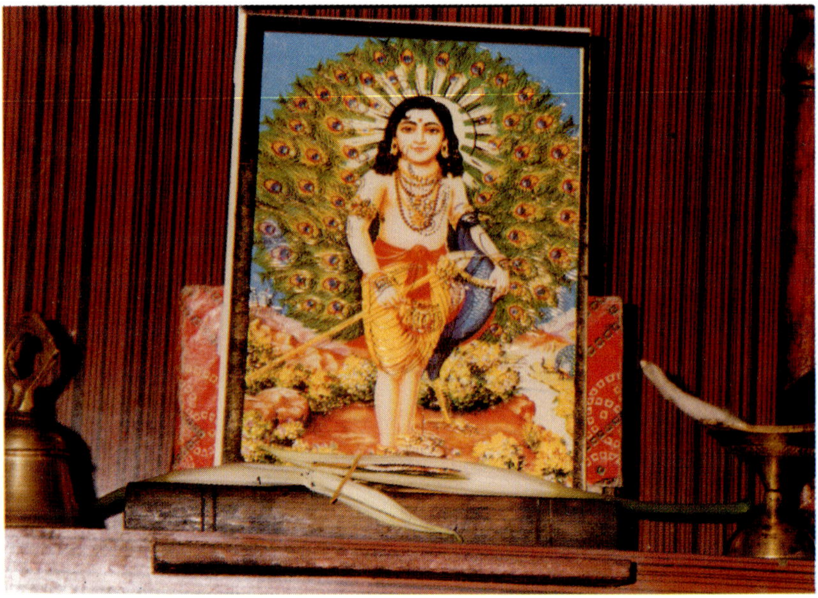

30. Warrior God, Kartikeya

31. Kartika Deepam Puja

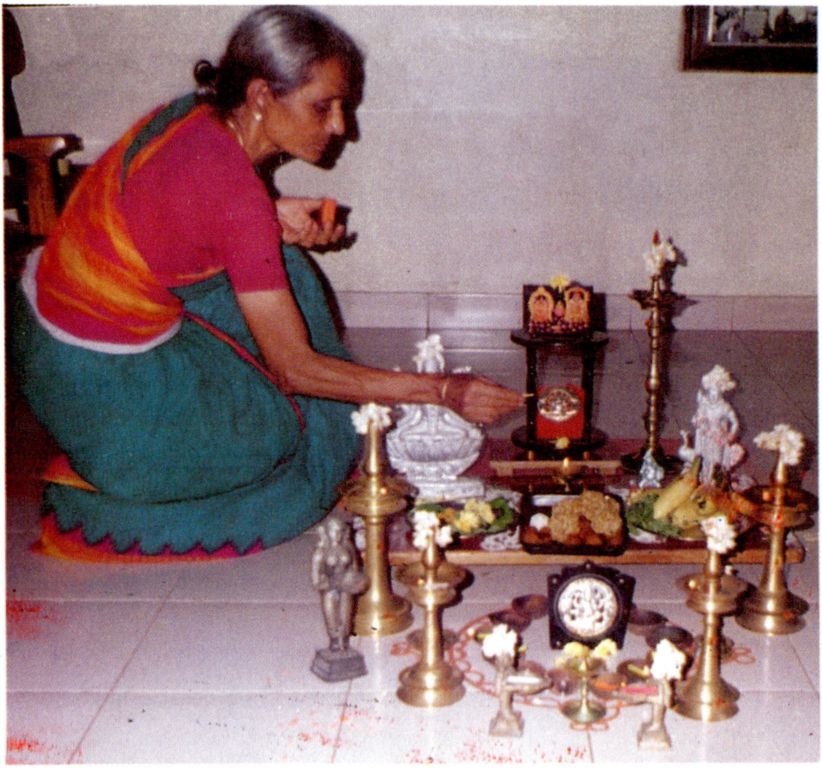

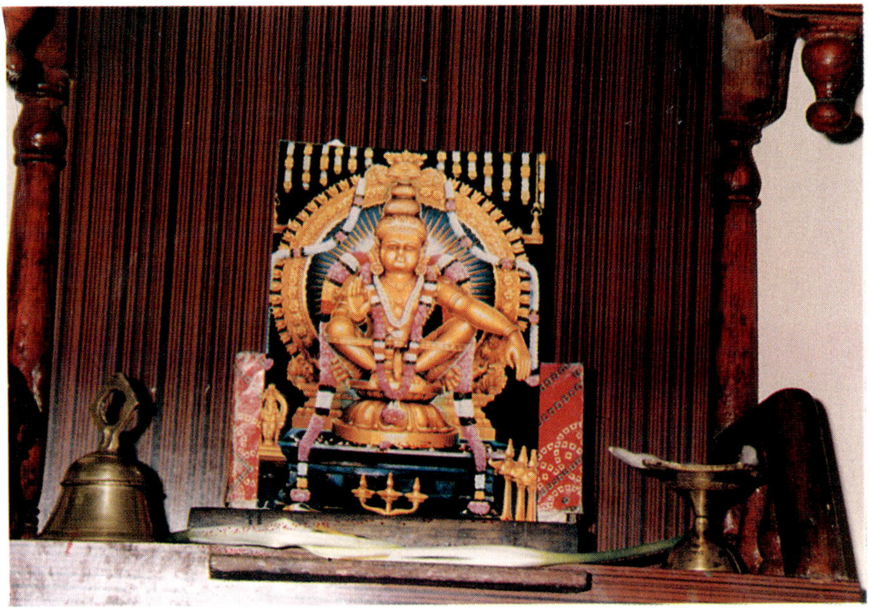

32. Swami Ayyappan

38. Sri Satyanarayana

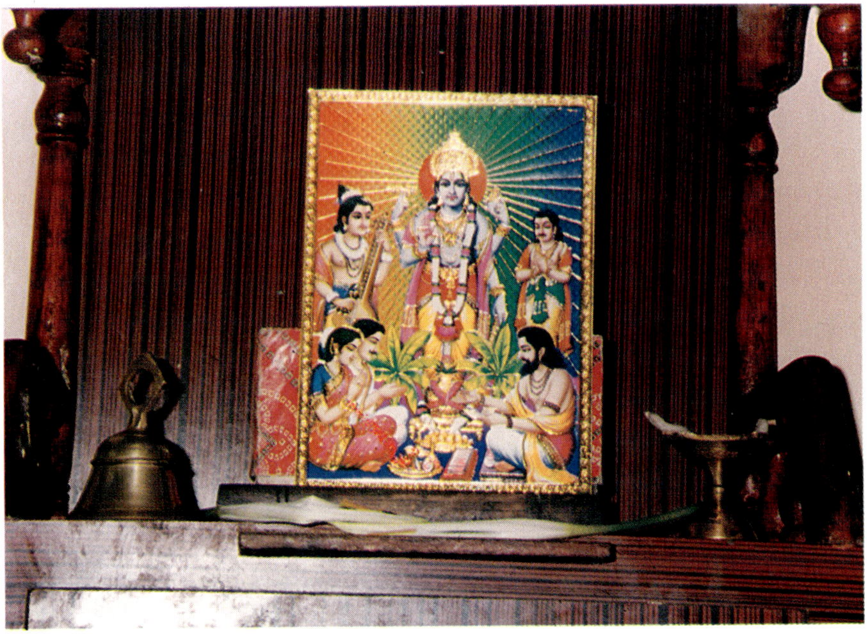

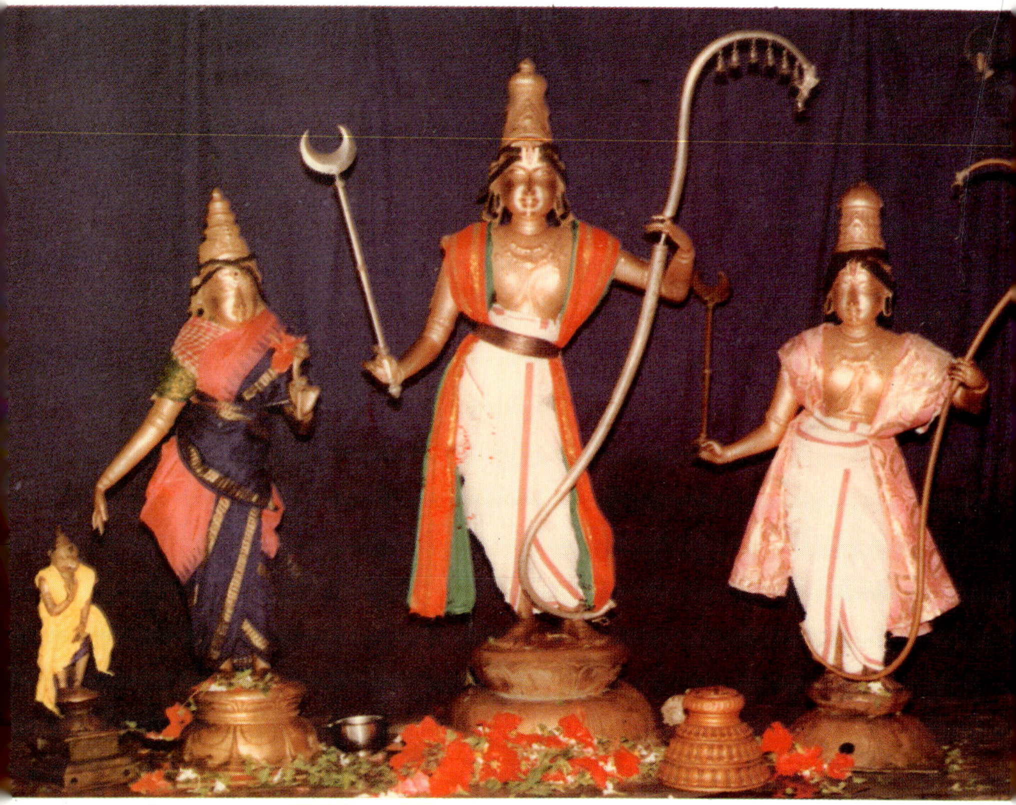

35. Rama, Sita and Lakshman

36. Hanuman

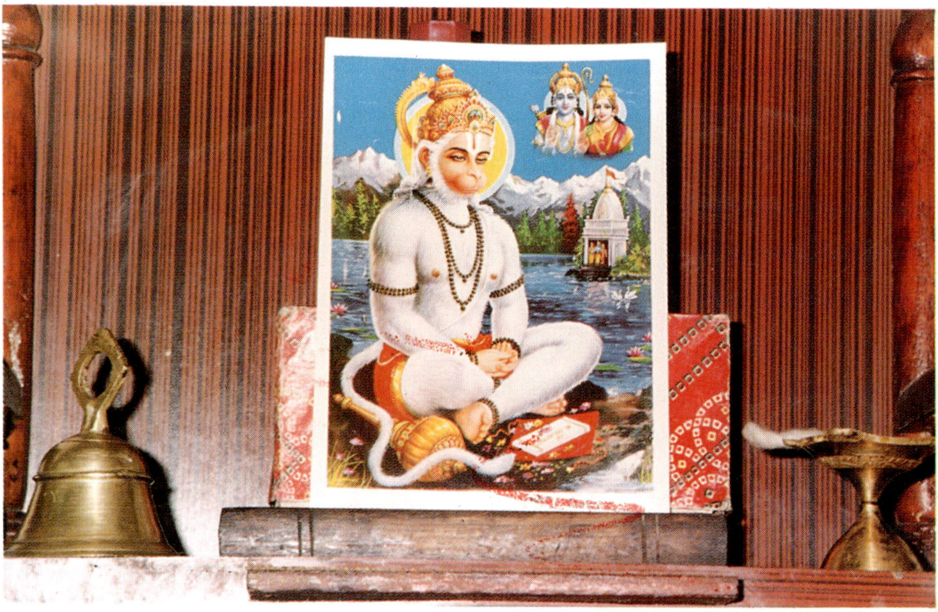

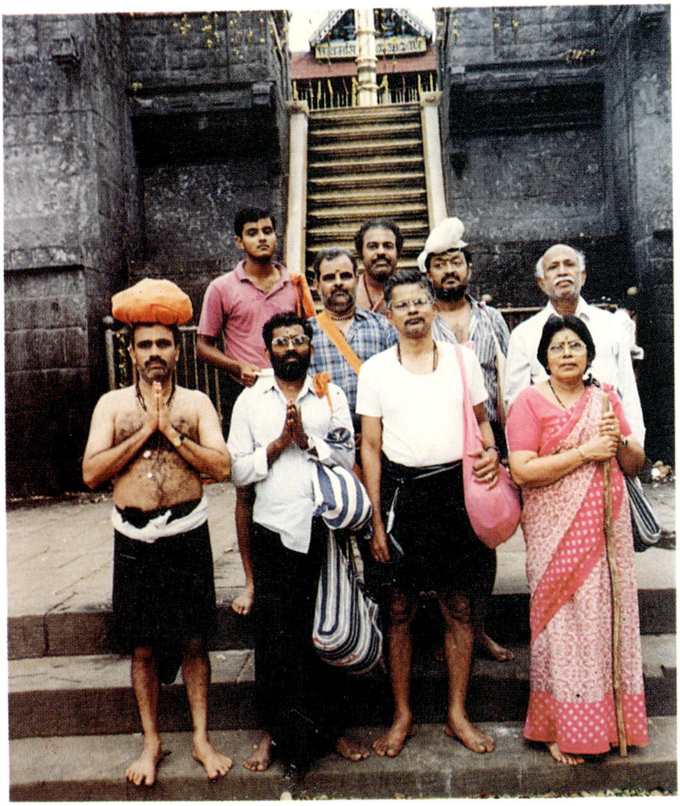

34. Annual Yatra to Sabarimalai

33. Annual Yatra to Sabarimalai

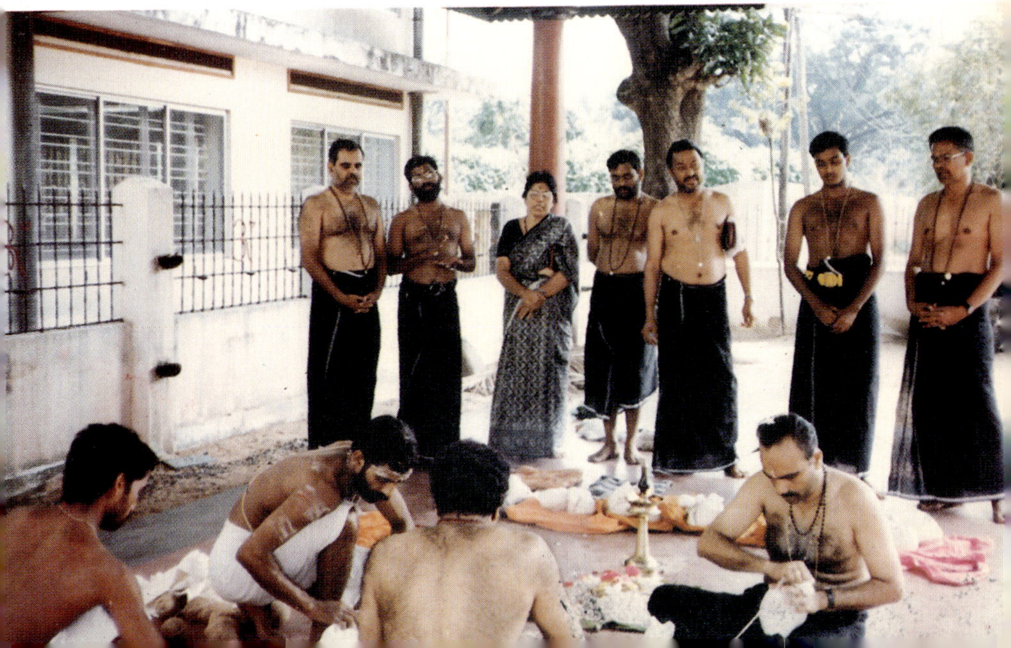

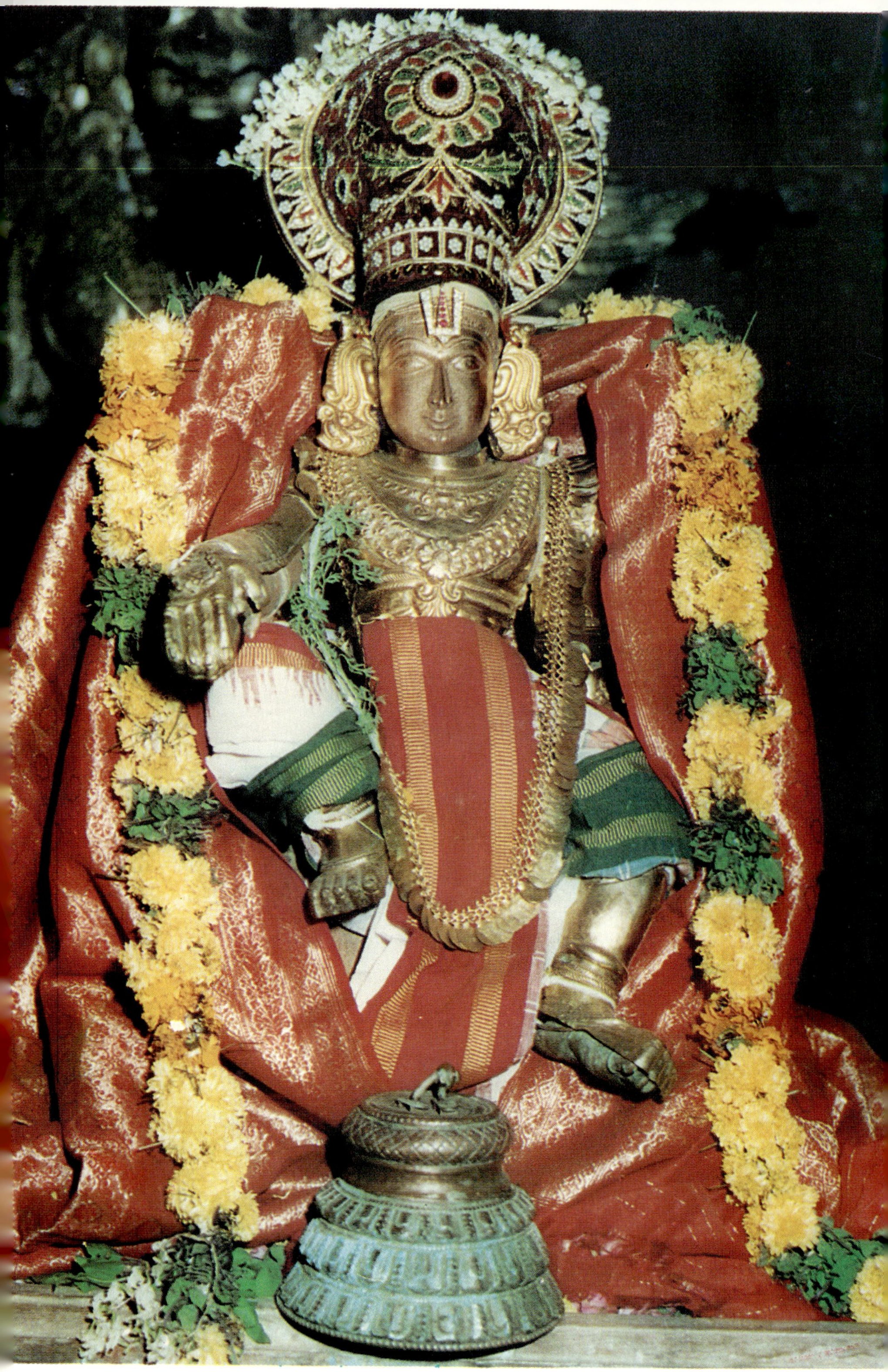

37. Sri Vaikunthanath

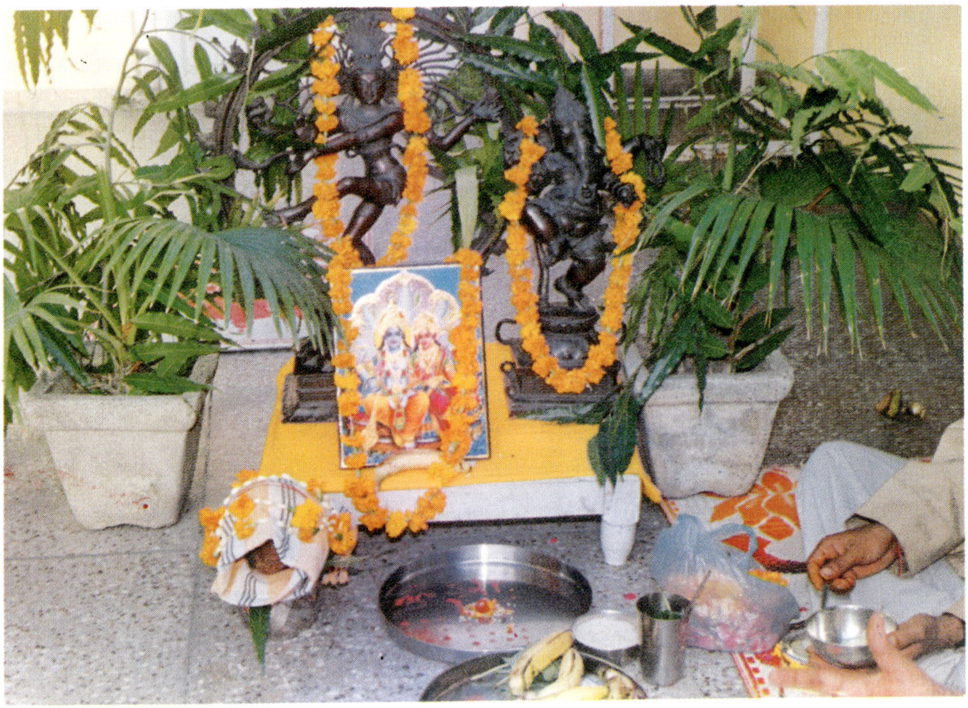

39. Satyanarayana Vrata

40. Lighting Oil Lamp for Sani

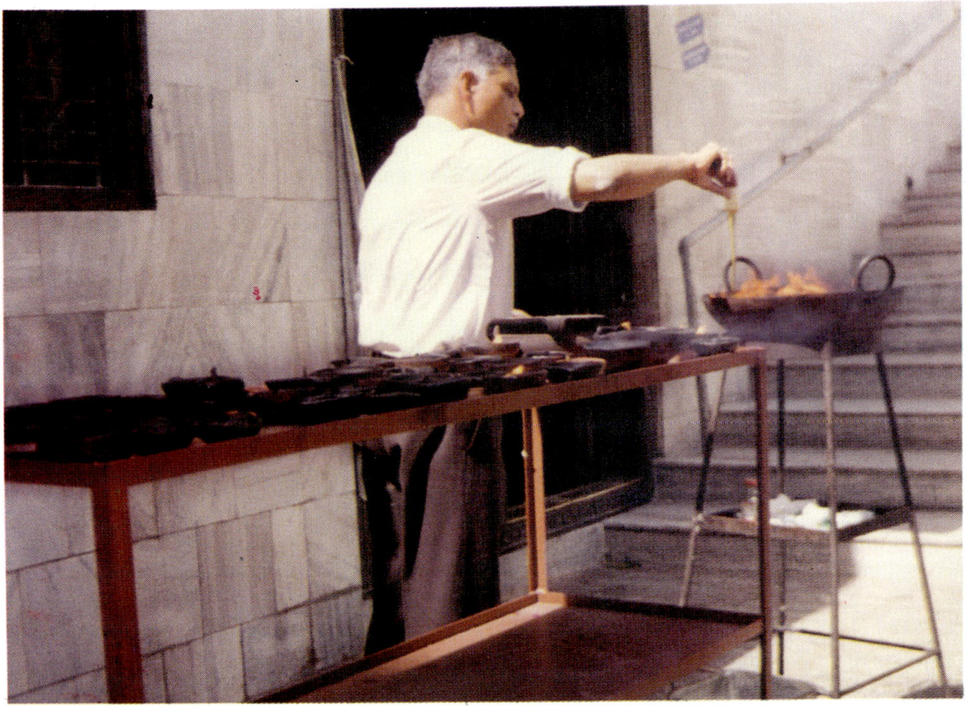

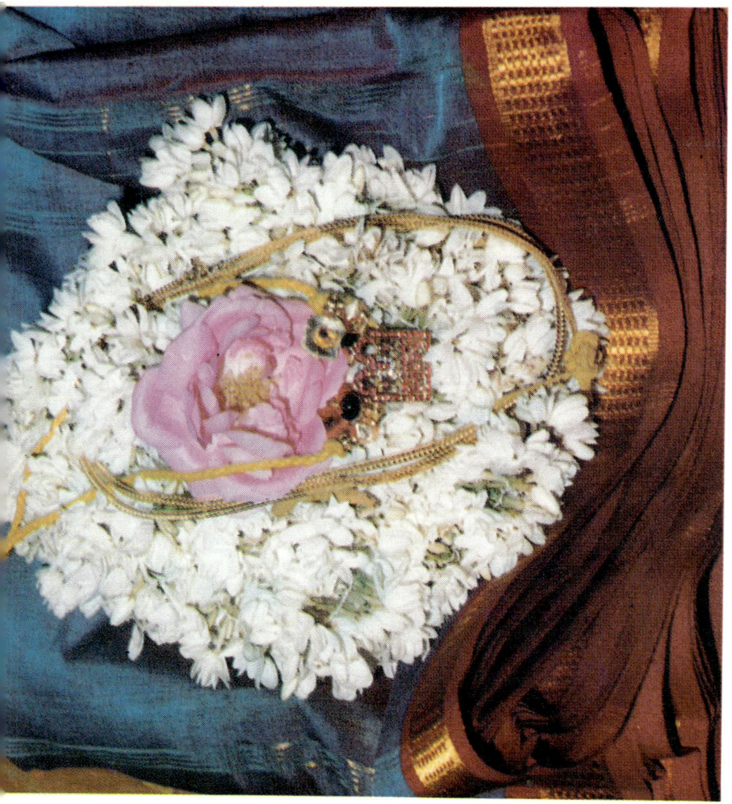

43. Mangal Sutra

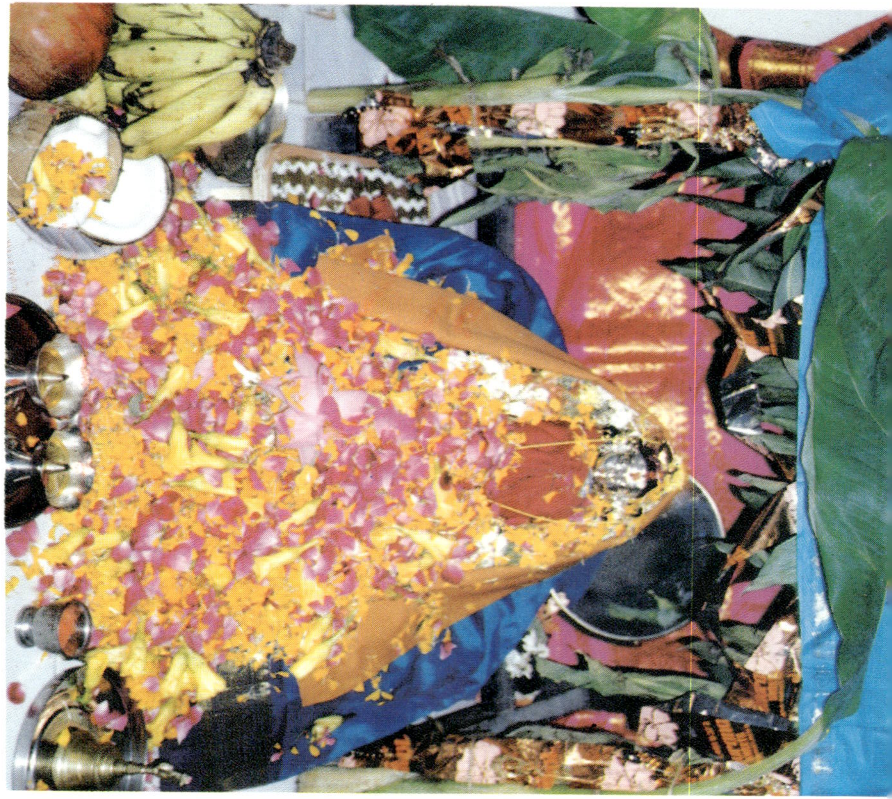

41. Mangala Gouri Vrata

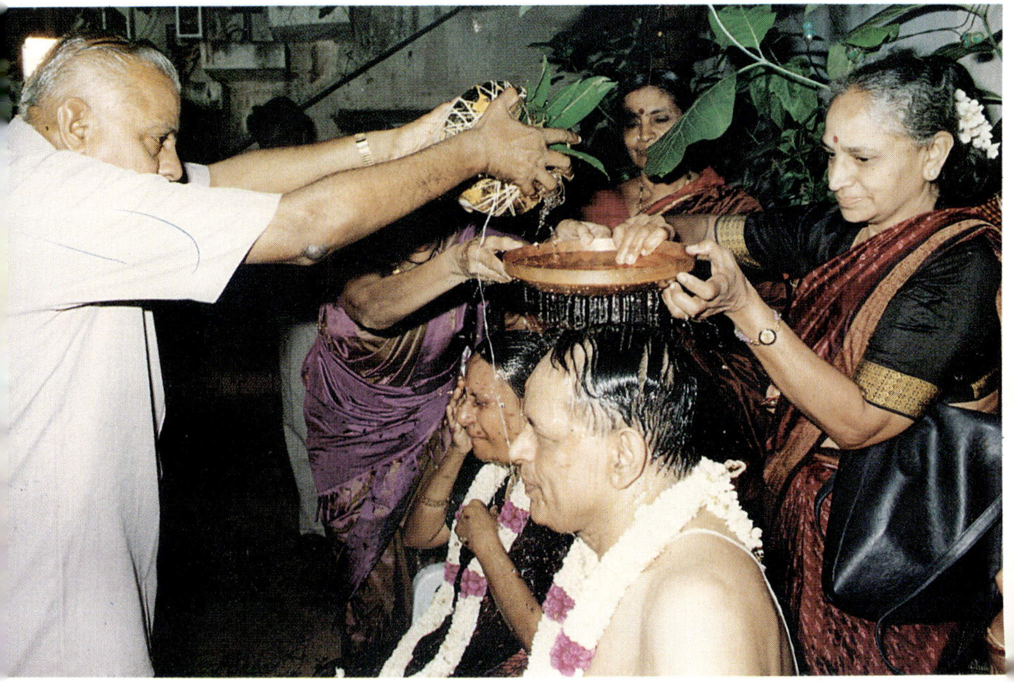

42. 60th Birthday Shower

44. Wedding Ceremony

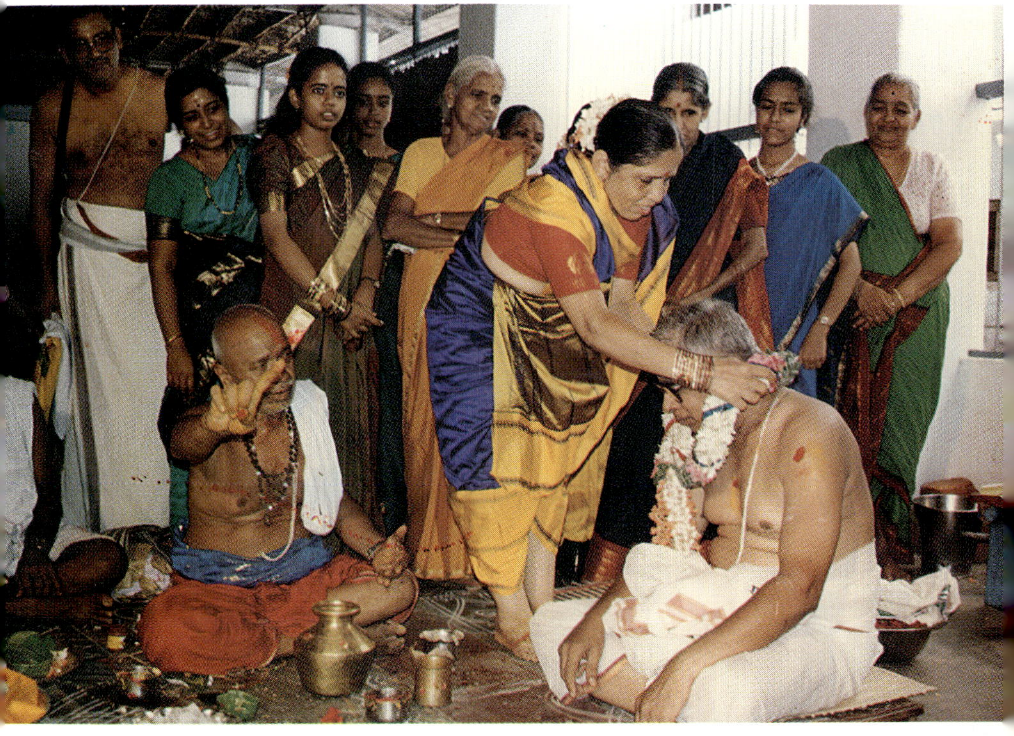

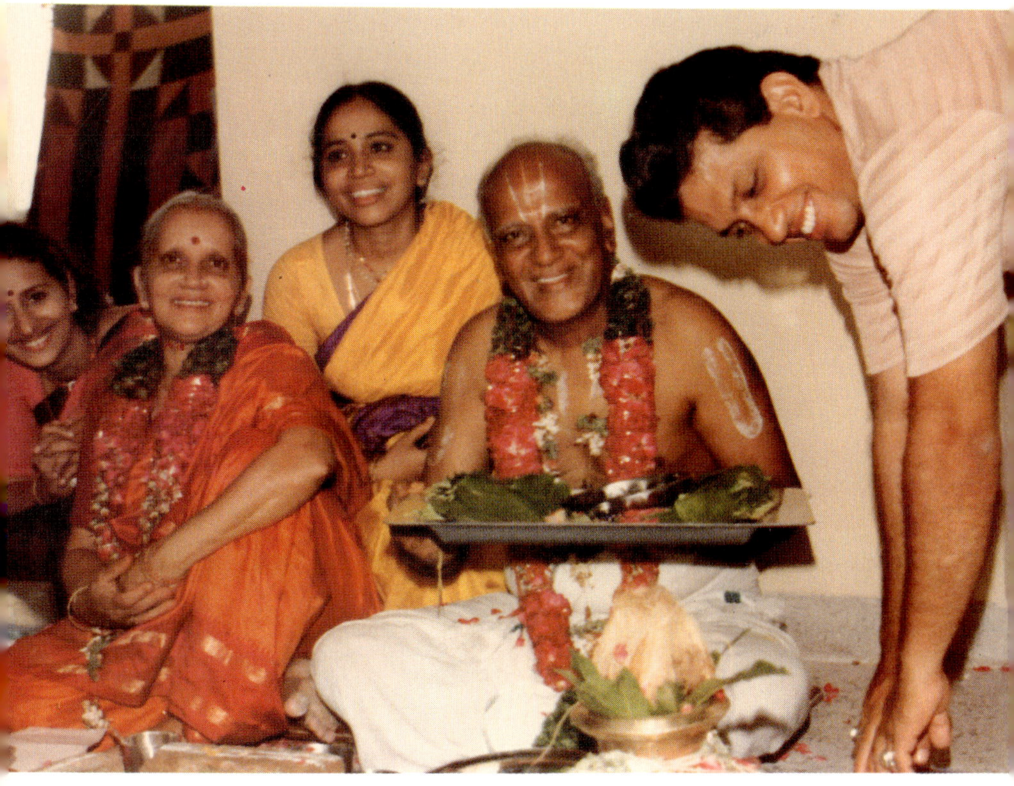

45. Taking Blessings from the Couple

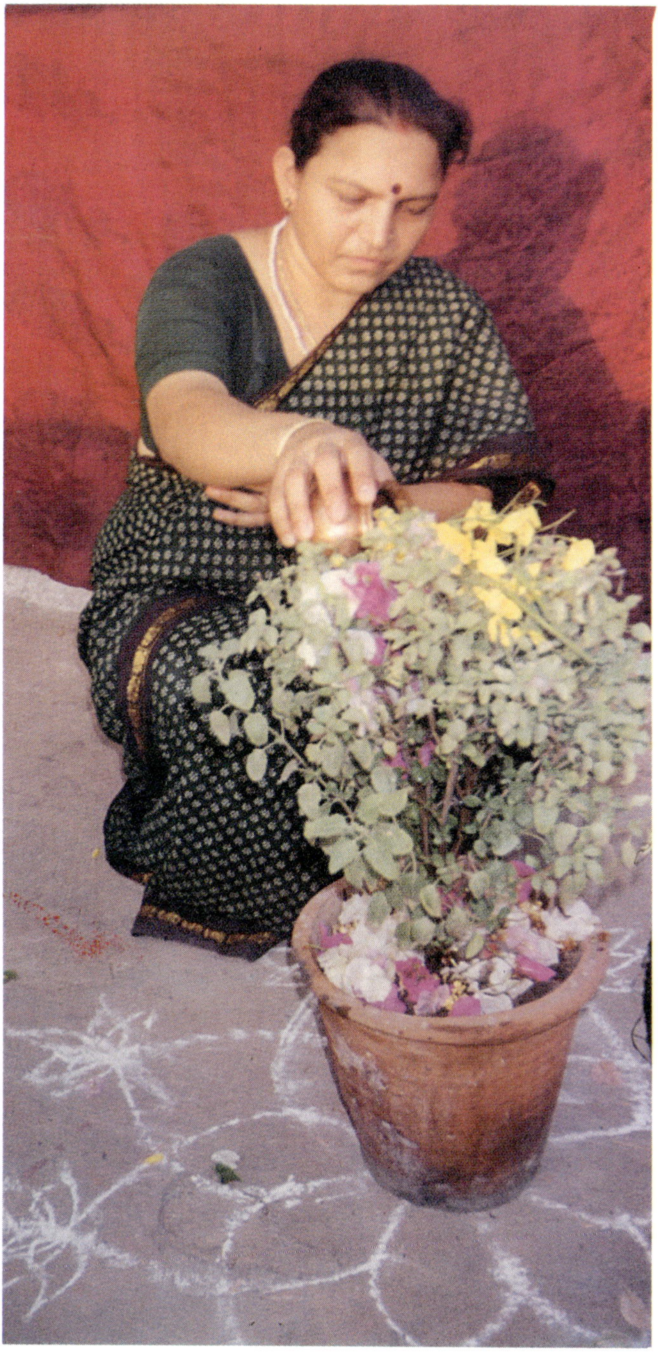

46. Tulsi Puja

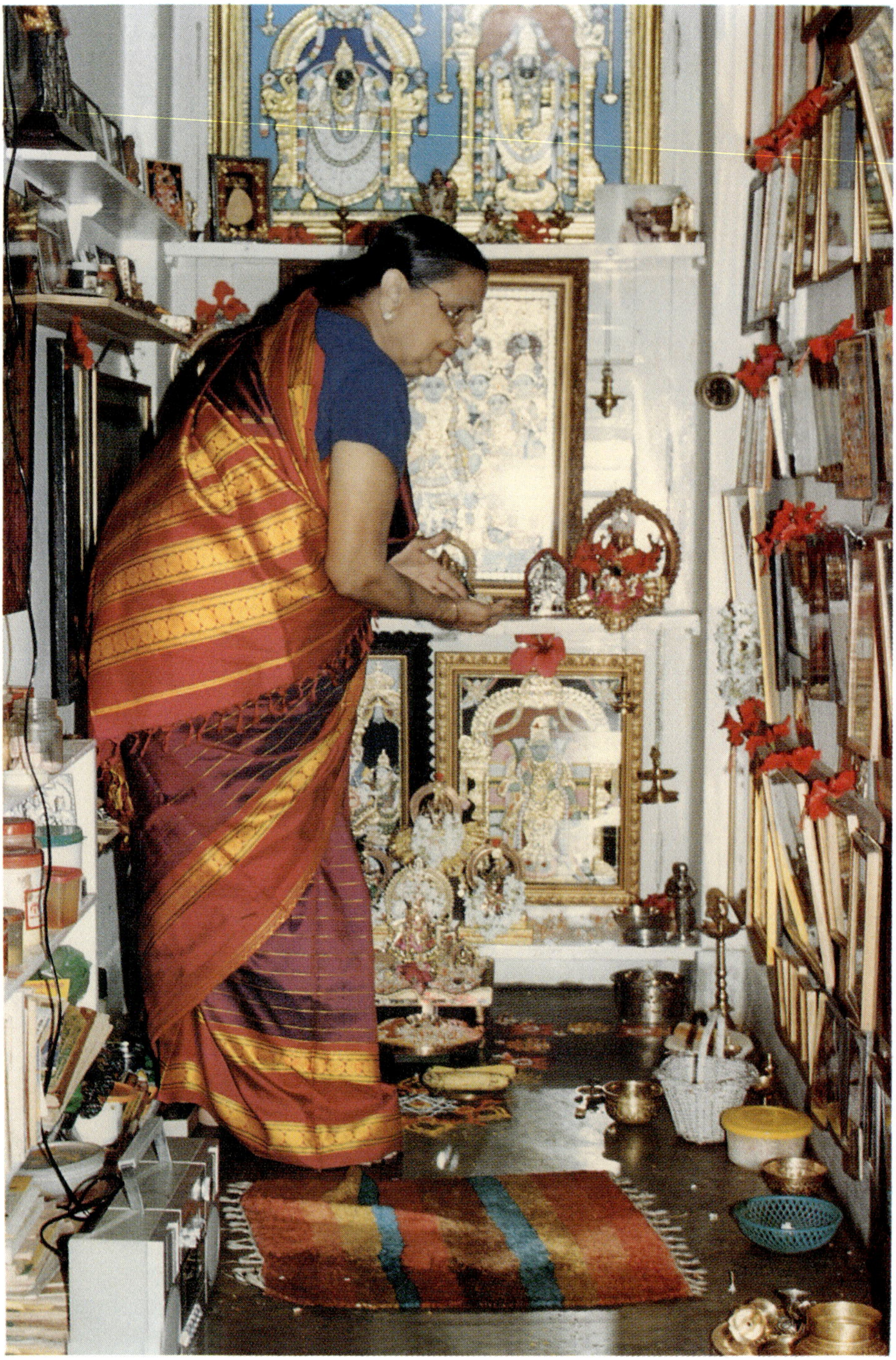

47. Puja at Home

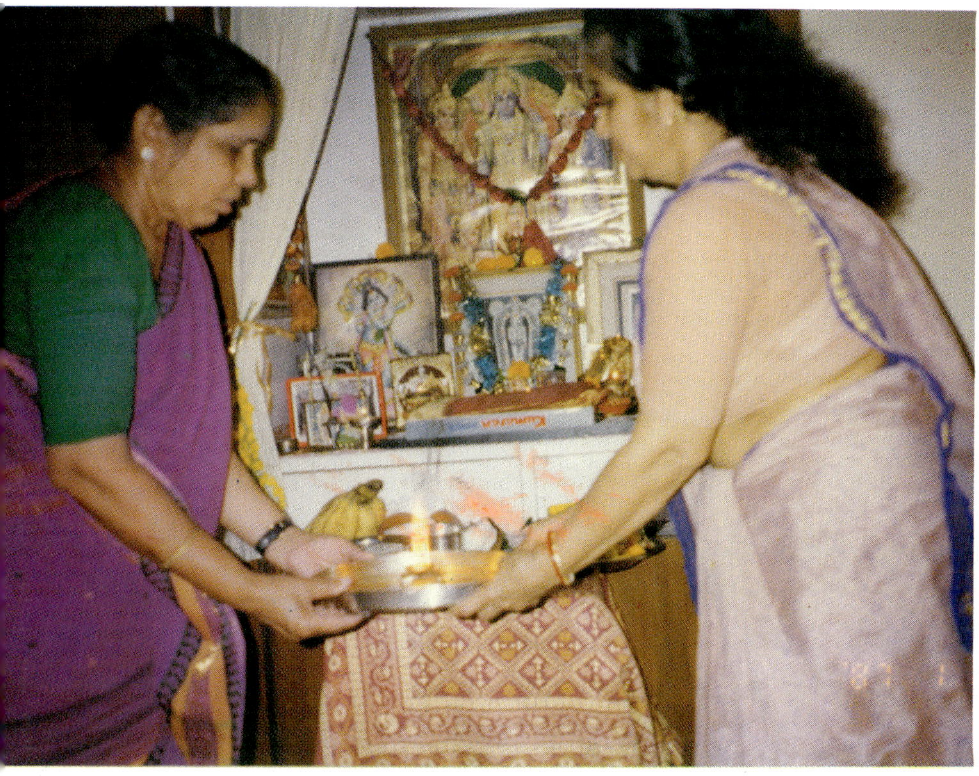

48. Arati after Puja

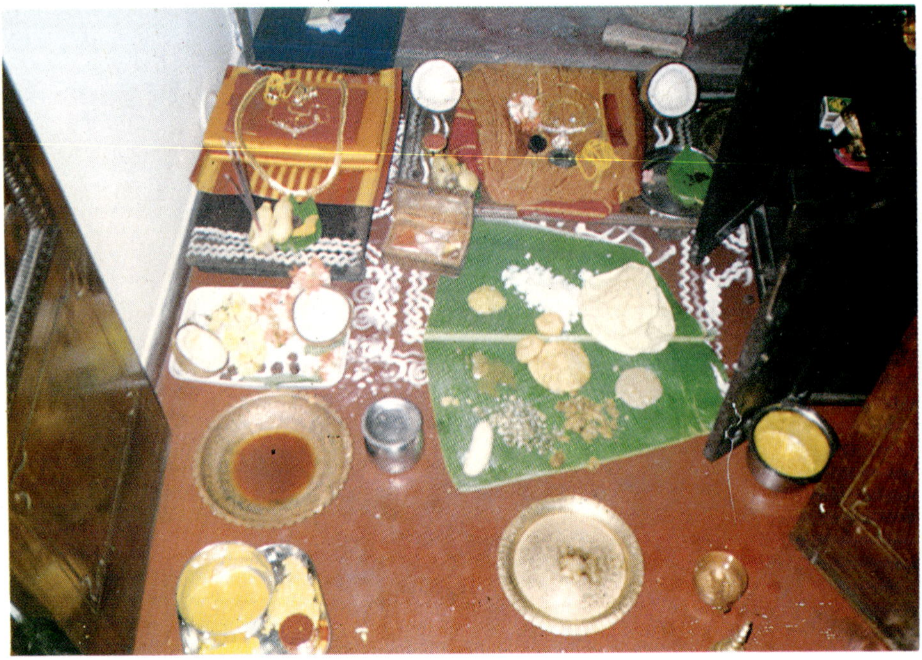

49. Sumangali Vrata

50. Traditional Feast

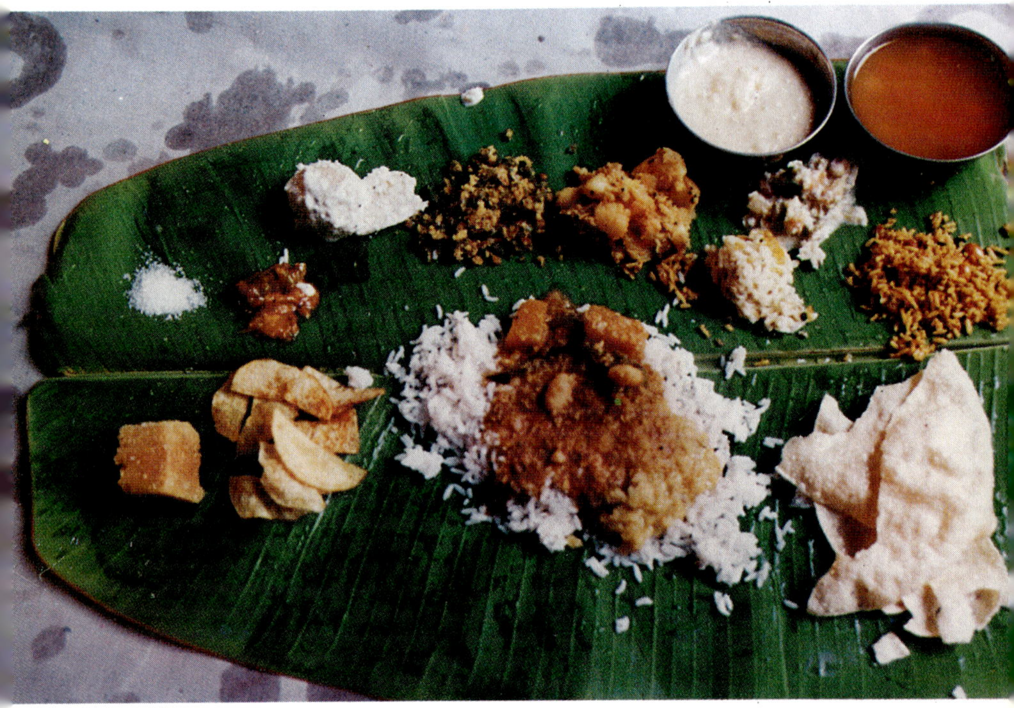

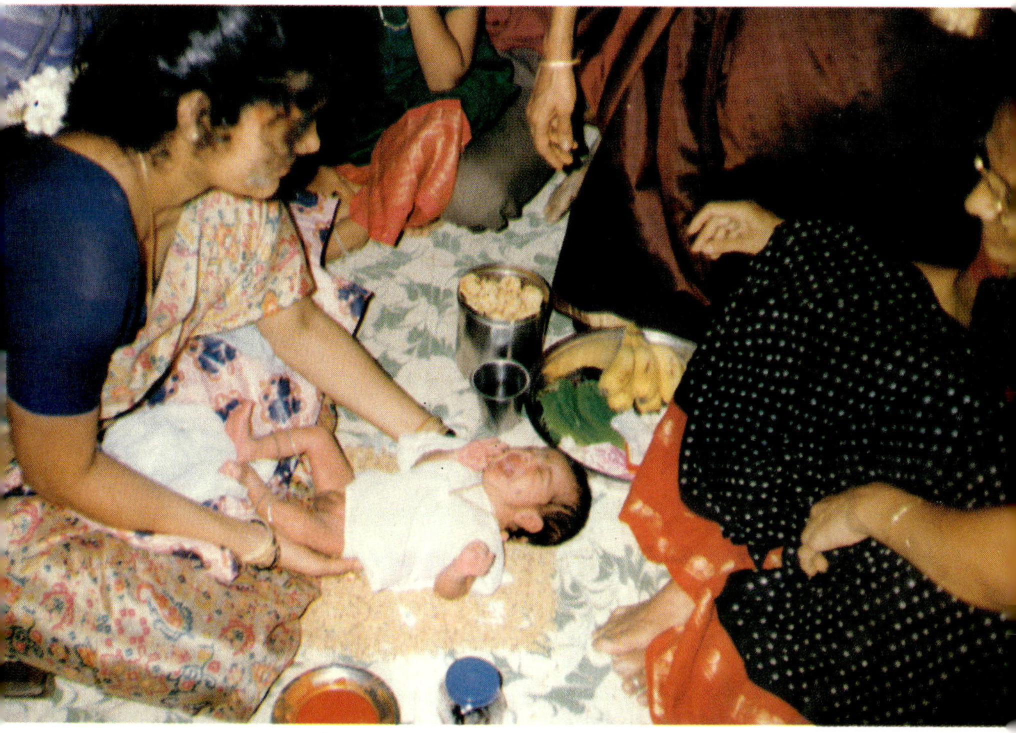

51. Jata Karma

53. Upanayaman

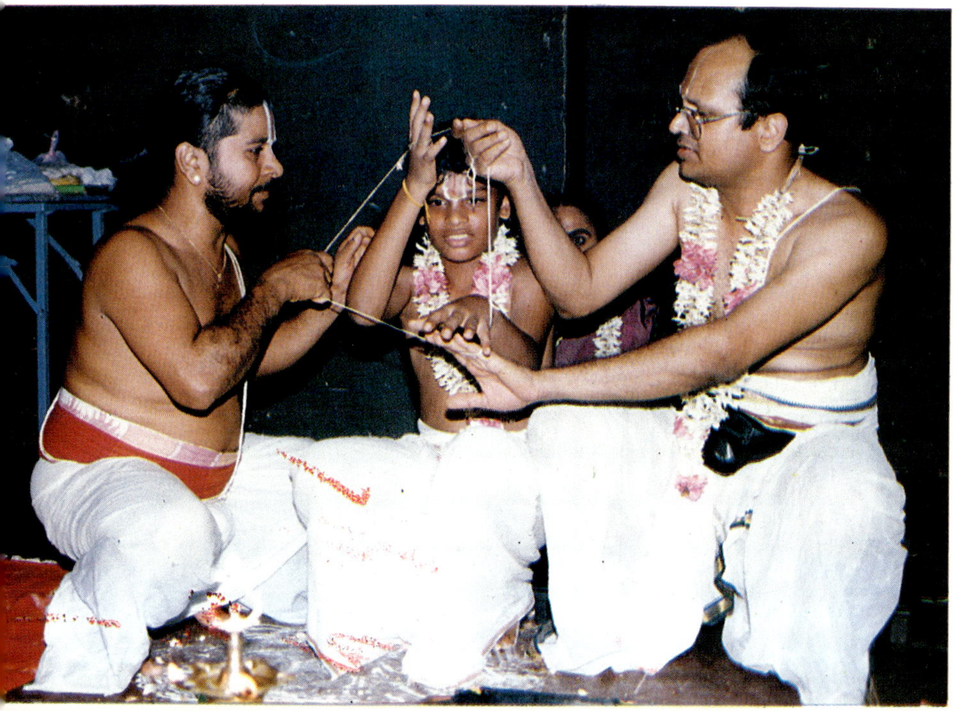

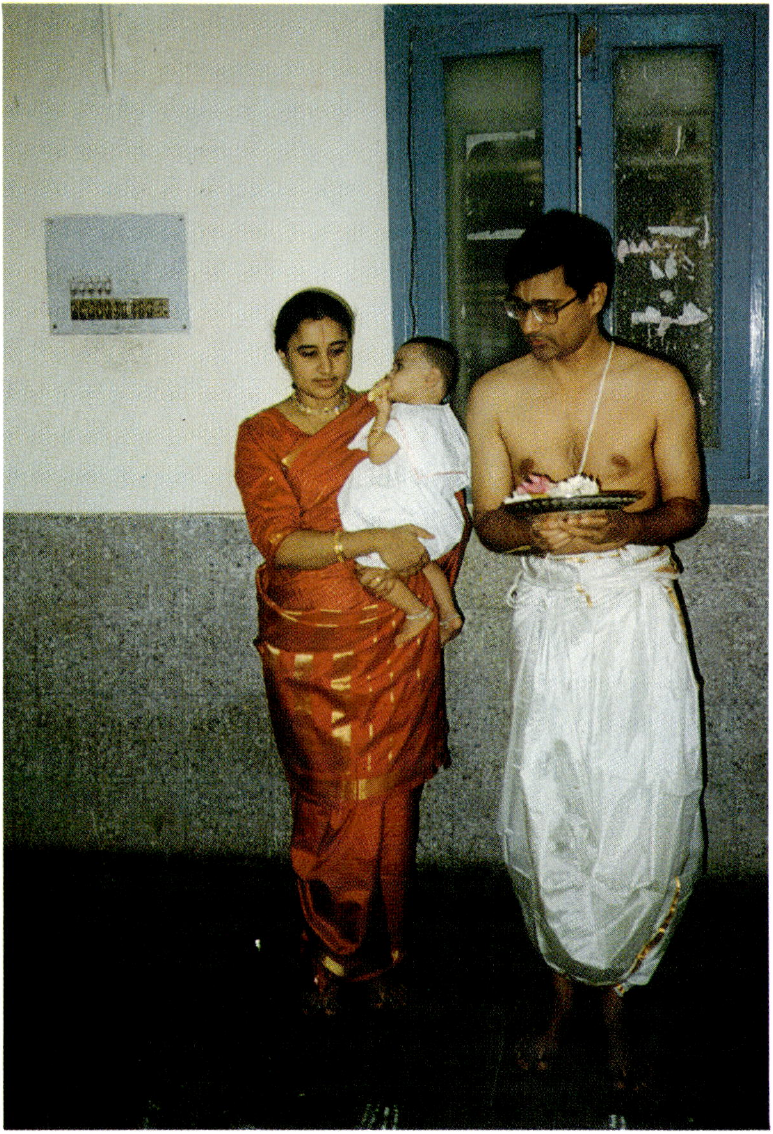

52. Nama Karma

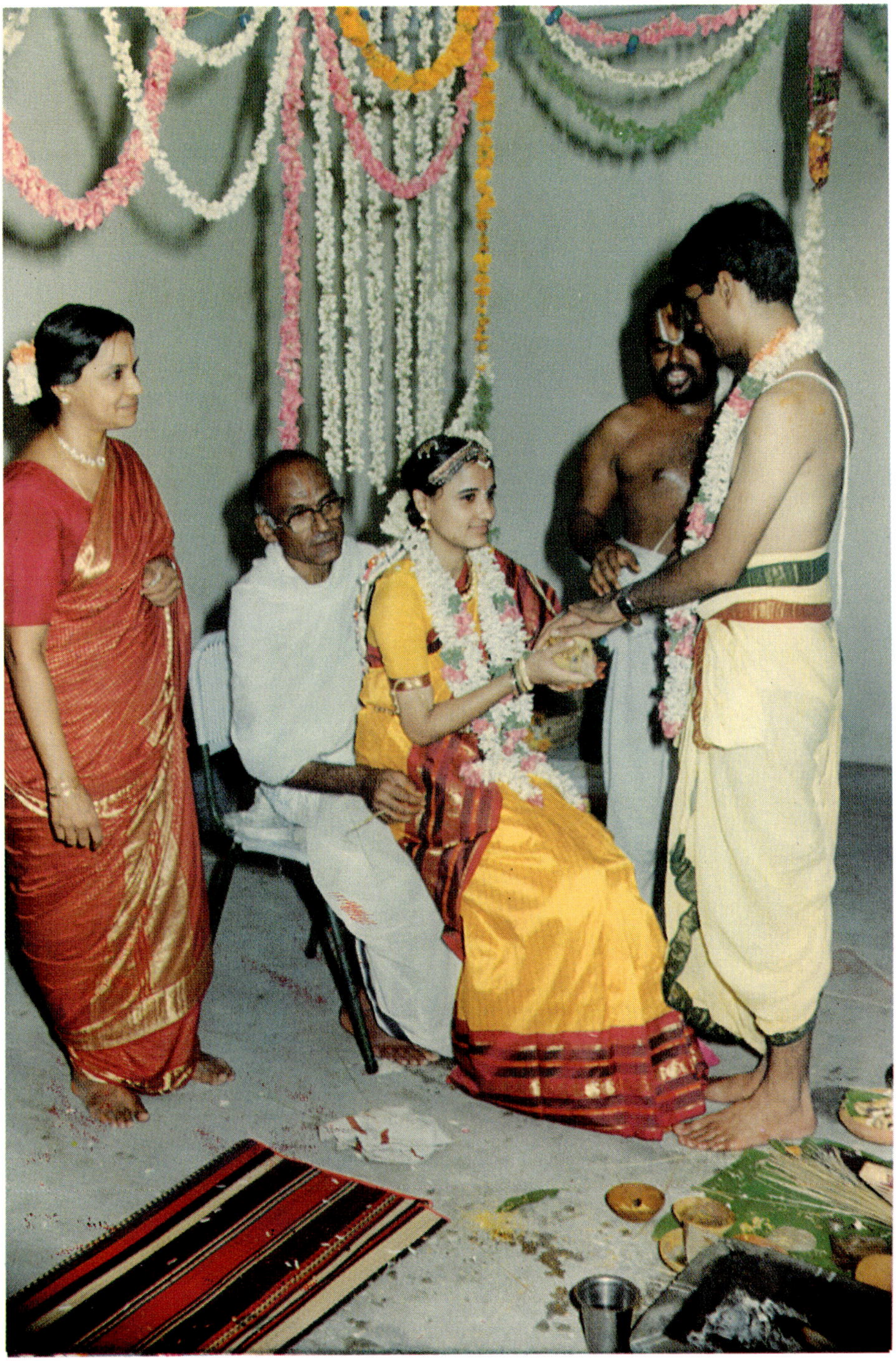

54. Marriage Function

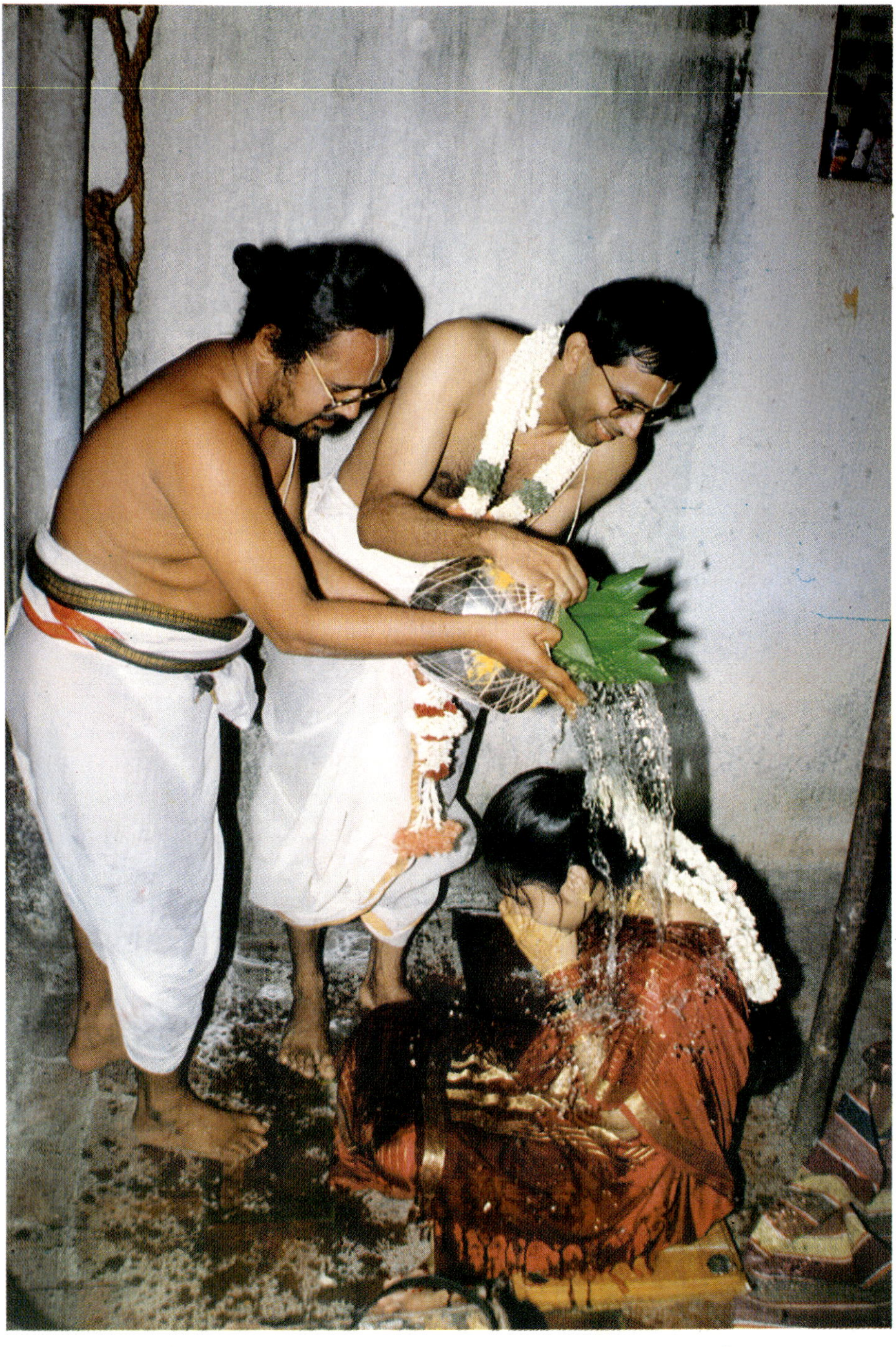

55. Seemantam

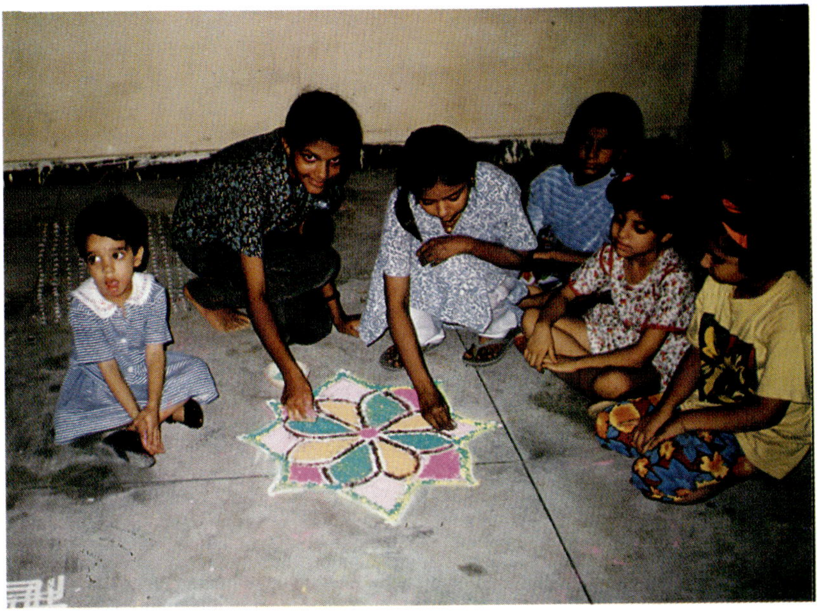

56. Rangoli by Children

57. Starting a Rangoli

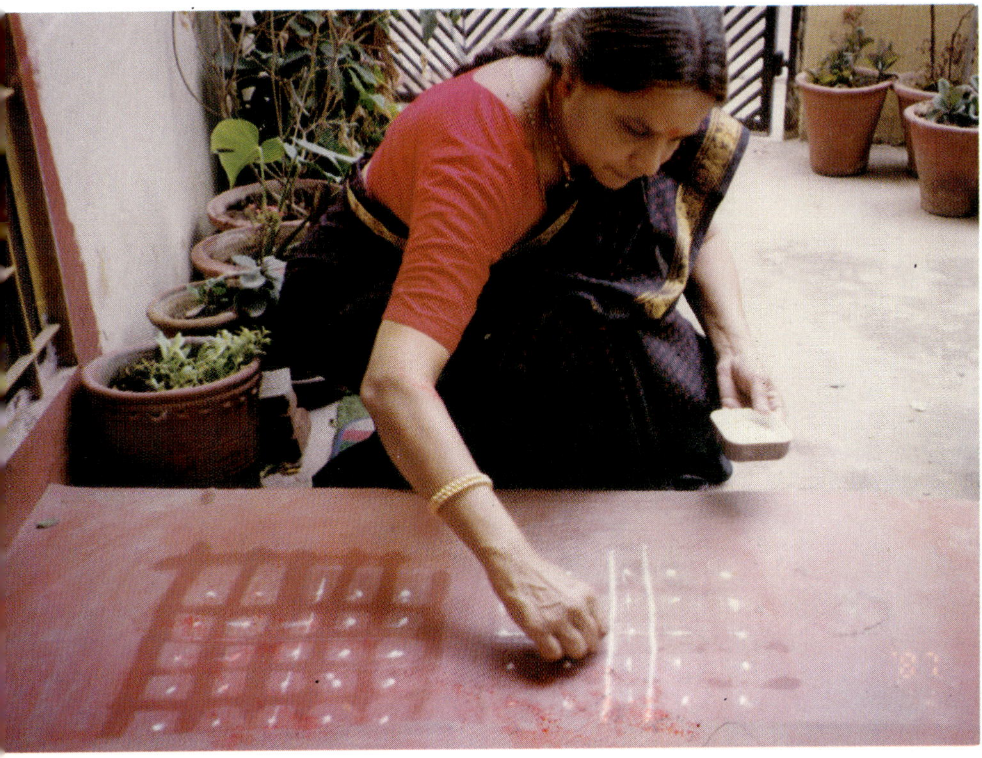

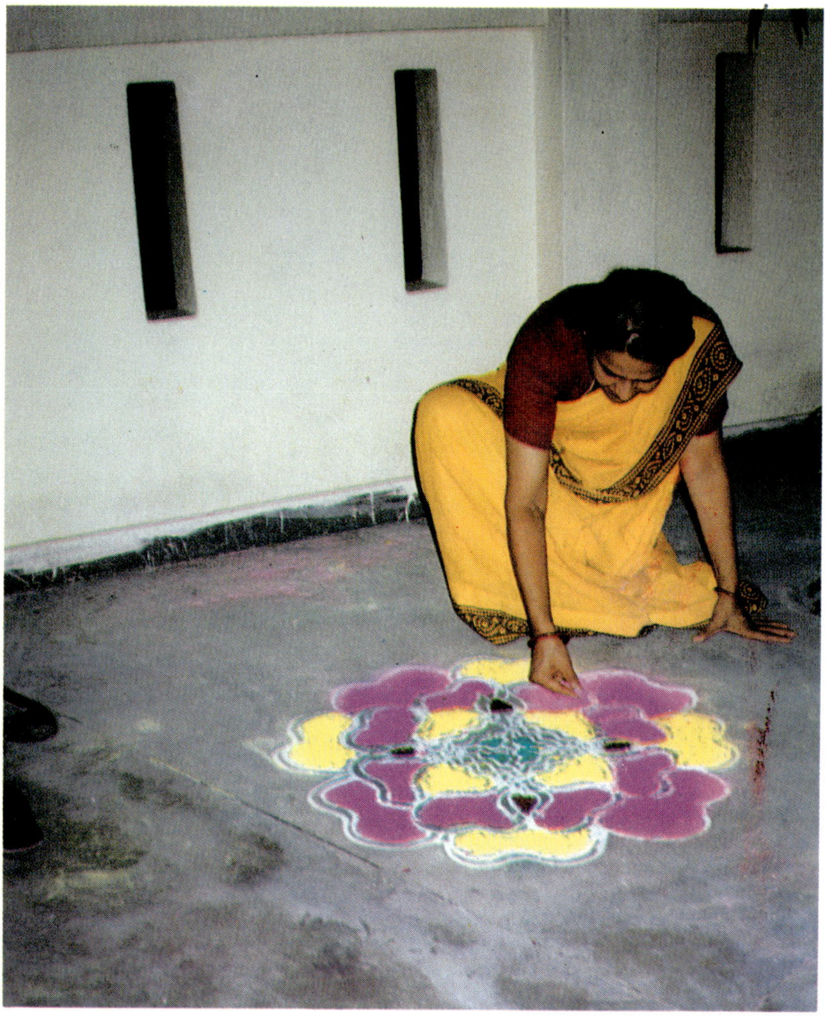

58. Starting a Colour Rangoli

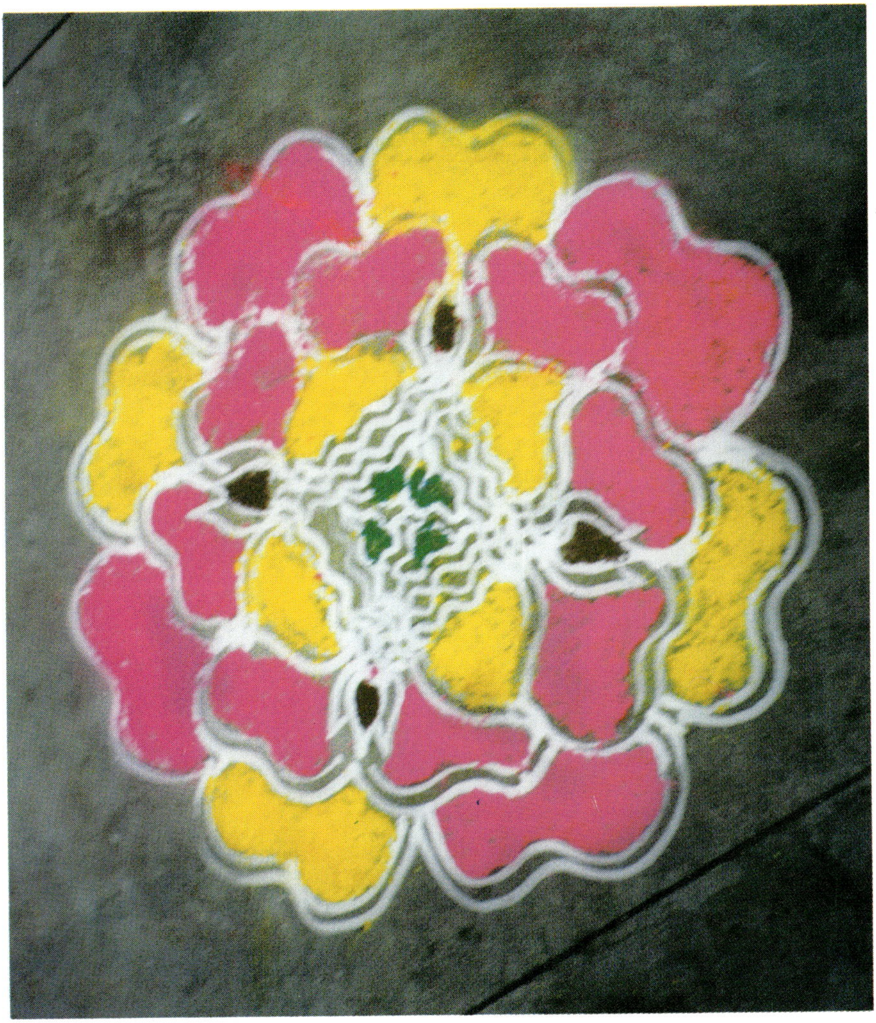

59. Completed Colour Rangoli

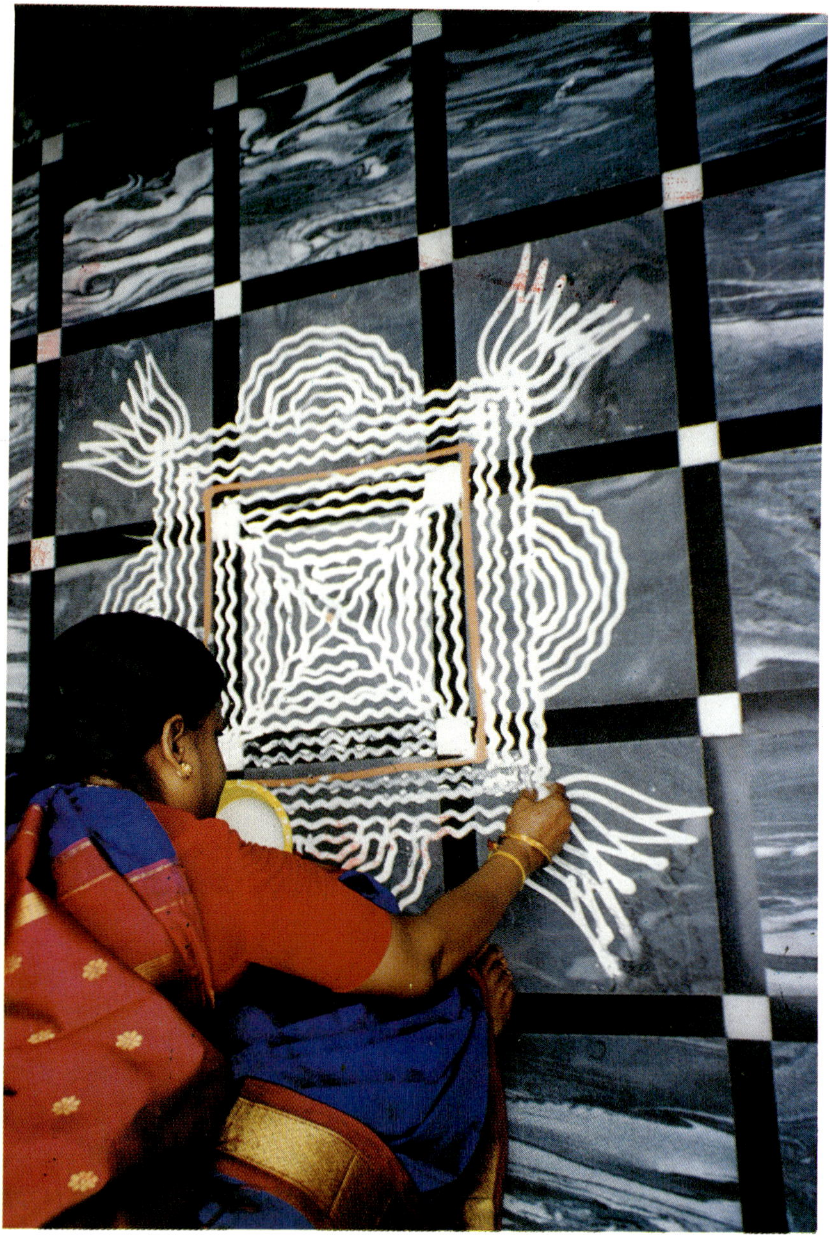

60. Starting Wet Rice Flour Rangoli

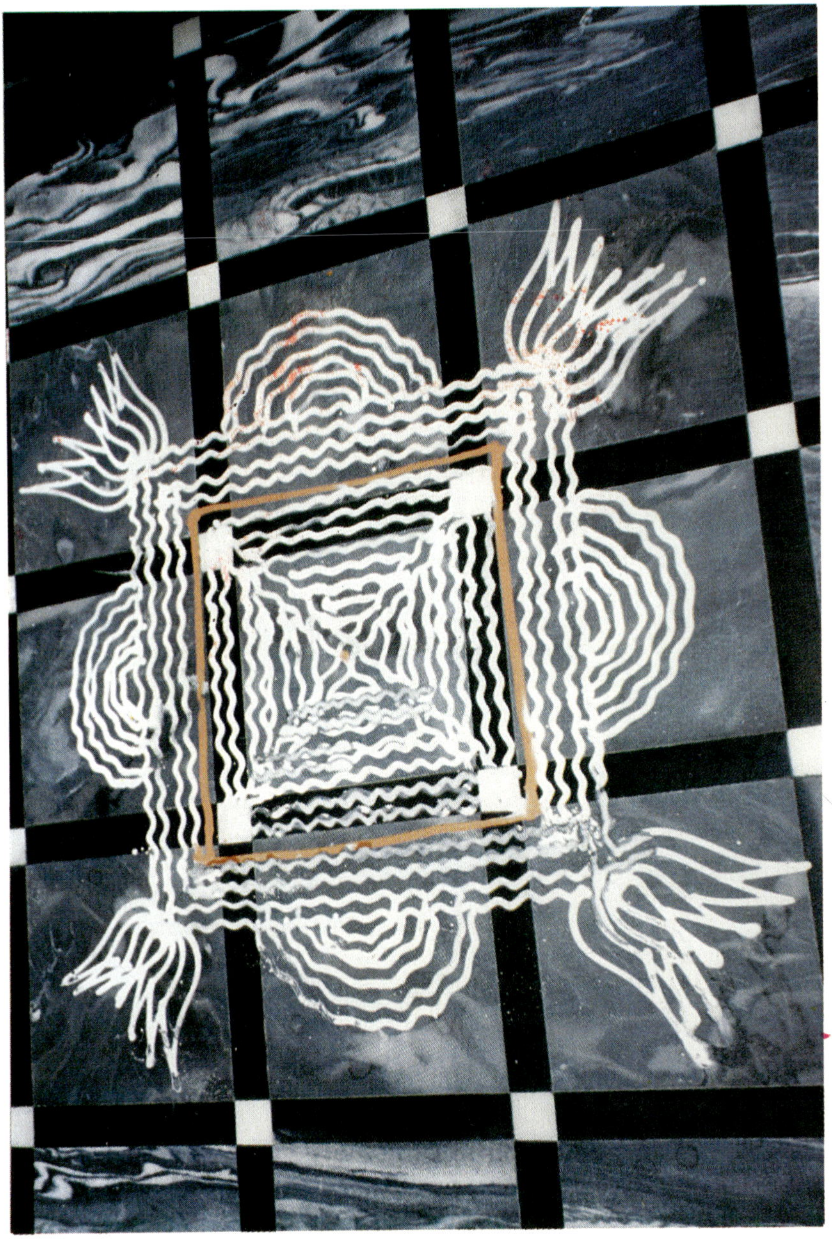

61. Completed Wet Rice Flour Rangoli

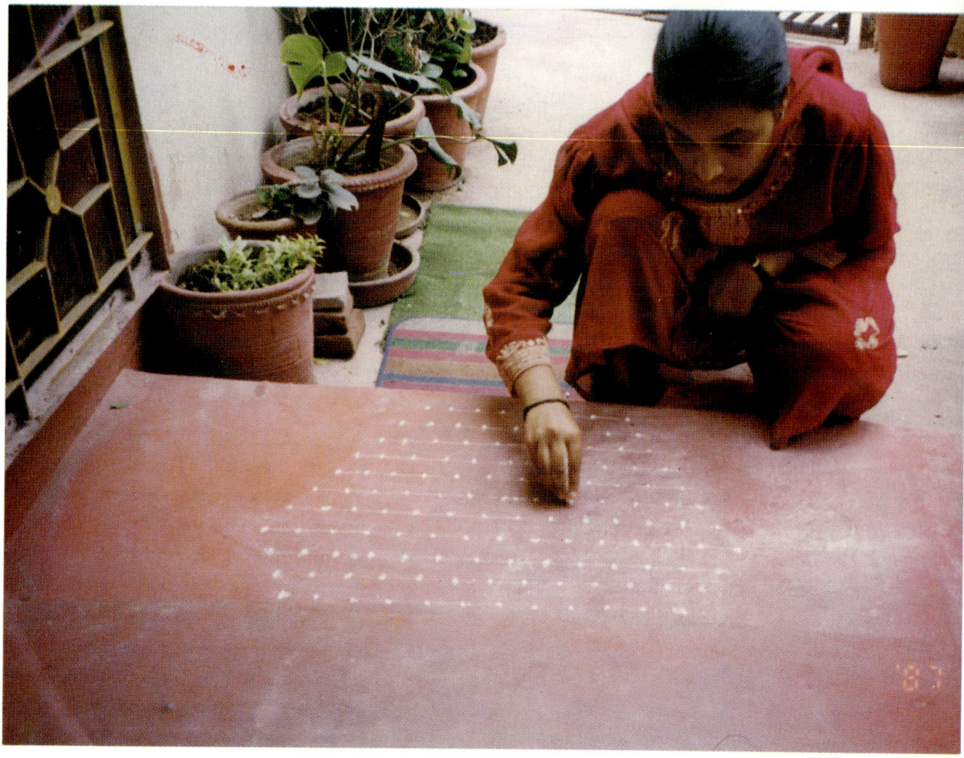

62. Starting Dry Rice Flour Rangoli

63. Completed Dry Rice Flour Rangoli

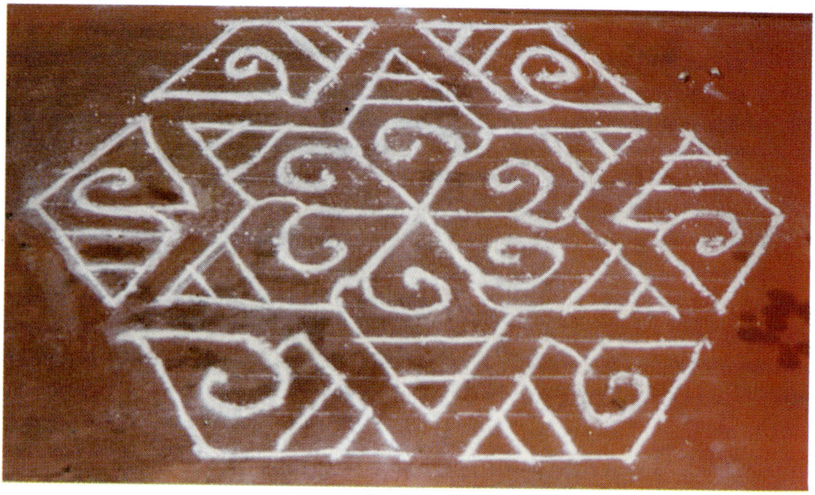

SECTION I

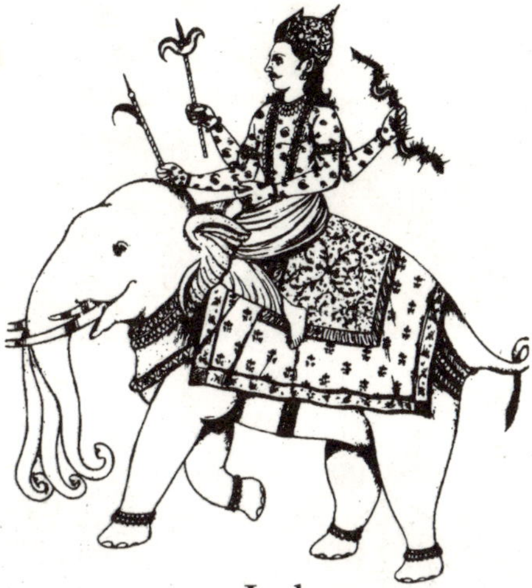

Indra

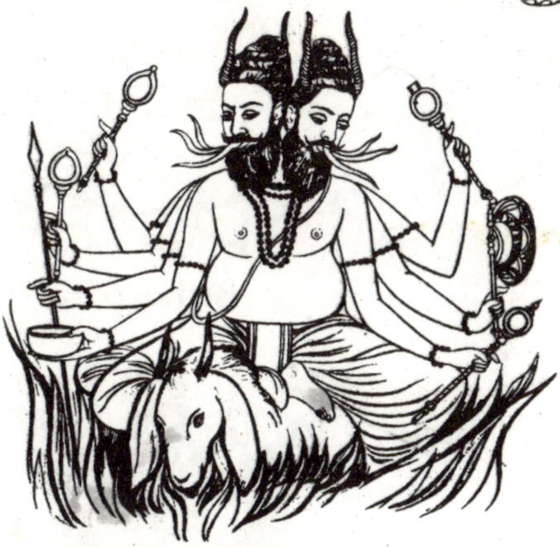

Agni

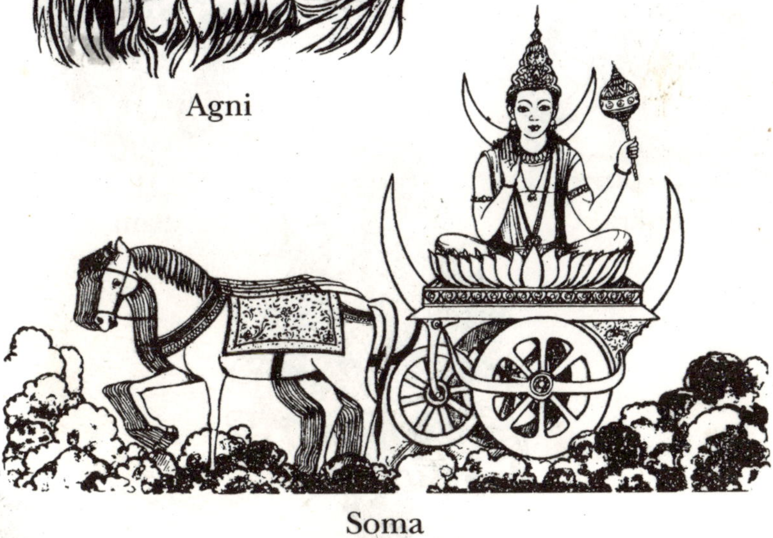

Soma

THE WEEKLY DEITIES

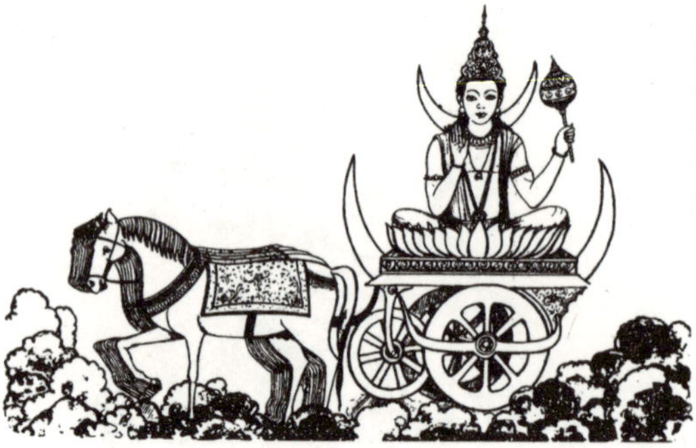

Soma

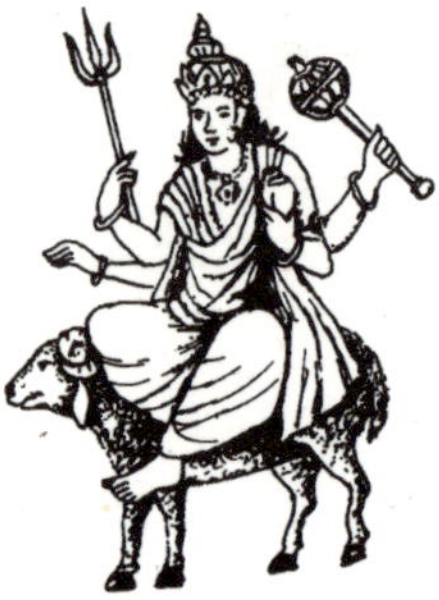

Mangal

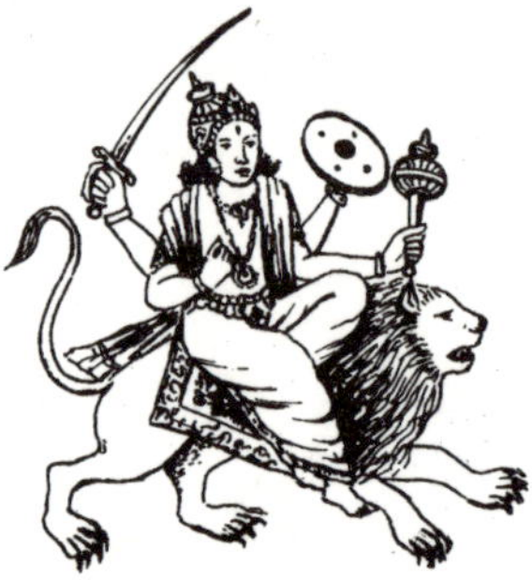

Budh

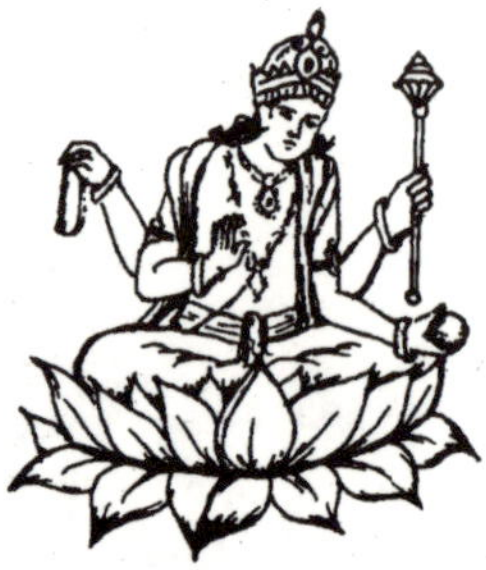

Brihaspati

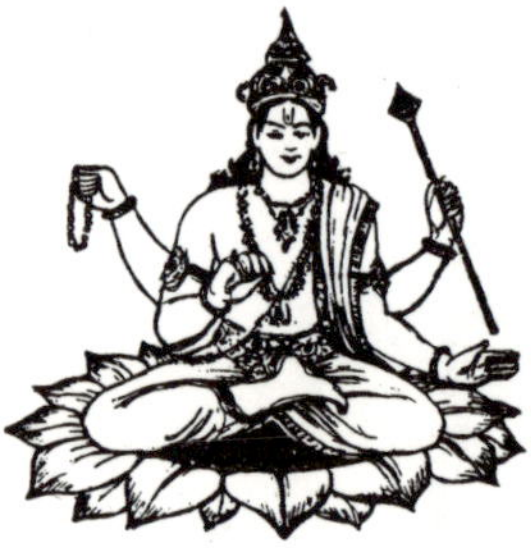

Sukra

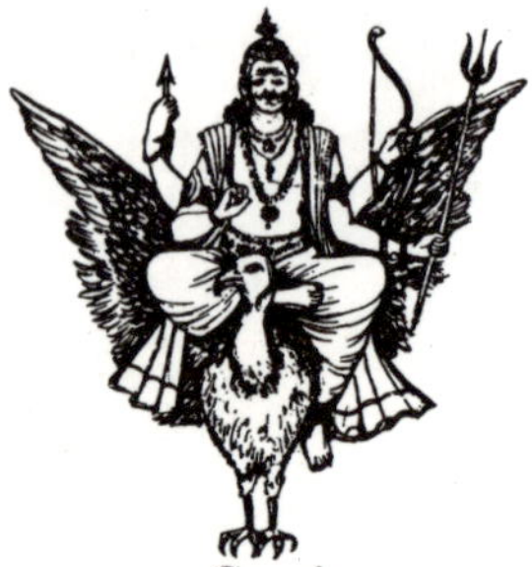

Sani

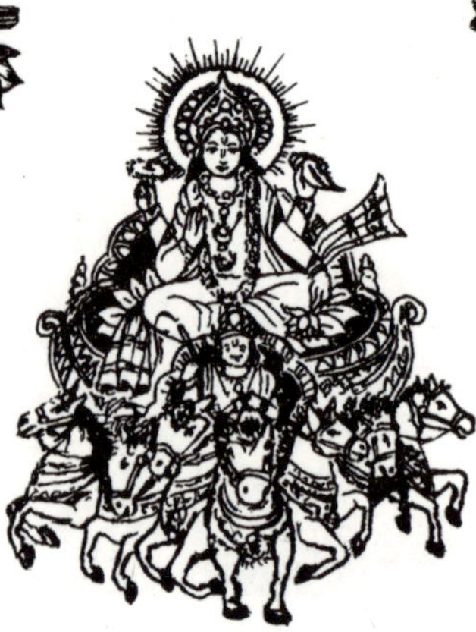

Ravi

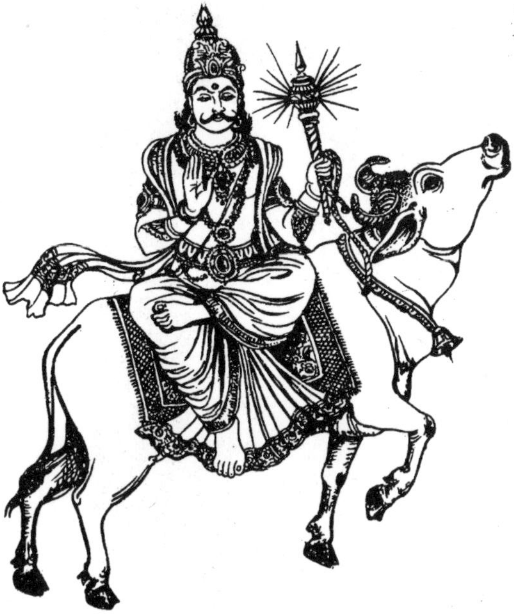

Yama

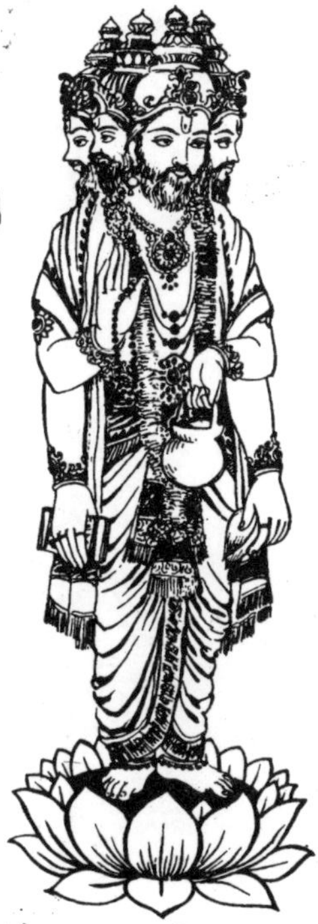

Brahma

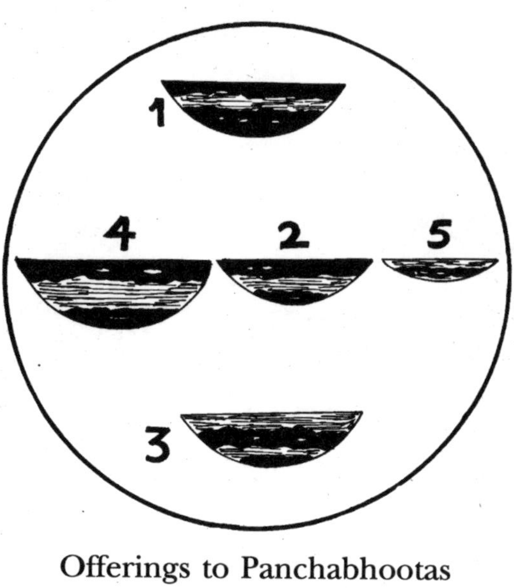

Offerings to Panchabhootas

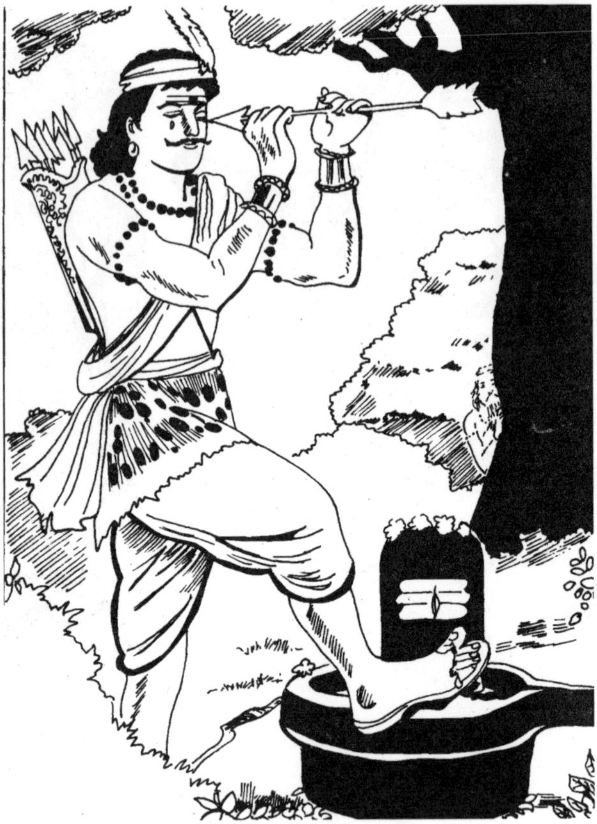

Bhakta Kannappa

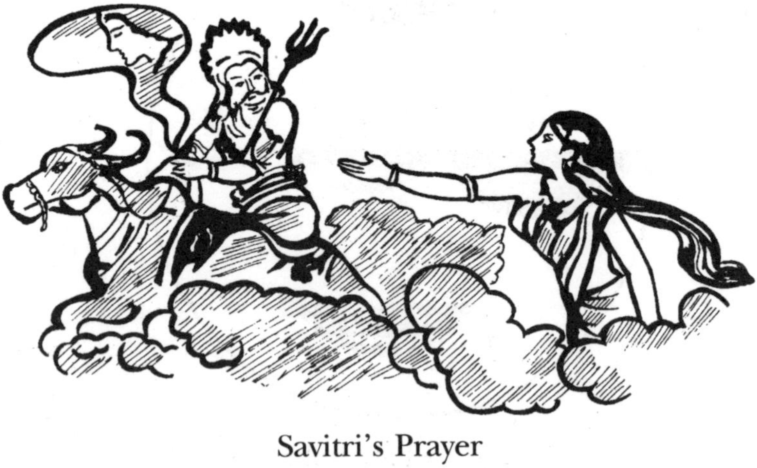

Savitri's Prayer

SECTION I

Rituals Directing the Journey of Life

Chapter 1

ZODIAC SIGNS, RULING PLANETS AND RASIS

The individual's life is taken care of spiritually and physically by karmas of life, pujas, fasts and vratas etc. during and after the life cycle. Man is considered to be an atma, an individual soul which is also part of the paramatma or Brahman, the universal soul. Hence he has to lead a wholesome life with balanced physical, mental, and spiritual growth. To achieve this balance, the ancient seers have given certain traditional patterns of behaviour in everyday life and observances during special occasions. Many of these are to be observed with reference to the zodiac signs, stars and planets.

Nine planets, 27 stars, and 12 rasis or zodiac signs influence good and bad phases in our lives. Each of the planets is the lord of 2 or 3 rasis, and its characteristics and phases influence the thoughts and actions of individuals born under the rasis when the planet is most powerful. The characteristics ascribed to the planets vary from fiery and hot-headed Mars to fastidious and artistic Mercury.

Just as important as the planets is the position of the sun, and the phases of the 27 stars. The stars are divided under the zodiac signs, each sign (rasi) having 2¼ stars under its influence. Each day, the moon goes into one of the stars (called a lunar mansion). Thus the moon remains in the same rasi for 2¼ days. The phase of the moon in the birth star and rasi at the time of birth are taken into calculation for predictions and casting the horoscope.

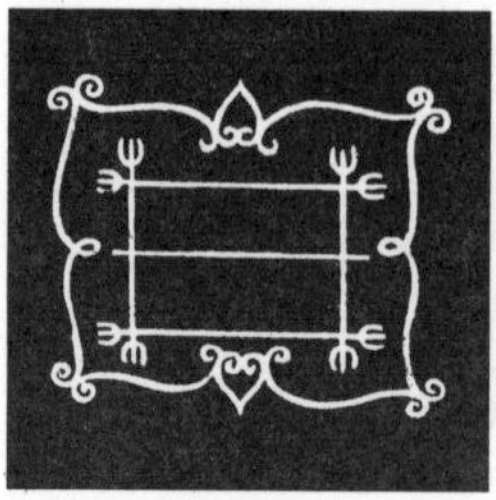

Budh
(Mercury)

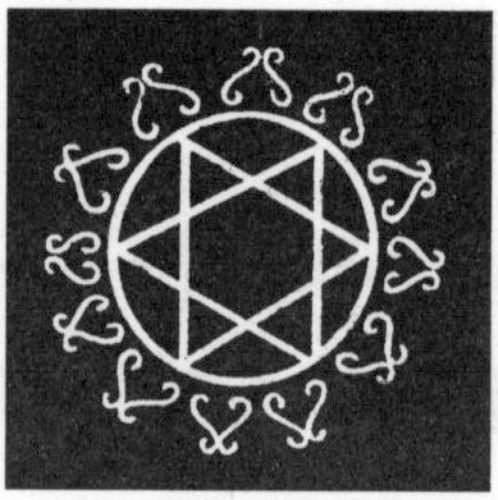

Shukra
(Venus)

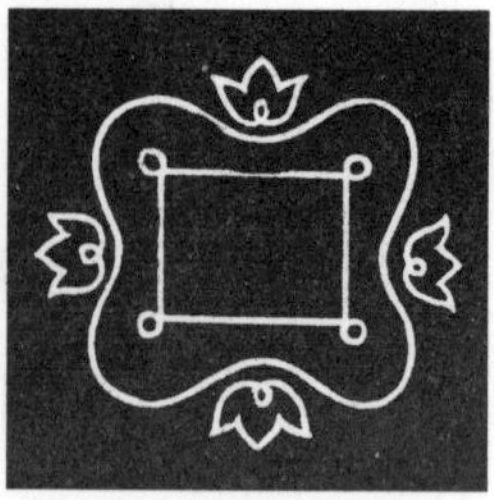

Chandra
(Moon)

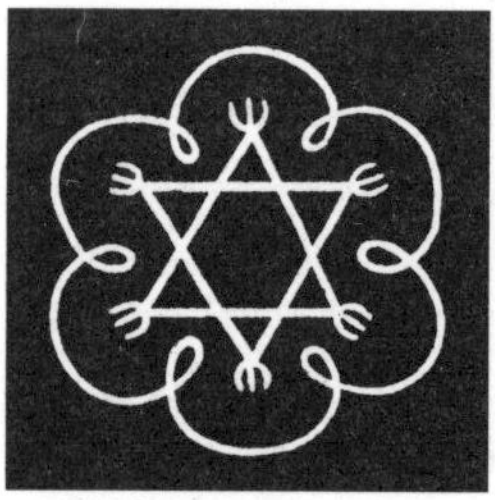

Guru
(Jupiter)

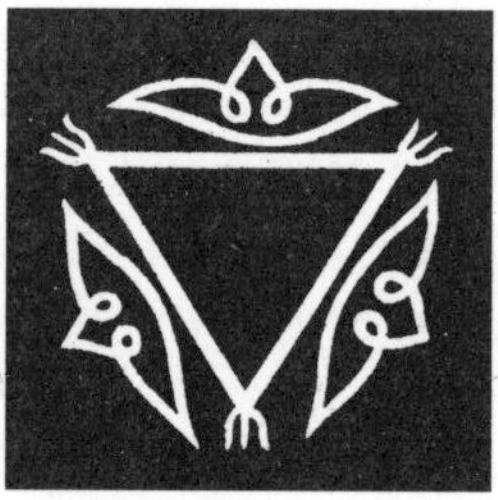

Surya
(Sun)

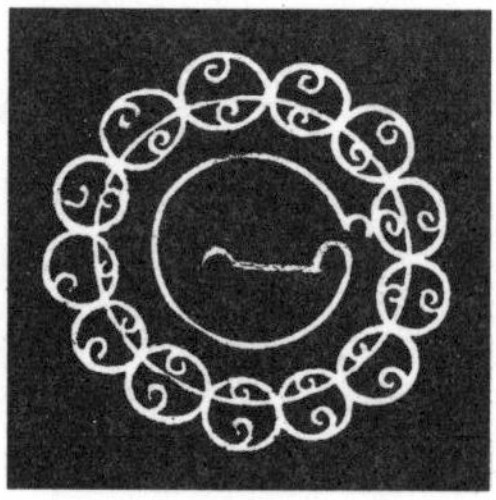

Mangal
(Mars)

Ketu
(Shadow Planet)

Sani
(Saturn)

Rahu
(Shadow Planet)

NAVAGRIHA KOLAM
Portrayal of nine planets through Rangoli for Navagriha Puja

SECTION II

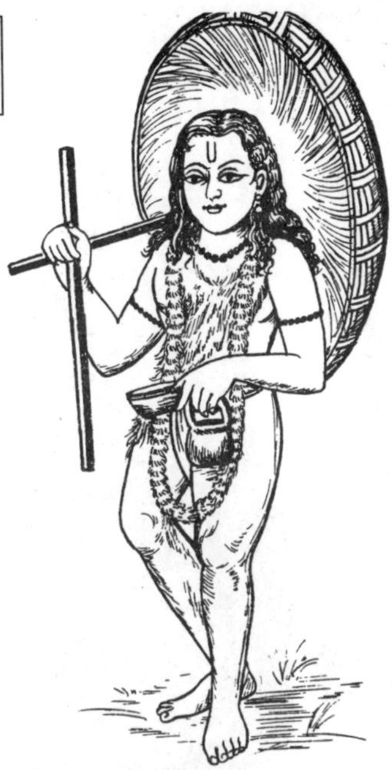

Vamana Avatar

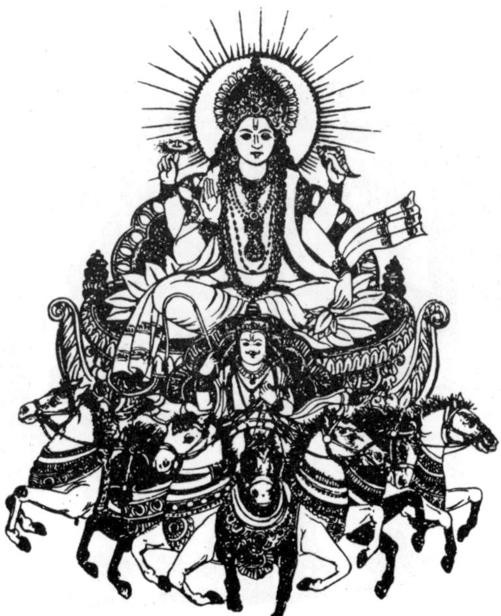

Sun God Surya

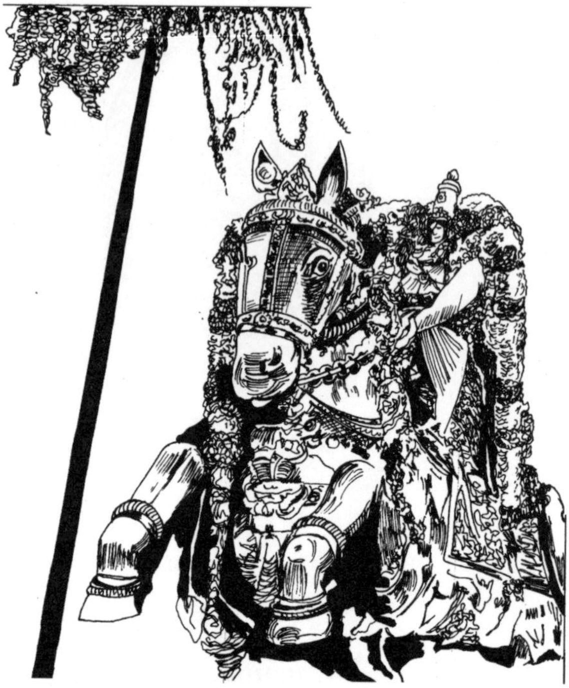

Procession of Goddess Kaveri

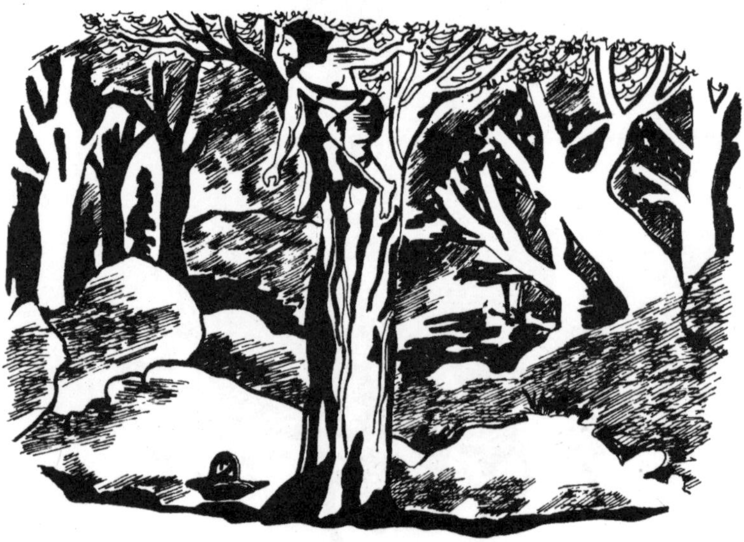

Legend of Sivaratri

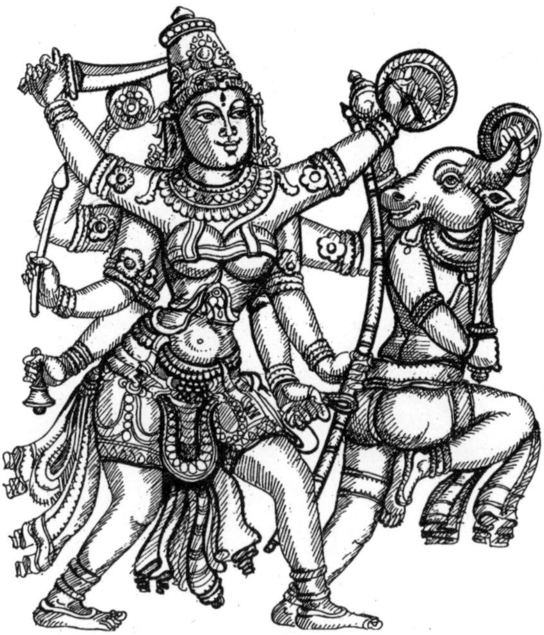

Durga Killing Mahishasura

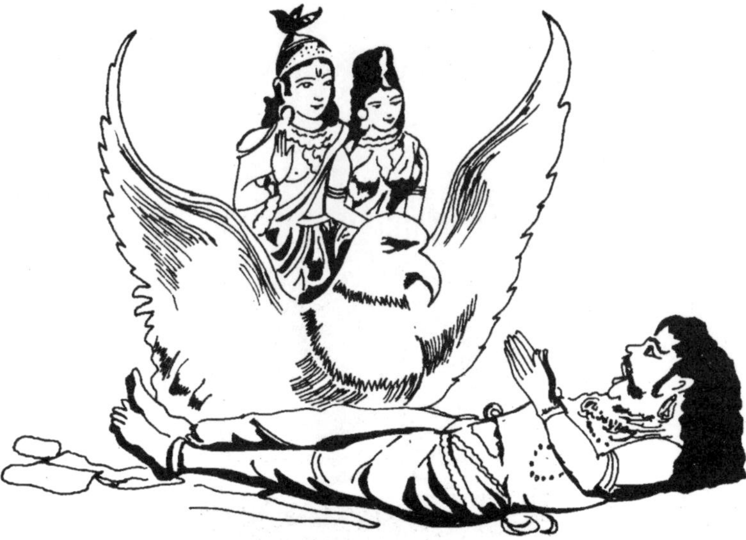

Legend of Deepawali

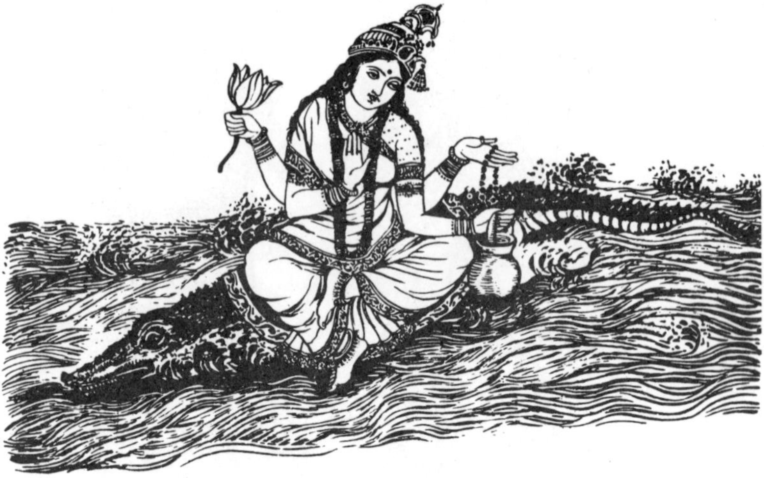

Goddess Ganga

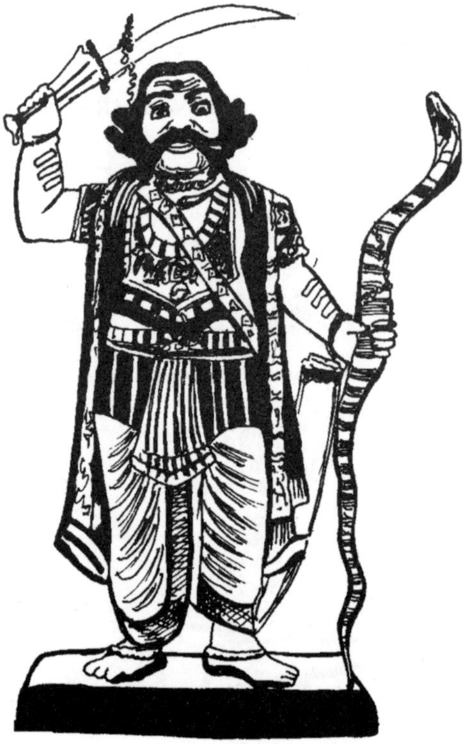

Statue of Mahishasura

Hindu religious practices are timed primarily with reference to the lunar months which include a complete lunar phase. In the case of the calendar of three southern states, Andhra Pradesh, Karnataka, and Tamil Nadu the phase is from one new moon to the next, a period of 29 to 30 days. In Kerala the name of the rasi or zodiac sign is given to the solar month. In the case of the north Indian calendar, the phase is calculated from one full moon to the next. Hence a festival may be celebrated on the same day but will fall on different calendar months, or it may be celebrated on different days in southern and northern India in accordance with the calendars.

Each lunar month is divided into 30 tithis, each tithi measuring the time taken for a twelve degree rotation of the moon around the earth. Astrological predictions and calculations, days for ceremonies and festivals are based on the tithi, lunar month, and the current year's almanac. As the lunar month is only of 354 days, tithis are added and adjusted to complete the 365 days of the solar calendar.

Thus each individual's predictions are made from the birth star, the zodiac sign, the ruling planet, and the phase of the moon in the star.

Order of Planets for Making Calculations

Tamil	Sanskrit	English
Surya	Surya	Sun
Chandra	Chandra	Moon
Chevvai	Mangal	Mars
Budhan	Budh	Mercury
Guru	Guru	Jupiter
Shukran	Shukra	Venus
Sani	Sani	Saturn
Rahu	Rahu	Nil
Ketu	Ketu	Nil

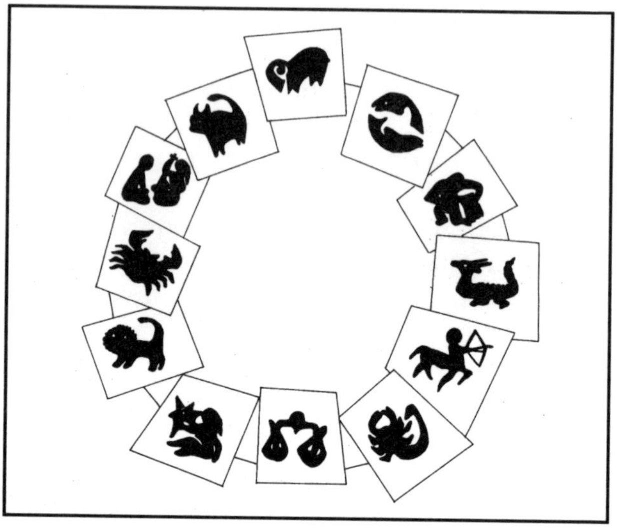

ZODIAC SIGNS

Zodiac Sign	**Ruling Planet, Rasi & Griha**	
Indian Name	**Sanskrit**	**European**
Mesha	Mangal	Mars
Rishabha	Shukra	Venus
Mithuna	Budh	Mercury
Kataka	Chandra	Moon
Simha	Surya	Sun
Kanya	Budh	Mercury
Tula	Shukra	Venus
Vrishchika	Mangal	Mars
Dhanur/Chopa	Brihaspati	Jupiter
Makara	Sani	Saturn
Kumbha	Sani	Saturn
Meena	Brihaspati	Jupiter

27 Stars and Corresponding Constellation (European) Names

Tamil	European
Ashwini	Part of Aries
Bharani	Musca
Karthikai	Pleiades
Rohini	Hyades
Mrigashirisham	Head of Orion
Tiruvathirai	Part of Orion
Punarpusam	Part of Gemini
Pusam	Part of Cancer
Ahilyam	Part of Cancer
Maham	Part of Leo
Puram	Part of Leo
Uthiram	Part of Leo
Hastham	Part of Corvus
Chitrai	Part of Virgo
Swathi	Part of Bootes
Visakam	Part of Libra and Scorpio
Anusham	Part of Libra and Scorpio
Kettai	Part of Scorpio
Moolam	Part of Scorpio
Puradam	Part of Scorpio
Uthiradam	Part of Sagittarius
Thiruvonam	Part of Sagittarius
Avittam	Part of Aquila
Sathayam	Part of Dolpin
Poorattathy	100 stars of Aquarius
Uthirattathy	Part of Pegasus

Revathy	Part of Andromeda 32 stars in Pisces

South Indian Annual Calendar of Rasis/Stars

The dates mentioned may change according to the calculations of movements of the sun in the particular year.

14 April–14 May (Chitrai—Chaitram)

Rasi	Mesha
Stars	Ashwini—4 qrs
	Bharani—4 qrs
	Karthikai—1 qr

15 May–14 June (Vaikasi—Vaisakham)

Rasi	Rishabha
Stars	Karthikai—3 qrs
	Rohini—4 qrs
	Mrigashirisham—2 qrs

15 June–14 July (Ani—Jeshtam)

Rasi	Mithunam
Stars	Mrigashirisham—2 qrs
	Tiruvathirai—4 qrs
	Punarpusam—3 qrs

15 July–14 August (Adi—Aashadam)

Rasi	Katakam
Stars	Punarpusam—1 qr
	Pusam—4 qrs
	Ahilyam—4 qrs

15 August–14 September (Avani—Shravanam)

Rasi	Simha
Stars	Maham—4 qrs
	Puram—4 qrs
	Uthiram—1 qr

15 September–14 October (Purattasi—Bhadrapadam)

Rasi	Kanya
Stars	Uthiram—3 qrs
	Hastham—4 qrs
	Chitrai—2 qrs

15 October–14 November (Aipasi—Aaswinam)

Rasi	Thulam
Stars	Chitrai—2 qrs
	Swathi—4 qrs
	Visakam—3 qrs

15 November–14 December (Karthikai—Karthikam)

Rasi	Vrishchikam
Stars	Visakam—1 qr
	Anusham—4 qrs
	Kettai—4 qrs

15 December–14 January (Marghazi—Aagrahayanam)

Rasi	Dhanus
Stars	Moolam—4 qrs
	Puradam—4 qrs
	Uthiradam—1 qr

15 January–14 February (Thai—Pausham)

Rasi	Makaram
Stars	Uthiradam—3 qrs
	Thiruvonam—4 qrs
	Avittam—2 qrs

15 February–14 March (Masi—Magham)

Rasi	Kumbham
Stars	Avittam—2 qrs
	Sathayam—4 qrs
	Poorattathy—3 qrs

15 March–14 April (Panguni—Phalguni)

Rasi	Meenam
Stars	Poorattathy—1 qr
	Uthirattathy—4 qrs
	Revathy—4 qrs

Comparative South, North and European Calendar

The annual calendar of North India has lunar months of 27 or 28 days. Every four years it is adjusted to the solar calendar so that variations are reduced. For astrological calculations the daily movements of the moon into each of 27 stars are taken into account. Compared to the lunar calendar of North India, South Indian calendar months are two to three weeks behind. The names of the months, name of the era, approximate comparative Gregorian (European) months are given below.

Calendar of Months according to South Indian, North Indian (lunar months), and Gregorian (solar months)

Tamil	Sanskrit	Telugu	Malayalam	European
Chitrai	Vaisakh	Chaitram	Kanni	Mid-April–Mid-May
Vaikasi	Jeshta	Vaisakha	Tulam	Mid-May–Mid-June
Ani	Aashada	Jyeshta	Vrichigam	Mid-June–Mid-July
Adi	Shravana	Aashada	Dhanur	Mid-July–Mid-August
Avani	Bhadrapada	Shravana	Makaram	Mid-Aug.–Mid-Sep.
Purattasi	Aaswina	Bhadrapada	Kumbam	Mid-Sep.–Mid-Oct.
Aipasi	Karthika	Asweja	Meenam	Mid-Oct.–Mid-Nov.
Karthikai	Aagrahayan	Karthika	Medam	Mid-Nov.–Mid-Dec.
Marghazi	Paush	Aagrahayan	Edavam	Mid-Dec.–Mid-Jan.
Thai	Magh	Paush	Mithunam	Mid-Jan.–Mid-Feb.
Masi	Phalguna	Magh	Karkadagam	Mid-Feb.–Mid-March
Panguni	Chaitra	Phalguna	Chingham	Mid-March–Mid-April

Uttarayanam and Dakshinayanam

The sun's journey towards the Tropic of Cancer is the Uttarayana. Starting from the winter solstice, the period Jan. 15–July 15 is considered auspicious for feasts, festivity, and celebrations. The sun's journey southwards, towards the Tropic of Capricorn, is astrologically not considered auspicious. A number of religious practices, fasts, and pujas are customary in the period June 22nd onward. This is based on the legend that the region north of the equator is the region of Devas, who became powerful during the winter. The region south of the equator belonged to the Asuras or demons, who wielded power in the next six months.

The beliefs were also based on the position of the sun, which symbolized prosperity and survival of all living beings. In Uttarayanam, the sun became stronger as it journeyed northward. Harvest ripened fruits and vegetables abounded.

It was a time of prosperity. In Dakshinayanam, the waning period of the sun, shorter days and longer nights, made it agriculturally a lean season.

On the first day of the sun's northern journey, Sankranti, newly harvested grains are cooked and offered to the sun. At Ganga Sagar in Bengal where the Ganga enters the sea, a grand fair is held. Hundreds of thousands of people go by boat to Ganga Sagar island for a dip in the sea.

Rahu Kalam—The Inauspicious Time

In Hindu astrology, the movement of the stars and planets caused by the gravitational pull, affects all living beings. The stars and planets as well as the karma (the action in the previous birth) influence our thoughts, emotions and behaviour.

The hours when Rahu is in power every day are considered most inauspicious for any venture, journey, or important activity.

The Legend

Rahu and Ketu, the planets with a negative influence, are shadow planets or "chhaya griha" which cause eclipse and cast dark shadows on human beings. The legend goes back to the epic age when the ocean was being churned by Devas and Asuras and priceless treasures were distributed between the two. When amrit or nectar giving immortality was churned out, there was a struggle between the two groups to possess amrit. Vishnu in the form of Mohini, a beautiful woman, intervened. She distributed the nectar first to the gods. The demon commander-in-chief Rahu hid between the Sun and the Moon and managed to drink the nectar before Sun and Moon gods raised a cry. Vishnu's chakra beheaded Rahu, who cursed the sun and moon with periodic eclipses. But Rahu and Ketu, the head and body of the demon, were immortal and took their place among planets exerting negative forces on living beings.

The Timings of Rahu

Sunday	4.30–6.00 p.m.
Monday	7.30–9.00 a.m.
Tuesday	3.00–4.30 p.m.
Wednesday	12.00–1.30 p.m.
Thursday	1.30–3.00 p.m.
Friday	10.30–12.00 p.m.
Saturday	9.00–10.30 a.m.

These times are avoided for new ventures, activities, ceremonies or journeys and for all auspicious occasions.

Chapter 2

STAGES IN THE SPIRITUAL JOURNEY

KARMAS OF LIFE

(Spiritual aspect of an individual's life)

The living faith of Hinduism is expressed through the cycle of Karmas marking different stages of life. Of these, one is for boys that is Upanayana Karma; the rest being common to boys and girls.

The Karmas or sanskaras are sacraments that start before birth, and continue up to the ceremonies performed after death.

The sanskaras enhance the individual's status and values in life, help him to avoid negative thinking, and equip him to reach the goal of a spiritual life or divine life.

The sanskaras are said to have been developed and institutionalized over a long period, in order to give stability to the community and meet the needs of the time. To this day, they help to give positive directions to an individual's growth. They answer the individual's need to give the chief events of his life a deeper spiritual significance and to find a continuity and purpose in the journey of life.

There are over 40 sanskaras both religious and social in nature. Of these, six are commonly undertaken and mark important stages in life. Along with sanskaras are birth anniversaries and observance of amavasya and purnamashi (new moon and full moon).

Jatakarma and Namakarma—The Sanskara after Birth

It is the ceremony of giving an infant (both boy as well as girl) a name and identity and is performed on the 11th or 22nd day after birth.

DESCRIPTION

A priest purifies the house by sprinkling holy water (made sacred by mantras) in all the rooms of the house. Then the havan (fire) is made ready. The couple sit before the havan, with the infant on the mother's lap. The priest announces the year, month, date, place and time of birth, star of the child (nakshatra), the ruling planet of the star and the rasi, or zodiac sign. Then the name of the child is whispered into the right ear of the child by the father and/or mother.

On a banana leaf, baked rice is spread out, betel leaves, arecanut, and fruits are kept. Mantras are chanted and ghee is offered to the sacred fire invoking all deities to bless the child. The cooked rice is offered to gods as neivedyam. A spoonful of the same rice is then fed to the baby as prasadam.

At the conclusion arati is taken. Elders, friends and relatives bless the infant with akshada and give presents.

Cradle Ceremony

Both the ceremonies, that is naming and cradling, one religious and the other social ceremony, can be performed either on the same morning or one in the morning and the other in the evening of the 11th or 22nd day. Friends and relatives are invited for the ceremony.

DESCRIPTION

A place in the room, facing east, is selected. Kolam or rangoli is drawn. Two planks for seating the couple are kept next to the rangoli. The planks are decorated with lines drawn with rice flour. Then a tray or banana leaf filled with whole wheat or paddy is kept on the kolam.

The aunt or uncle of the infant writes down the three names of the infant on the paddy with the forefinger. After each name is written, the grain is smoothened with the hand. Generally, the parents and the two grandparents after consultation among themselves suggest the names. The mother then whispers the names into the infant's right ear.

A cloth is placed on the grain and the infant is placed on the tray. A black coloured cord decorated with a small bell for boys and small leaf for girl child made of either silver or gold is tied around the infant's stomach. This cord is known as "arana" which is meant to protect the child from any harm by evil forces. Then the mother takes the baby on her lap and feeds a few spoons of milk and honey mixture.

A decorated cradle is kept ready for the baby. A stone is placed in it first, symbolically to draw evil forces away from the child. Then the stone is removed and the baby is put in the cradle and rocked and lullabies are sung.

Sweets, savouries like sundal and hot and cold drinks are served to all guests and relatives. Then the ceremony concludes with traditional feast.

Annaprasanam

The ceremony takes place when the infant is three months, or six months old or a year old. The first feeding of staple (solid) food (anna literally meaning rice/wheat) is done. This is the second important Karma for the infant.

The parents are seated on two planks and the infant is placed on the mother's lap. A mixture of honey and milk is kept ready. The mother gives the infant three sips of the mixture.

Chuda Karma

Traditionally the first haircut was done before the child was one year old or during the age of three years. The offering of hair is done to the deity of the family or to any ishta devata. The father sits with the child before the havan. He does havan, repeating the mantras recited by the priest, then with a pair of scissors he cuts a little hair from different parts of the head. First at the front, then at the right, then at the back and lastly from the left. He washes his hand and does prokshana, completing the ceremony.

Akshara Abhyasam

When a child completes four years, on Vijayadasami day, his father or teacher chants the mantras of akshara abhyasa by writing the mantra "Om Namo Narayana" or "Om Namah Sivaya" on whole wheat or paddy grain piled on a banana leaf placed in front of the puja. Then the father or teacher holding the hand of the infant in his hand starts writing the mantra at first and then the alphabets of the language on the grain. Later the child is taken to the regular school for admission.

Upanayana and Yagyopavita

In Vedic times the upanayana or donning of the sacred thread initiated a boy of five or six years into the disciplined life of a brahmachari, who attained the highest gyana, the brahma gyana for the good of all. Brahmacharya is the first of the four ashramas into which a man's life is divided. The other three being grihasta, the life of a householder performing all activities for the good of his family and society, followed by vanaprastha, the retirement into a forest for a self-sufficient life free of social obligations, and the final stage, sanyasa, which was a time for prayer and meditation for the good of all.

The yagyopavita ceremony practised in a few communities is done on an auspicious day, for a boy of 11 years or more. On the day of the ceremony, he undergoes all the karmas undertaken after birth, so that he is deemed to have taken birth a second time, starting a new pure life after wearing the thread sanctified by the recitation of mantras before a sacred fire or havan.

The boy is initiated into Brahmagyana through mantras and learns the Gayatri japa from his guru. He promises to wear the sacred thread and devote himself to the attainment of gyana, not for his own material gain, but for attaining the spiritual knowledge and power to do good to all. Thus he accepts his role and responsibility in society.

Vivaham (Wedding)

One of the most important karmas of Hindu sacraments is the marriage or vivaha karma. The ancient Dharmashastras and Grihasutras describe marriage as the second stage after the student life of Brahmacharya when the duties of a householder are assumed. The objective of marriage as described in the scriptures is to unite a man and a woman mentally, physically and spiritually in a commitment to raise a family, serve society, continue the race and maintain the spiritual heritage. Marriage

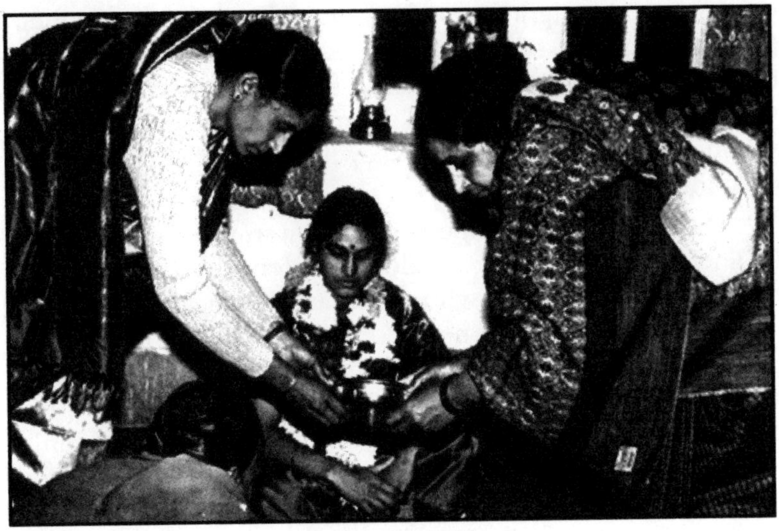

Arati to the Bride

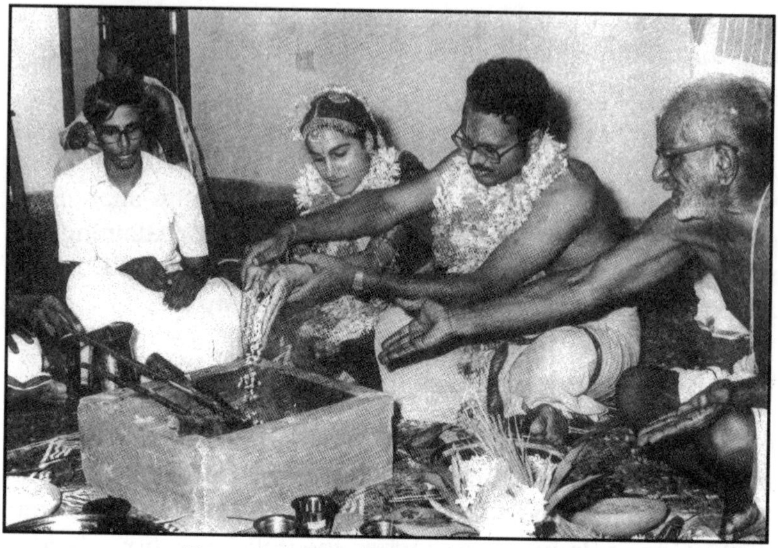

Homa invoking the guardian Deities

enables the couple to fulfil religious duties and rituals which can only be undertaken jointly by the couple. This includes yagyas, pujas, pilgrimages, fasts and observances. By their joint performance of duties, the couple becomes a powerful motivating central force in society, the wife has an equal role with the husband as the sahadharmini. As the couple fulfils spiritual and social obligations, they move together on the path of spiritual progress.

Matching of horoscope is important in the vivaha karma. In ancient times, when a child was born, the parents went to seers and holy men who made astronomical calculations and predictions for the new born child. The birth star, the position of the planets at birth, their ascendance or descent at birth, the zodiac sign are all important for making the calculations. Thus it is necessary to know the place of birth, its latitude and longitude which will help to determine the ruling planet, the phases of the moon, the birth star, the lagna and rasi or zodiac sign.

Horoscopes of a boy and a girl are matched before marriage and a minimum of 5 compatible aspects are considered essential for a happy marriage. The horoscope helps to fix the time and date of important events in life such as an engagement, a career, purchase of a house or a start of a new venture and the astrological birthday every year. As each planet and rasi is associated with a particular colour your horoscope helps in selection of stones and jewels which will be beneficial to health and welfare.

A south Indian marriage follows most of the vedic rituals including exchange of garlands, and exchange of marriage vows during the saptapadi or seven rounds made around the sacred fire. The vows include promise of right conduct, respect and love for the partner, setting up of a good home, raising children, care of parents, charity and hospitality to others.

In a south Indian marriage, great importance is given to the mangalyadharanam during kanya dan or giving away of the bride. The mangalyam commonly known as thali is a kind of marriage talisman for the bride and is an essential

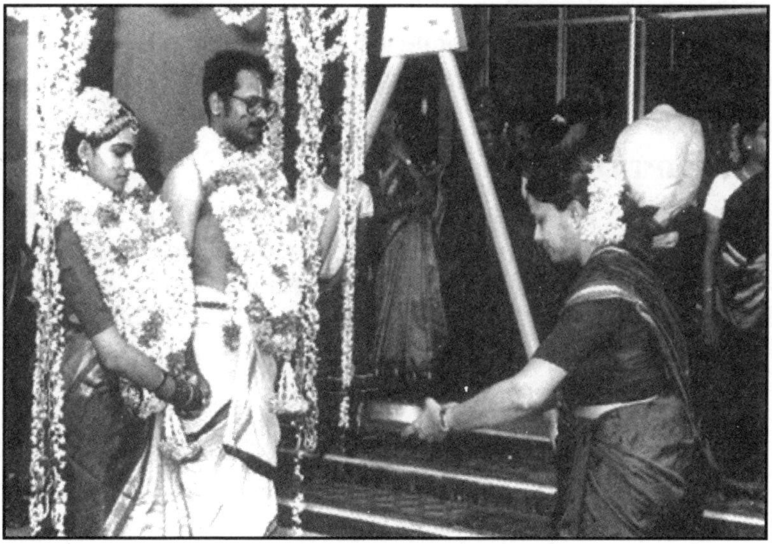

Arati to Bride & Groom

jewellery for all married women. The golden thali with gold or stone studded symbols and pendants is blessed by the chanting of mantras, blessed by all the assembled elders, and then tied round the bride's neck by the groom. Three knots are tied; the first two are tied by the groom and the third knot is tied by the groom's sister. The first is for Brahma, the couple are committed to raise a family and live a long and happy life. The second knot is for Vishnu, the couple are committed to shelter and protect the family. The third knot is to do away with all negative thoughts, base actions and instincts like anger, greed and lust.

In the boy's or girl's life wedding is the important ceremony leading to poochootal or ceremonial flower decoration and seemantham (blessing of the new comer before birth).

Poochootal, Valaikappu—Ceremonial Flower Decoration

The ceremony takes place on a suitable day during the sixth month of pregnancy. It is an occasion for a social get-together to raise the morale of the would-be mother and enable her to receive the blessings and goodwill of all for a safe confinement and a healthy baby.

DESCRIPTION

Traditionally poochootal was performed in the maternal home, but any convenient place can be selected. A priest selects the date and time. Women, relatives and friends are invited.

For arranging a poochootal you need:

1. Glass bangles, various colours and sizes—3 dozen
   (for presenting a pair of bangles to all lady guests)
2. Fancy bangles and sets of bangles—2 dozen
   (for the would-be mother)
3. Gold and silver wire twisted to form a bangle—1 pair each

4. Black sari and blouse—1 set
5. Three neem (margosa) stalks twisted in a circle
6. Puja items like kumkum, flowers, bowl of akshada (rice mixed with turmeric), a small bowl of darba grass
7. Small items like pencil, eraser, small Bhagwat Gita, baby's feeding cup, cowries (sea shells), wooden doll etc.
8. Blouse pieces for giving as gift to 5 or 7 sumangalis
9. Wooden plank for seating the would-be mother.

Seemantham—The centre parting on the head ceremony

The ceremony usually known as Pumsavana Seemantham is performed at the end of the 7th month of the first conception. The objective is to purify the womb in which the child's physical and mental traits are evolved. By means of the puja, the growing child will develop best qualities and characteristics. In days gone by the puja was performed in the third month, for ensuring the birth of a son.

DESCRIPTION

Husband and wife participate in the ceremony. They wear the traditional style of dhoti and sari for the function. The start is with the Udaga shanti (udaga meaning water). A Kalash is filled with water, mango leaves are tied to the neck, and a coconut is placed on top. The husband does japa and recites mantras with darba grass in his hand. He touches the Kalash at intervals with the darba grass. After japa is over, the water charged with mantras is poured over the couple, to the chanting of mantras—the husband draws a rekha or line on the forehead of wife symbolizing the transfer of gyana or knowledge to the unborn.

The couple change their clothes and are seated before the sacred fire for performing homa. Then seemantham is done in the centre parting by drawing the darba grass dipped in holy water thrice along the parting. The husband does homa, pouring ghee into the fire, 5 varieties of flower buds are given to two girl children (who are before the age of puberty) to mash together on a stone. When homa is over the mashed buds are tied to the saree end of the wife by the husband. A cloth is draped around the couple. The saree end is squeezed and a drop of flower essence is put into the wife's nostrils. Mantras are chanted. Then the wife's parents give gifts of new clothes to the couple and arati is done to conclude the ceremony.

The ladies in the group assemble around the wife who is seated on a chair, special songs for the occasion are sung. The husband's sister presents flowers and sari to the wife. All invitees participate in a traditional feast.

Chapter 3

CELEBRATIONS AND OBSERVANCES

The 60th and 80th birthdays are celebrated by children and grandchildren, who organize the celebration, and invite family and friends for a grand get-together, and receive the blessings of the couple. The celebration is really thanksgiving to the creator for giving a long life span to the couple.

Sashtiabdapoorthi—The 60th Birthday Celebration

The celebration of the 60th birthday is like a marriage ceremony. An auspicious time in the morning is selected. A new "thali" which may be strung on a yellow thread or gold chain is made. Before the day of the celebration, a pot or Kalash is filled with water, mango leaves are tied round the neck and a coconut is placed on top, and by recitation of mantras, the water is made holy. Varuna, the god of water, is invoked by the mantras by priests holding Kusa grass in their hands. The sacred water is believed to be charged or magnetized with spiritual energy to remove mental and bodily impurities.

The Kalash or pot is placed on a rangoli covered with paddy or rice or on a wooden plank on which rangoli is drawn and covered with rice. The sacred water can be used for purifying a room or a house by sprinkling of drops of water. It is used before ceremonies like upanayanam, or after child birth to purify the household, and the family.

In the 60th birthday celebration the udaga shanti is done by pouring the water magnetized with "japa" and "akshara shakti" over the couple. Then the wife is decorated like a bride. Her feet are anointed with turmeric paste, and hair is braided with flowers. The couple wear new clothes, and the sister or daughter-in-law ties the third knot of the new thali on the wife's neck, after homam is done. The couple are believed to acquire divine spiritual powers and their family and guests do namaskar to receive their blessings. A traditional feast and giving of presents mark the occasion.

Sathabhishekam—The 80th Birthday Celebration

The 80th birthday of a man or a woman who has seen a thousand moons is an even more auspicious occasion for the family. The celebration starts with the udaga shanti, pouring of sacred water, for which japa had been done earlier. The water is poured on the couple by relatives and children through a sieve with big holes in it. Then the couple change clothes and are seated before the homa. After chanting of mantras, arati is done. Then the family and all invitees do namaskaram to the couple and receive their blessings.

Kanakabhishekam

The celebration is for the birth of a son's son's son (great-grandson through sons). The celebration is similar to that of the satabhishekam. However small gold coins and precious stones are placed in the Kalash of holy water. Later these are distributed to grandchildren and relatives. The holy water is poured on the couple by the grandson and his wife and great-grandson. It is a happy occasion for a family gathering and for receiving the blessings of elders.

In addition to all the above, girl children have two more karmas performed in their lives.

Sumangali Prarthna

A sumangali is a woman whose husband is alive. She is believed to have immense spiritual force, even after her death.

The Puja is done to invite and get the blessings of a mother, grandmother, paternal grandmother or grand-aunt or other relatives who passed away in their husbands' lifetimes (as sumangalis). Sumangali Puja is done before or after celebration of a wedding, before an upanayanam or seemantham. It is also done before the shraddha, the annual ceremony observed after the death of an individual, particularly a mother or grandmother. The tradition of sumangali puja is an unbroken one in many families and is continued by each generation without fail.

The Puja is done to invoke the good wishes and blessings of the departed sumangalis for the function, and for the couple (if it is a marriage) or mother-to-be in case of a seemantham. The offerings made to the departed sumangali also help her to attain moksha or liberation from re-birth.

The Legend

The story is told of Sri Raghavendraswami who renounced the world and became a Sanyasi. Unable to bear a life of solitude, his wife Lakshmi committed suicide. Her spirit could find no rest and appeared before the saint, seeking guidance. He blessed her and said that on her path to moksha she would be helped by the "punya" (or virtue) gained by Sumangali Puja done before or after family functions and observances. The Puja done in the name of his wife gradually became a family tradition for invoking the continuing good-will and blessings of departed sumangalis.

DESCRIPTION

Two usual ways of Sumangali prayer are described below, these are modified according to family customs.

One way of doing the prayer is to select the main living sumangali in the family, who may be the eldest married daughter or aunt. One of them is the main sumangali. If neither is available, a close relation may be invited for the Puja. In addition, five to seven other married relatives or friends are invited. The main sumangali is presented with a sari, blouse piece, kumkum, flowers, a small mirror and comb, with pan supari, coconut and dakshina or coins. The others are given the same items except the sari, in place of which a blouse piece is presented.

The sumangalis assemble outside the Puja room at the auspicious time. Their feet are washed and anointed with turmeric. The start of the Puja is "announced" to the departed soul by a few claps with both hands. After this invocation, the sumangalis enter the room and partake of a traditional feast in memory of the departed sumangali.

They first do namaskar to the wooden plank on which a new sari and blouse piece is kept (in case of a wedding, the bridal sari and jewels are kept on the plank). Then the guests are seated and partake in a feast. One banana leaf is kept before the plank. Food is first served on this leaf as an offering to the departed sumangali. The food is then eaten by the main sumangali present at the function symbolizing its acceptance by the departed soul. Afterwards pan supari is given and gifts are presented.

The other method is to have the day and time selected by a priest. Then select five to seven married relatives and girls who have to send their saris and blouses in advance. These are dipped in water, then dried and kept in separate plastic bags, for wearing in the Puja, after a bath. A new sari, preferably of the traditional nine yards, is similarly washed and kept for the Puja.

In the morning of the Puja, select a place facing east inside a room. Draw a rangoli, place a wooden palaha (plank or takht) on it and draw a kolam in front of the plank. You can draw a kolam with rice flour and water in front of the house. Now place the new sari, blouse piece, and pan supari, turmeric, banana, flowers, small mirror and comb, kumkum in a container. On the wooden plank keep a small tray near the kolam, and light an oil lamp and agarbatti, keep akshada and flowers. (If the Puja is being done before a marriage, the wedding sari, thali and trinkets are kept for the Puja.) Containers with gingelly oil, shikakai powder or shampoo, sandal paste or perfumed powders etc. are placed in the Puja.

When the ladies are assembled outside the room, they are ushered in after clapping of hands to invoke the presence of the departed sumangali. Then the hostess invites each lady, places some oil on her head, anoints her neck and hands with sandal paste, her face with turmeric. A tilak or kumkum mark is placed on the forehead. Then each is given some shampoo or shikakai powder, oil and perfumed powder for the bath, along with the clothes washed the previous day.

Next, banana leaves with pointed ends are placed in a row (pointed ends towards the left), the leaves may all face north, one leaf is placed in front of the Puja plank. When the ladies return from the bath wearing their washed saris, their feet are anointed with turmeric paste and washed. Flowers are given for their hair. Then the hostess calls out the names of the departed sumangalis and invites them to the feast. A little sandalwood paste is placed on the sari kept in the Puja as a token of honouring the departed ones. The invitees all place some akshada and flowers on the Puja sari, and do namaskar. Then they are seated and the feast is served in a traditional anti-clockwise order as follows:

> A spoonful of three fruits cut and mixed, raita (pachadi), two types of kootu (vegetables cooked with green gram and spices), sweet pachadi (sweet raita), two vegetables, a spoonful of payasam, sweets, vada, followed by sambar, rasam, curds and payasam.

After the feast, the ladies sit on a new rug or mat, and are served dried ginger and jaggery syrup, buttermilk, betel leaves, arecanut and lime. Before leaving, kumkum and sandalwood paste is applied and gifts are given.

After departure of the sumangalis, the rest of the family can be served with the feast. The hostess then eats food served on the banana leaf kept in the Puja.

When the Puja is done on occasions other than a marriage, in place of the wedding sari, a new sari, blouse piece and other items are arranged on the plank.

In the traditional feast for sumangali prayers, the menu is as for the shraddha or annual ceremony for parents and ancestors, and consists of payasam, sweet mango pachadi, vada, cucumber with soaked green gram, curd pachadi, four vegetables, two kootus, sambar, cumin seed-black pepper rasam, black gram vada, wafers, papad and pickles. Adirasam, Semolina appam, gingelly laddu in addition to payasam are served.

The sumangali prarthana is associated with both happy and sad events. It is done either before kanyadan i.e. a marriage, or if the lady of the house dies in the status of sumangali.

Ceremonies after Death

The ceremonies after death are performed in the belief of existence of atma (soul) after death. The purpose of the ceremonies is to enable the soul to break its earthly bonds, merge with the Supreme Being and achieve moksha or liberation from the cycle of re-birth.

The ceremonies are generally performed by the eldest son, or another male member from the paternal side who does all the rituals from lighting the funeral pyre to the various rituals which conclude on the 12th day, when the soul finally breaks its bondage and leaves the earth. Hence the importance of the son who is to give agni to the dead parents and do the shraddha i.e. annual ceremony for parents along with three generations of ancestors on both sides, helping them in the pitri loka or abode of ancestors.

The priests performing the ceremonies after death do not perform other ceremonies or vratas. The thirteenth day after death is a day of rejoicing—the house is purified and the entire family comes together for a grand feast blessed by the departed soul. New clothes are worn. It is a day of thanksgiving.

Shraddha

Shraddha is reverence to the parents and ancestors by way of annual ceremony. It is observed according to the astrological thithi or date of death. The shraddha is not a funeral ceremony, but reverential homage paid by all relatives to the departed soul. The pinda or offerings of rice, flour, gram and water sprinkled with darba grass are nutrients for the soul which has undergone the numerous ceremonies after death.

The sastras have minutely described the performing of shraddha. The reason given for the ceremony is that until it is performed, the soul is torn by its negative forces, its longing for worldly life. The shraddha strengthens the soul and gives a firm and positive spiritual force by which it can attain the blissful abode of the Divine fathers—the pitri loka.

In the shraddha ceremonies, repeated exhortations are made by the priests to the departing soul: "May this funeral offering be acceptable to thee." The exhortation is repeated for offering of cloth, pot of water and til seeds (sesame). On the tenth day, the spirit is strong and whole and reaches the doors of Yama, the lord of death. It is a day of joy. The shanti homa is done to purify the home. On the 12th day, it is believed that the spirit joins the souls of the ancestors. The family gets together on the 13th day. Kolam is drawn. The family wear new clothes and partake a grand feast.

The annual shraddha is performed for parents, grandparents and close relatives. Gaya in Bihar is mentioned in the ancient texts as a place where reverent offerings to ancestors are most acceptable. If a man is too poor to afford cooked food, he may offer raw rice or just lift up his hands in devotion to his ancestors.

A special shraddha is performed on Mahalaya amavasya on the 15th day after the full moon, in the Tamil month of Purattasi. On this day the offerings are made together to the souls of all ancestors, who may not have been liberated and are awaiting release from the world through the offerings made with piety and reverence by their descendants.

DESCRIPTION

After early morning bath, a sankalpa or resolve to undertake shraddha is made, giving the year, month, date (tithi) and person in whose name the shraddha is undertaken. Mantras are recited and pinda, or balls of rice flour and gram are offered along with water and til (sesame) which is sprinkled on darba grass. In conclusion, the prayer is made so that the offerings be accepted by the spirit, who will bless the bereaved family and depart.

Tarpan (meaning satisfaction) is a periodic offering to ancestors on the day of their death, i.e. it starts with sankalpa. Taking a little water in the hand, the year, month and astrological day of shraddha (tithi) is recited. Ancestors of both parental houses are invoked and water is sprinkled on the darba grass along with til. Tarpan may be done on 12 new moon and 12 full moon days. It is done at the start of the month, or on the Indian new year's day, at the start and end of lunar and solar eclipses. The blessings of the ancestors give strength and solace to their families, help them survive and flourish.

Etiquette in visiting a bereaved family

The house of bereavement is a place of reverence for the dead person who is now an atma or immortal soul. When a death occurs, family members are not expected to spread the news of death. Friends and acquaintances are to convey the news to all who knew or had dealings with the deceased. The cooking fire is not lit in the bereaved house till the body is disposed of. Generally neighbours supply food to the family. The concept is that no fire should be lit in the home, until the cremation fire is extinguished. Elder members of relatives and friends visit the bereaved house and convey their condolences. No flowers or gifts are taken. The members of the bereaved family receive them silently without greeting them as is done on other occasions. The visitors offer sympathy and remain seated for a while in silence. Then they depart without the customary farewell. Any convenient time, preferably the morning, is selected for the visit. It is customary to take a bath after the visit to the house of a bereaved family for cleaning all negative feelings and forces. Usually Monday, Tuesday and Friday are avoided. Visitors do not eat anything in the bereaved household till the thirteenth day is over.

Chapter 4

FASTS, VRATAS AND BELIEFS

(Physical and spiritual control of individual during life)

Fasts or Vratas are undertaken as a means of purifying mind and body, preventing impure thoughts and negative forces from entering the mind, and developing ethical, moral and spiritual forces which lead the individual on the path of salvation. The system of fast is akin to yoga in that it helps to increase one's will-power and control over the mind. Hence the saying that what is a fast to the body is a feast to the mind.

Fasts differ from ceremonies and festivals as they are not part of community activity. It is left to the individual to select any fast or no fast at all. Similarly, the number of fasts, and the deity or concept on which the fast is undertaken are from a person's own choice. A person undertaking a silent, solitary fast has lower stress levels, reduced blood pressure and a positive and stronger mental capacity. The ancient rishis describing the need for fasts or vratas have said that only if the gross elements (sthool sharir) of body and mind are controlled and slowly reduced, can the finer or subtle elements and powers (sookshma sharir) gradually gain ascendance, helping the individual towards self-illumination and self-realization. The immediate purpose is thus the gradual awakening of the 'Kundalini' the inner energy of the individual, depicted as a snake coiled around the centres of thought, action and will-power.

DESCRIPTION

The fast can be of any duration. It can be repeated in weekly, monthly or yearly cycles. It can be daily for each day of the week for a certain period. The period of 48 days forming a 'Mandala' or circle can be selected. A periodic fast can be undertaken seven times or more frequently. The fast may be kept very strictly even without drinking of water. It can be kept avoiding certain foods like cereals, sour foods; if for health reasons a total fast is not feasible, you can take, say, non-cereal foods, milk, fruits which will be easily digested. In general foods such as spices, meat, or strong flavours of onion, or garlic are avoided, as they create Tamas or negative forces they do not allow the body to relax in meditation and thus defeat the purpose of the fast.

Importance is given to the sincerity of the fast and prayer, once undertaken, the vratas must be completed without fail.

Once the mind wavers, the devotee will not be able to reach the goal.

After early morning bath the devotee sits on an asana (a seat of cloth or wood) in the pose for meditation. Holding some water in the cup of his hand, he makes a vow or sankalpa describing the nature of the vrata and the purity of mind and body with which the vrata is undertaken. In the case of a fast for a deity or a planet, the relevant slokas and stories are narrated. After prayers and meditation, arati is done. At the conclusion of the vrata the deity is invoked again and the puja is concluded. Mantras are recited to seek divine blessing for breaking the fast. Meditation and daily prayers are continued after the fast.

The Days of the Week

Each day of the week is named after a planet which is believed to have both beneficial and harmful effects on human beings. The prayers offered on each day invoke the blessings of the ruling planet and the presiding deity. A fast is kept, and the story of the planet is narrated before meditation and prayer.

Observing a fast on the day of the week

As on most vratas there is no obligation to observe fast on a particular day of the week. But once a decision is taken to meditate on a selected day of the week, the fast is continued for a seven week period or the fast may be for every Monday or any other day in a particular month of the year. The fast may be for half a day or full day.

DESCRIPTION

Fast is kept on the day of the puja. After the morning bath light the oil lamp in the puja, offer flowers and incense. The sankalpa invoking the deity on whom you are to meditate is recited. The mantras (Pravacha) of the deity are recited a number of times and meditation is done. Avoiding all negative thoughts and actions; practising ahimsa and eating vegetarian food after the fast are essential for a person observing a vrata.

After prayers, offerings of prasad, fruit, coconut or gold and silver are made. The three essential aspects are japa (meditation), homa (offerings to God) and dana (giving gifts or prasad to others). Before puja is completed, the story of the planet or deity is repeated and arati is done.

The purpose of silence, solitude and meditation during a fast is to avoid expressing our own ego during the fast and restore the power of inner spirit through concentration and meditation. It is a means of straightening out our lives, developing self-control, and setting forth on an inner journey which can bring rich rewards of peace and contentment.

The Legend

Many legends narrate the success of vows undertaken with sincerity and devotion by people from all walks of life. Lives of Savitri, Anasuya, Andal, Meerabai, Karaikkal Amma and others show that unattainable goals can be attained by channellising the consciousness towards an objective.

The story of the naming of the different days of the week is interesting. According to ancient Indian astronomers, planets are fixed in their order of placement in the sky and rotate in their own orbits around the sun. In the first dawn the sun was visible in the 'hora' or hour of dawn and hence the first day of the week was named Ravivar after the sun (Sunday). In the 24th hora the moon rose on the horizon and the second day was named Somvar after the moon. Similarly, subsequent days were named Mangalvar, Budhvar, Brihaspativar, Shukarvar and Sani, the planet seen on the 7th day, gave his name to Sanivar (Saturday).

DAYS OF THE WEEK IN TAMIL

(Ruling Deities and Fasts)

Fasts are kept in the name of the planet of the day as well as the associated deities whose special qualities and powers are invoked by prayer and meditation.

GNAYIRU *(Sunday, Ravivar)*

The sun is the ruling deity, Aditya Hridayam, the mantras invoking the sun are recited nine times at dawn. Rama avatar, descended from the sun, is worshipped. Red flowers and red sandalwood are offered. Prayers are offered to the sun for ensuring good health, strong eyesight, and preventing or curing skin ailments.

THINGAL *(Monday, Somvar)*

The ruling planet is the moon. It is a special day for meditating on Lord Siva with whose blessings happy marriages take place, and family life brings fulfilment. Meals are taken once a day, generally in the afternoon. Fasting on the amavasya or night of the new moon has a special significance.

SEWWAI *(Tuesday, Mangalvar)*

The ruling planet is Mars. It is the day special to Hanuman, powerful protector from danger and disaster. In south India, it is the day of Murugan or Subramania, the warrior son of Lord Siva. He protects devotees from diseases of all kinds.

BUDHAN *(Wednesday, Budhvar)*

The ruling planet is Mercury. It is the day for Hayagriva, the horse-headed avatar of Vishnu who dived into the ocean and rescued the Vedas. Prayers on the day are for scholarship and sacred learning.

VYAZHAN *(Thursday, Brihaspativar)*

Jupiter is the ruling planet. Hanuman, son of the Wind God Vayu, who protects the weak, gives courage in the face of a crisis and strengthens will-power, is worshipped. It is a special day for worship in the famous shrine of the child Krishna at Guruvayoor in Kerala. Ayyappan the warrior son of Vishnu in the form of Mohini and Siva is worshipped at Ayyappa temple. In Karnataka, it is the special day of Raghavendraswami who showed the way to achieve spiritual powers. For Sai Baba devotees, Thursday is a significant day for prayers and meditation.

VELLI *(Friday, Shukarvar)*

The day is of the planet Shukra (Venus). It is a day to remember all forms of Shakti, and Lakshmi goddess of wealth. The goddesses are worshipped and prayers are made for family affection, love and prosperity. White clothes are worn and offerings of rice and white flowers are made.

SANI *(Saturday, Sanivar)*

The day of the powerful planet Saturn is also the day for the worship of the navagriha, the nine planets that influence our destiny. Black is the colour associated with Saturn. Offerings of til and oil are made. Black clothing is worn. The influence of Saturn on an individual's Zodiac sign can be from 2½ years to 7½ years. During this period special prayers are made to Saturn, and navagriha puja is done. The powerful planet is invoked to remove all obstacles and mental and physical sufferings. Navagriha puja is done in temples to the nine planets whose icons are arranged in a group at one side of the temple. Devotees do "homa" and offer nine kinds of grains. They pray for protection from all harmful influences of the planets. Saturday is an important day at Tirupati, where splendid ceremonies are held for Lord Venkateswara.

Ekadahi Fast

The fast and prayers on Ekadashi, the eleventh day after the full moon, have special sanctity. They add to the positive spiritual energy of the individual and help him towards the goal of liberation of the soul.

There are 26 Ekadashi and Purnima (full moon days) fasts, each with its own significance.

The Vaikuntha Ekadashi occurs in the Tamil month Margazhi soon after the start of the northern journey of the sun (uttarayana). This is the time when heavenly beings (devas) are closer to human beings. In all Vishnu temples, predawn prayers are held, prabandhas, slokas of great saints invoking Vishnu are recited for 20 days. On the day of Vaikuntha Ekadashi a small door in the sanctorum is opened. Chanting slokas, devotees throng through the doorway to heaven or "Bhooloka Vaikuntha" as it is known, believing that they have achieved the goal, and will no longer go through the cycle of re-births. The Vaikunta Ekadashi fast is believed to have the power of 12 ekadashi fasts kept round the year. Hence it has a special sanctity for the devotee.

Ekadashis specially sacred to Vishnu occur on the 11th day of the bright fortnight of June–July, or Ani month, and on the 11th day of the bright fortnight of October–November or Kartikai month. In the intervening period the Lord is said to be in slumber. This coincides with the rainy season, which was a time for meditation and solitude. The Ekadashi fast fulfils the need for the digestive system to take rest and helps periodically clear the digestive tract of food, oils and spices.

Hari-utthan Ekadashi

This important Ekadashi occurs on the 11th day of the bright fortnight in the month of Aipasi (Kartikai) (mid-November–mid-December), after the Chaturmas the four month period of solitude and prayer, when Lord Vishnu is said to be resting. The Ekadashi at the start of Chaturmas 11th day of Ani (Ashada) is equally significant and sacred. Another story told of the power of Ekadashi is about king Rukmangada. The practice of Ekadashi by the king and his people throughout his kingdom made the inhabitants healthy and long-lived. Puzzled by the sudden decrease in the incoming souls of the dead into Yamaloka, Yama, the Lord of Death, went to Brahma for restoring the normal span of life. In order to break the pious practice of Ekadashi, Brahma sent an enchantress Mohini, who won Rukmangada's affection. The king forgot his responsibilities as a ruler and spent his time with Mohini. He obeyed her wishes in all respects except one, and that was in breaking the Ekadashi fast. Mohini forced him repeatedly, in desperation the king agreed to grant any wish of hers except the breaking of his fast. Mohini angrily demanded the head of his son. Rukmangada's son readily agreed to keep the word of his father and put his head on the block. In the nick of time Vishnu appeared and saved Rukmangada's son. He blessed the king and all the inhabitants of his kingdom.

The Legend

The story is also told of Vaikanasan who lived in Kambam near modern Madurai. He was troubled by dreams of a line of ancestors suffering agony because they could not reach the Eternal Brahman. He begged sage Manipunger to help the departed souls. The sage told him that souls were held back because of their past karmas or actions. They would be released only if Vaikanasan kept a strict fast of Vaikuntha Ekadashi and in memory of all his ancestors, made offerings of sesame (til) and water. The positive forces generated by his prayers would take his ancestors to their goal. Since then the Vaikuntha Ekadashi has been the most important Ekadashi for devotees. In all Vishnu temples a small door symbolizing the door to heaven, 'bhooloka vaikuntha dwar (gate)' is kept open for devotees.

Satyanarayana Vrata

Generally observed on a full moon day it can also be observed on Sankranti, Ekadashi, or Amavasya. The puja is done to overcome any crisis or calamity in the family. Performance of the puja is believed to show the way out of a difficult situation, give the family peace, happiness, health and prosperity. It is a puja for family and friends.

The Legend

Satyanarayana, Lord of Truth, is another name for Vishnu. There are many interesting legends associated with the puja. Once Narada told Vishnu that human beings suffered misery throughout life and could not find happiness. Vishnu sent to the world the message that by observing a strict fast and listening to the story of Satyanarayana and by meditating on his name they could overcome hardship and sorrow.

Another story illustrating the spiritual significance of the puja says that there was once a poor brahmin who lived on alms, taking pity on him Vishnu came before him as a learned scholar and advised him to do Satyanarayana Puja. The brahmin started the puja the very next day which was a full moon day. He made an offering of flour and sugar, and after worshipping Narayana distributed the offering. Soon he became prosperous. A woodcutter who heard the story was inspired to do the puja with all devotion. His family prospered and when death came, his soul was liberated to reach the lotus feet of Vishnu.

After puja each person is served adai, with a pat of butter and offered betel leaves, coconut, fruit and flowers.

DESCRIPTION

After early morning bath and prayer a small pavilion is made with the help of banana leaves and trunks. A picture of Satyanarayana is placed amidst the green leaves. Worship is offered with camphor, fruits, lamps, incense, betel leaves and flowers. A time is fixed and a priest is generally engaged to narrate the five stories of the vrata to the people assembled in the house. The couple organizing the vrata observe a strict fast and do not even sip a glass of water. After the reading out of each story, an offering is made of 5 bananas and 5 parts of rava halwa and arati is done to the picture. When all the stories are over, and arati has been done, the puja is completed and prasad is distributed to all. The priest is given gifts of grain, fruits and sweets. In the afternoon the couple break the fast.

Pranava Mantra OM

The Mandukya Upanishad describes OM as the container of the Supreme Brahman. The three sounds in OM, a, u and m, represent three states. A is the first stage of consciousness, the waking state, U is the second stage, the dream stage which is in between waking and sound sleep, M represents the third deep sleep stage. At the closing sound of OM the mind comes to rest in deep sleep. The silence after uttering OM is the fourth stage of the individual self-realization. The actual utterance of OM is for a limited span, but the silence abides. The philosophy of the tangible and intangible spheres is represented by OM and the silence after OM. The sages of the Vedas taught their students the way to realize the changeless, real inner self by going through three experiences, awakening, dream and deep sleep.

The word pranava means that which pervades life and is continuous in prana or breath. The mystic syllable OM was selected by the sages to represent the infinite Brahma and OM was added to every mantra giving power and vitality to the sacred syllables. Hence the sloka OM ithi brahma, OM itham sarvam. The sacred sound OM is the Brahma.

Panchabhoota Puja: Invoking the five elements

Before the start of a ceremony, the five elements are invoked for removing all barriers and negative forces so that the mantras can be most effective.

The panchabhoothas or five elements are represented within the human body as well as the world outside. They are:

Earth	:	The physical body of man and his material needs.
Water	:	The flowing emotional continuity in man and nature.
Fire	:	The thinking faculty, urges and passions which motivate actions.
Air	:	The breath we take, and the unseen spirit within the body.
Inner vision	:	The fifth element at the core of the being.

The prayers to the elements also are invoked. The moon sphere and the sun sphere symbolizing the creative power of the conscious being, both as a reality (the sun) and as a reflection of being (the moon).

The sages believed in the efficacy of meditating near panchavati, or five trees harmoniously grown into one, each tree representing an element present in the human body.

In ritual worship five, seven or nine types of sprouted grains are arranged in a circle and mantras invoke Indra, Lord of the Air, Yama (Lord of Death), Brahma (the Creator), Varuna (Lord of Water) and Soma (the Moon god), the grains include mustard, green gram and other common grains.

Common Beliefs and Practices

Namaskar, a mutual salutation

The salutation is done by raising the joined hands either upto the chest or the forehead when greeting one another. Namaskar to a deity is done by raising the folded hands above one's head. The namaskar is done with the formal words of greeting. Underlying this is the belief that every human being has a positive soul force vibrant in important centres of the body like the heart and the mind. The salutation is thus addressed from the soul of one person to that of another, and is a symbolic action implying recognition and reverence to the divine spark present in every being.

Asirwad, the benediction

Great value is attached to receiving blessings from deities, gurus, and elders by bowing down or prostrating at the feet. This is done at the conclusion of almost every ceremony, puja or ritual. At the conclusion of a marriage, the couple seeks the benediction of the congregation. Children seek the blessings of parents, young and old seek divine blessings and blessings of the gurus. After the shraddha ceremony, the blessings of the departed soul are sought by the entire clan.

Like the namaskar, the blessing is also believed to emanate from the soul force, giving positive vibrations which benefit the recipient, building so to say a protective circle of energy and goodwill. The person saluted also puts aside negative thoughts and feelings, and becomes charged with affection and conveys this in his benediction. The blessing given may be for a long and happy married life, for a long life, for good health and prosperity, or for spiritual enlightenment, depending on the occasion.

Tilak, the mark on the forehead

All rites and ceremonies start with a vermilion mark made with the thumb and index finger on the forehead. The custom is followed while welcoming or seeing off guests or relatives. The mark is generally made with kumkum a red powder made with turmeric, camphor, alum and other elements. Perfumed sandalwood paste is also used. On some occasions and pujas sacred ash or vibhuti is used symbolising the sacrificial fire of renunciation.

In terms of yoga, the centre of the forehead is the psychic location where the sixth chakra, the ajna is located. It is also called the third eye which is the eye of enlightenment. Opening of this eye is symbolic of the merging of the subconscious and conscious self, and attaining the universal being. The tilak marks the centre of meditation and wisdom.

Taking gifts when visiting

There are many proverbs on the need to take gifts while going on a visit. Going empty-handed to visit children, pregnant women, elders or to the temple is against social etiquette. The gift may be simple like sweets for children, flowers, saffron, or fruits for elders, or coconuts, flowers and fruits for the temple deity. Taking gifts which are auspicious, acceptable and give joy are an act of merit. The gift is not only a tangible symbol of affection and benediction but also shows self-denial and thought for others, which results in similar feelings and thoughts in the recipient. By taking suitable gifts to a guru, the sishya or would-be disciple shows that he is not greedy or selfish but will imbibe knowledge for the benefit of others.

In the same spirit, a host will not let a guest or a visitor leave empty-handed. Customary gifts of coconut, betel leaves, arecanuts, turmeric, and fruits are given along with the prasad if the occasion is a festival or puja.

Growing Tulsi or Basil in the home

The tulsi is believed to be the home of Bhagyalakshmi, the goddess of good fortune and prosperity. Hence the tulsi is planted outside the house, in a decorated stand or an earthen pot. Of all plants, tulsi receives the most respect because it symbolises the welfare of the family. The tulsi is also considered the beloved plant of Vishnu. Housewives observe Tulsi dwadashi in the month of Karthikai by fasting and prayer. The tulsi is worshipped every day by applying turmeric and kumkum to the plant, lighting a lamp, and watering the plant as well as the surrounding area. After evening prayers, and lighting a lamp for the deity, a lamp is also lit for the tulsi plant. The green serrated leaves of the plant are useful for treating inflammation of the throat and nasal passages, a decoction made of tulsi leaves helps to prevent infections, and is a useful remedy for infants and small children.

Averting the Evil Eye

The metaphor of the evil eye is used to describe the ominous negative forces flowing towards a person because of jealousy, hatred, or other negative thoughts. The ancient belief continues that these negative forces are caused by achievements, success or good fortune. Some persons especially vulnerable are infants, newly-weds, or young mothers. A variety of methods are adopted to ward off the evil eye. This includes reciting the drishta dosha mantra in which Ganesa is invoked for protection. Wearing birthstones or stones like coral is another method. Infants, brides and young mothers remain in partial seclusion. When infants are taken out, a black mark is made on the cheek with collyrium, to draw away the evil gaze. A newly built house has an ugly pumpkin face hung outside. When a person has achieved success in an activity, he or she is encircled with burnt chillies and salt, and this is thrown into a fire signifying the destruction of the negative force. In case of sickness or any other affliction, lemons and green chillies are strung together and hung outside the house for protection. The drawing of rangoli and lighting of oil-lamps is believed to attract benevolent forces and divert negative forces from the household. Almost all communities have their methods of averting the subtle negative forces which affect a person at a vulnerable point of time. Due to this age-old belief it is considered proper to avoid giving direct praise or compliments on someone's good health, success, or family prosperity.

Chapter 5

DAILY PUJA IN THE HOME

(Physical involvement and materialistic life of the individual during the cycle of life)

Puja is a general term for ritual worship. It includes lighting a lamp, meditation, chanting hymns, and making offerings to the deity. Puja done in the home is generally performed in the morning. After lighting the lamp, kumkum and turmeric is applied to the deity. Flowers and fruits are offered, on occasions kheer or payasam is offered with betel leaves and nuts, and coconut, mantras are recited to the accompaniment of ringing bells. Then 'dhoop' or agarbatti is offered, followed by arati.

To make arati, dissolve a little lime in water and add turmeric. The water will become dark red. The arati is done by two ladies holding the bowl of arati and making three circular movements before the deity. The arati is then thrown in a clean corner outside the house or in a pot. This signifies the end of the puja. After the puja, prasadam is distributed.

The Legend

The power acquired by the pure at heart devotee is illustrated in many popular legends. The story of saint Kannappa Nayanar is an example. Once upon a time, a hunter with a dead animal on his shoulder came to rest in an old half-broken stone structure. In the middle was a long black stone on which two eyes were painted. Not aware that it was a forgotten Sivalinga the hunter tried to sleep in a corner. But he was disturbed by the sight of tears flowing from an eye of the

Sivalinga. "What can ail this stone? Why do tears flow from its eye?" he wondered. Unable to sleep, he went to wash the dead animal. He returned with his mouth full of water, which he offered to the Sivalinga with the thought that the stone was perhaps weeping for thirst.

But even the drink of water did not suffice, tears continued to flow, unable to bear the sight the hunter pulled out an eye and placed it on the tearful eye of the Sivalinga, "There now we have one eye each, so please stop weeping." "Now what should I do?" wondered the hunter. "Perhaps it also has need of the other eye. Why should I deny this old stone neglected for many years in this corner of the forest?" He plucked his other eye. Then sightless, he balanced himself with one foot on the Sivalinga. Adi Shankara narrating this story adds that at this juncture, Lord Siva appeared before the hunter and liberated his true devotee. Thus the simple hunter, all of whose actions were impure but with motives pure, achieved what great sages could not achieve after years of penance.

The ancient temple of Mahakal at Ujjain in Madhya Pradesh is founded on the devotion of a cowherd named Sikar. The boy tended the cows playing his flute and wandering in the forests beside the river Sipra. One day, the lad came upon a group of Brahmins offering homa to a Sivalinga. The prayers were done in secret to avoid the wrath of a demon king who ruled the place. The chanting of Om Namah Sivaya fascinated the lad. He went for a bath in the river and found a big stone magically coming out of the water. He rolled it up the shore and sitting before it with eyes closed, recited the mantra "Om Namah Sivaya". It was evening and Sikar did not return home—nor was he back in the morning. The anxious parents found him sitting by the side of a big black stone, with a group of cowherds all reciting the sacred mantra—Sikar and his friends would not leave the spot despite all efforts by the cowherd families.

In desperation they tried to roll back the stone into the river but failed to move it from the spot. The demon king sent his soldiers to punish the boys, but they were struck by lightning emerging from the stone. The stone took the form of a Sivalinga and a voice from heaven said that the spot was sacred to Siva and his devotees. Henceforth Siva would be worshipped as Mahakal the timeless one.

From the devotion of the little cowherd sprang the majestic temple of Mahakal, which draws hundreds of thousands of pilgrims throughout the year.

Puja and Prasadam

Puja or prayer can be done through a service or rituals as in a temple or it can be as simple as a namaskar, a salutation to the divine power. Puja can be the chanting of 108 names of God. Or by uttering the syllable OM, and meditating in silence following the utterance.

The ancients gave great importance to reaching out to the Supreme Brahman through silence and meditation. The individual who sets out on the inward journey can reach the trouble spots of life, change attitude, and behaviour, develop a positive outlook, can overcome all obstacles and restore physical and mental health.

Meditation, to the sages, was the only food which could restore the health of man, help him understand the unexplained laws of nature, and realise his own latent powers. Hence the saying that knowledge from the scriptures was like the flame of a small oil lamp, while knowledge through meditation gave the mind the illumination of the sun.

Stages of Puja in Temples

The puja in temples is done in different stages. At the end of each stage the blessings of the deity are invoked, arati is done and prasad is distributed to devotees. At each stage the spiritual essence is enhanced by mantras, circling of oil lamps, incense and camphor flame, and offering of flowers and flower garlands to the deity. The stages are:

Agya	:	Inviting the spiritual presence of the deity at the puja
Padya	:	Washing the diety's hands and feet with milk and water
Achamaneeyam	:	Giving a sip of water
Alankara	:	Adoring with sandalwood paste, clothes and ornaments
Archana	:	Chanting of mantras and meditating on the names of the deity
Bhoga	:	Offering food, fruit and flowers to the deity and later distributed to devotees
Pankha	:	Fanning with a palm leaf
Darpana	:	Holding a mirror to the deity
Pariyamkasana	:	Putting the deity to sleep in yoganidra by chanting mantras and playing musical instruments

Puja done at home

Puja is done generally in the morning. After morning bath, the puja room is cleaned and kolam (rangoli) is drawn before the deity. Incense, camphor lamps and offerings are arranged. Bell and akshada are kept near a wooden plank or asana.

It is customary for the person doing puja not to sit on the floor but on a seat or asana as a mark of respect, as he is believed to be spiritually charged with the soul force of Brahman. The kurmasana or tortoise position is adopted for prayer and meditation.

There are no strict rules for puja done in the home. Generally, family or community traditions provide guidelines.

The stages of puja can vary from 10 to 16 or 32 according to the individual's perception.

The deities can be worshipped on any day and it is not necessary that puja should be done on a particular day of the week. The popular God Vinayaka is worshipped at all times with recitation of Ganesh Stuti. With his blessings, hardships can be overcome and obstacles in life's journey can be removed. The learned God is invoked for success in scholarship and career as well as other ventures.

In conclusion after namaskar to the deity, the naivedyam is offered, it is symbolically accepted by the deity and later on distributed as prasad containing divine grace and blessings of the deity.

Items for Puja (Kept in the Puja room)

Kumkum, turmeric powder, chandan powder or stick, joss sticks agarbatti, incense sticks, cotton wicks, oil for lamps, matchbox or lighter, camphor, bell, wooden plank, oil lamp (metal), tray for arati, bowl for akshada, bowls for offering food, honey or milk during puja, photos of Gods, kolam powder (rice flour), kolam trays or rollers.

Additional items on the day of puja

Coconut, flower garland, flower petals, betel leaves, arecanut, fruit, mango leaves for toranam for hanging above the front door, akshada (rice mixed with turmeric).

Preparation for Puja

Prasad

After puja and arati, prasad is to be distributed to all. This marks the conclusion of the cycle of puja and makes it effective spiritually. There are no fixed rules for prasad. Strong flavours, spicy and non-vegetarian food are not offered in puja or distributed as prasad. Prasad can be some sugar, fruit, milk or sweets.

After naivedya or offering to God, the prasad is accepted with reverence and eaten. It is not customary to re-cook or heat the prasad. If it is to be stored, it should be kept separately from kitchen and table dishes preferably in a clean tin in the puja room itself.

Arati

Arati has to be done at the end of the puja and at the conclusion of all auspicious occasions as well as for ceremonies like welcoming a bride, or celebrations like birthday or launching of new business etc.

To prepare arati for ceremonies, dissolve a little lime water and turmeric powder. The water will become dark red. For puja, dissolve kumkum in water and add turmeric and few grains of akshada. A few coins are placed on the arati which are later distributed among the two ladies.

Akshada

Akshada is thrown on the person performing the ceremony as a blessing by the elders during ceremonies and akshada is given to the deity as an offering. To make akshada, mix turmeric and rice in a small bowl, add few drops of oil and water and mix well till the rice becomes yellow.

Panchamritam

Panchamritam is prepared in all temples for anointing the deity and distributing as prasad to devotees. Many great temples have their special ingredients for adding to the panchamritam, such as vibhuti or raisins. You can make panchamritam for your puja by making a blend of ripe banana, crushed dates, ghee, jaggery, and honey. In place of jaggery, you can use powdered rock candy. The panchamritam which literally means five nectars will keep well and can be stored. It is useful as a general tonic for the system.

Puja offerings and their symbolism

Pushpa: Flowers grow from water, they symbolise the element of water and man's creative emotional life.

Gandha: Sandal paste symbolises mental powers. Its pleasant smell soothes the senses, subdues the animal or base instincts and impulses.

Dhupa: Incense is burnt and fumes rise in the air, symbolising reaching the realm of the spirit or soul.

Deepa: The lamp lit in the puja symbolises inner illumination caused by purity of thought in words and deeds.

The circling of the dhupa, deepa during puja is meant to drive away any impure and negative forces so that only spiritual powers and thoughts reach out to devotees.

Kolam: The floor decoration

The traditional kolam is a design drawn on earth with rice powder outside the doorstep. The morning ritual announces that all is well with the inmates of the house. The decoration at the entrance is believed to draw the blessings of Lakshmi, goddess of prosperity, on the house.

In practical terms, the kolam can be drawn only after the doorstep is swept and washed, hence it is a hygienic practice. Tradition says that the kolam provides food to myriad of ants and tiny insects, thus the day starts with charity to God's humble creatures.

There are specific kolams for the planets and for deities, festivals, marriages and so on. On occasions like death and annual ceremony for the dead (shraddham) etc. the house is not decorated with kolam.

The visual symbol of kolam creates an instant response in the viewer. The triangle signifying time space causation is vibrant with meaning and action. The simple chakra conveys the universal law, the unending cycle of life, death and re-birth. The spokes from the rim to the hub are many paths from action to peace, from sorrow to nirvana. The inner wheel is the psychic power in the individual which must be awakened and invoked.

Kolam can be drawn with the help of perforated trays and rollers. Oil paints and colours are used for elaborate designs on special occasions. Flowers, seeds, grains, charcoal, and turmeric are used for innovative kolams.

SECTION II

Calendar of Festivals

Chapter 1

TAMIL NEW YEAR

The Saka New Year day is heralded on the first dayof the month of Vaisakh, or Chitra around the middle of April. It is a day of thanksgiving and prayer. The new almanac (Panchang) is read on this day. Astrologers note the ascendant planet and signs of the Zodiac, and predict fortunes, crops and events of the year. Feasts, fasts, festivals and family events are planned for the year.

THE LEGEND

In the ancient text of the Vishnupurana, the king of the year is the planet in ascendance, and ministers are the stars. The blessings of the ruling planet are sought to bring good fortune for kings and commoners.

In most parts of the country, the New Year is the harbinger of spring, when nature is at its most joyous and colourful with promise of new life and prosperity.

DESCRIPTION

Early in the morning, a kolam (alpana) of red ochre and rice flour is drawn outside the front door. After the traditional oil bath, a fresh kolam can be drawn. This is followed by readings from the panchang. This can be done at home by calling a priest, or by going to a temple. Tarpanam in the memory of departed parents is done by the head of the household in many communities. A refreshing drink of diluted yoghurt is offered to all. Some special dishes made on the New Year's day are payasam, panakam, kosumbari and pachadi with six flavours of life: sweet, bitter, sour, hot (pungent), salty and astringent.

Vishu, New Year's Day in Kerala

Vishu occupies a unique place among various festivals and social celebrations in Kerala. Whereas almost all festivals are associated with some religious occasion, Vishu is significant by itself. Unlike other occasions, it is observed quietly and solemnly, without feasting, festivity, pomp and show.

Vishu is observed every year on the first day of the Malayalam month Medam (mid-April), generally 14 April.

DESCRIPTION

It is believed that the fortunes of the entire year depend on the nature of the object first seen on the morning of Vishu. To ensure an auspicious start, a number of auspicious objects are collected on the previous day. In a circular vessel of bell metal called 'uruli' about two cups of raw rice are placed. A newly washed good quality cloth is folded and kept on the rice.

The auspicious objects including betel leaves and nuts, yellow flowers, golden yellow ripe cucumber, a mirror, yellow flowers of the Konna tree (Cassia fistula) and a grantha or religious book of palm leaves are arranged decoratively on the folded cloth. A coconut is broken in halves. Each half is filled with oil and a wick is placed inside.

The coconut is placed with the other objects. When lit all the other objects are illuminated. A bell metal oil lamp is kept lighted at one side of the 'uruli'. The entire arrangement is called "Kani".

Before dawn on Vishu day one of the family members (generally a senior member) awakes and lights the lamps, and looks at the Kani. Then she or he awakes the others. One by one young and old see the auspicious "Kani". Great care is taken so that no other object is seen before seeing the auspicious "Kani". This is followed by the giving of gifts. The eldest member of the family distributes a few gold or silver coins to the younger family members.

The first day after the new moon in the month of Chitra, in end-March, or early April is the start of the New Year in Karnataka. It is believed that on this auspicious day Brahma created the world. Vishnu took his first avatar of "matsya", a fish, and rescued the world from flood waters.

Houses are cleaned and decorated with mango-leaf torans, and kolams. After the ritual morning bath, new clothes are worn. The family gathers for puja, an offering of "bewu bella" a special pachadi of neem flowers and jaggery is made to the deity and is then distributed as prasad. Youngsters do namaskar and receive the blessings of elders. There is a traditional feast.

In the afternoon, an elder member of the family reads the new almanac, predicting special events and festivals.

In many communities, on the day after Ugadi, there is a grand feast of vegetarian or non-vegetarian delicacies.

Ugadi—Andhra Pradesh and Karnataka

New Year day, the Ugadi in Andhra Pradesh and Karnataka is celebrated on the first day after the new moon of the month of Chitra, which occurs during end-March or early April.

The auspicious day is ushered by the cleaning and decorating of houses. New clothes are bought for the family, kolams are drawn, and mango-leaf torans adorn the doorways. After bath and puja a special pachadi (Ugadi pachadi) is offered to the deity, and distributed to the family and to all visitors on that day. The many flavoured pachadi symbolizes acceptance of many facets of the New Year. It also has medicinal and digestive properties. In the afternoon reading out of the new almanac is done in a temple or a meeting place. The auspicious and ominous portents during the coming year are read out, together with predictions of rainfall, crop production, earthquakes or floods. Ugadi day marks the start of the auspicious Vasanta Navaratri or nine days of the spring festival.

Chapter 2

CHITRA PURNIMA

(Full-moon night of the month of Chitra)

The first full-moon night of Chitra (April-May) is the occasion for a picnic, festival and community get-together.

THE LEGEND

The origin of this ancient custom is not known, but it is said to be in honour of Chitragupta, the record keeper of Yama, Lord of Death, through whose means millions of souls are born on earth and depart from it. The festival also expresses the spontaneous enjoyment of nature's beauty on a clear night of the full moon in early summer.

DESCRIPTION

In the morning, a kolam or drawing of rice-flour is done outside the south door of the house because it is believed that the Lord of Death lives in that direction. Inside the house, the figure of a moon is drawn on the floor. Nine kinds of grains are arranged around it to please navagrihas, rice is cooked, and a little ghee is added. Two plantains, two mangoes and a coconut with betel leaves and nuts are also offered to Yama. After puja and arati, the prasad is distributed.

Symbolic grains for Planets

For Sun—wheat, Moon—rice, Mars—whole red gram, for Mercury—green gram, Jupiter—whole bengal gram, Venus—mochai, karamani, string-bean, Saturn—sesame, Rahu—whole black gram, Ketu—horsegram. All these nine kinds of pulses along with betel leaves and nuts, plantain and cash are given as gift to brahmins after the navagriha puja.

Chapter 3

RAMANAVAMI

The birth of Sri Rama, the seventh incarnation of Vishnu, is observed every year on the navami (the ninth day) of the bright half of the month of Panguni. Ramanavami celebration gives us all an opportunity to invoke the divine grace of Sri Rama and imbibe the ideals and values of the "Maryada Puroshothama" into our own lives. Fasting, prayer, and chanting of the 100 names of Sri Rama helps devotees to cross to the shore of ultimate reality, hence the name of Rama is described as a taraka, or boat. The prayers on this day help to revive our latent powers to deal with the negative forces in the life, the disappointments and frustrations. To many devotees, the name of Rama is an unfailing panacea to cure all ills. The name of Rama is also compared to a wish-fulfilling tree (Kalpa Vriksha). Hence the name must be always repeated or recited. Tulsidas has said that uttering the name of Rama is like placing a jewelled lamp on the tip of the tongue. It gives light both within and without.

THE LEGEND

The great epic Ramayana has taken the story of Rama to many countries. It embodies in the character of Rama the highest ideals of human life. In the epic, poet Valmiki asks sage Narada if he had ever met a "sthitha pragyna", or an awakened soul of perfect harmony. Narada describes Rama as such a being. Rama is generally depicted as a warrior king. He carries a bow, and has a quiver full of arrows for defending the righteous and upholding the dharma.

The birth of Rama is described by Valmiki thus: "Then after the expiry of six seasons and on the completion of the twelfth month, on the ninth lunar day of the month of Chaitra, under the star Punarvasu with the Sun, Mars, Saturn, Jupiter and Venus at Aries, Libra, Capricorn, Cancer and Pisces and when the Moon with Jupiter entered the Zodiac sign of Cancer, Kaushalya gave birth to the great and auspicious Rama with mighty arms, rosy cheeks, and scarlet lips, the joy of Dasaratha and the adored one of all people. On his fair body were all the auspicious signs of a divine being."

The Festival

It is a day of fasting and meditation. There are readings from the Ramayana, devotional songs to Rama are sung. Lectures on Rama's life and teachings of the Ramayana help spiritual and moral evolution of people. Offerings are made of panakam, buttermilk, kosumbari, vada and payasam, which are distributed as prasad.

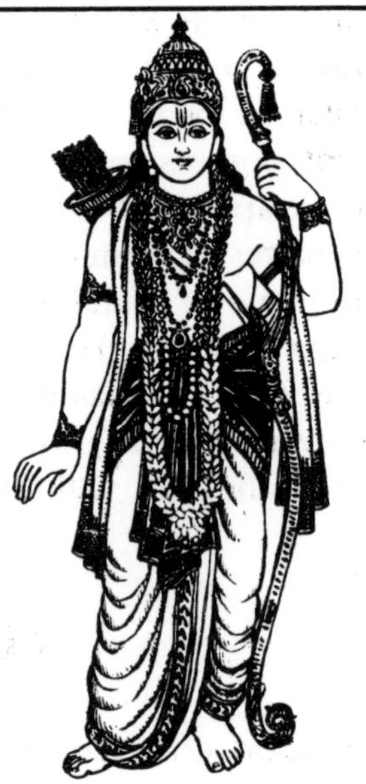

RAMA

In temples, there is special puja to Rama and recitation of the Ramayana. The deity is taken in a procession to enable all to receive blessings. In the "akhanda deepa" puja, the deity is brilliantly lit with garlands of oil-lamps which burn throughout the day and night. Devotees invoke the deity seeking strength to face a calamity or deal with a crisis.

Ramanavami comes at the and of the Vasanta Navaratri the spring festival of nine nights. A fast is observed on all nine days or on the first and last day.

Chapter 4

HANUMAT JAYANTI

The birth of the Monkey-god Hanuman, the embodiment of selfless devotion and power, is observed in Panguni (March-April).

In all temples of Rama, and all shrines of Hanuman, prayers are offered. Ramayana and Hanuman Chalisa are read. The deity is richly decorated. Fairs and festivals are held throughout the country.

The concept of Hanuman is described in the Ramayana in verses which are repeated daily by devotees. The opening verses rendered in English are:

"I salute the Lord of the Vanaras, the dear son of Anjana, the great hero, the destroyer of Aksha, terror of the city of Lanka, the remover of the sufferings of Sita."

"I salute the Ambassador of Rama, who is swift like the wind, who has conquered his senses, foremost among the intellectuals, the son of Vayu, and most wise of the Vanaras. Wherever the name of Rama is uttered, there folding his hands above his head, with tears of joy and devotion filling his eyes, stands Hanuman. Him I salute. In the great garland of the Ramayana, Hanuman is the jewel, he is the Mahamalaratnam."

In ancient illustrations and sculptures, Hanuman carries on his shoulders the vehicle (Dharma) on which are seated Rama and Lakshmana. He is a warrior in the cause of Dharma. He is the greatest, selfless and self-effacing devotee of Rama. By giving solace to Sita, he is a symbol of hope to suffering, oppressed humanity. He is described as sankatmochan, because of his heroic deeds of great strength and will-power. He is a true Brahmacharya, who has control over all the senses and chiranjivi, the immortal, or ever-living. These concepts of Hanuman are invoked during the puja.

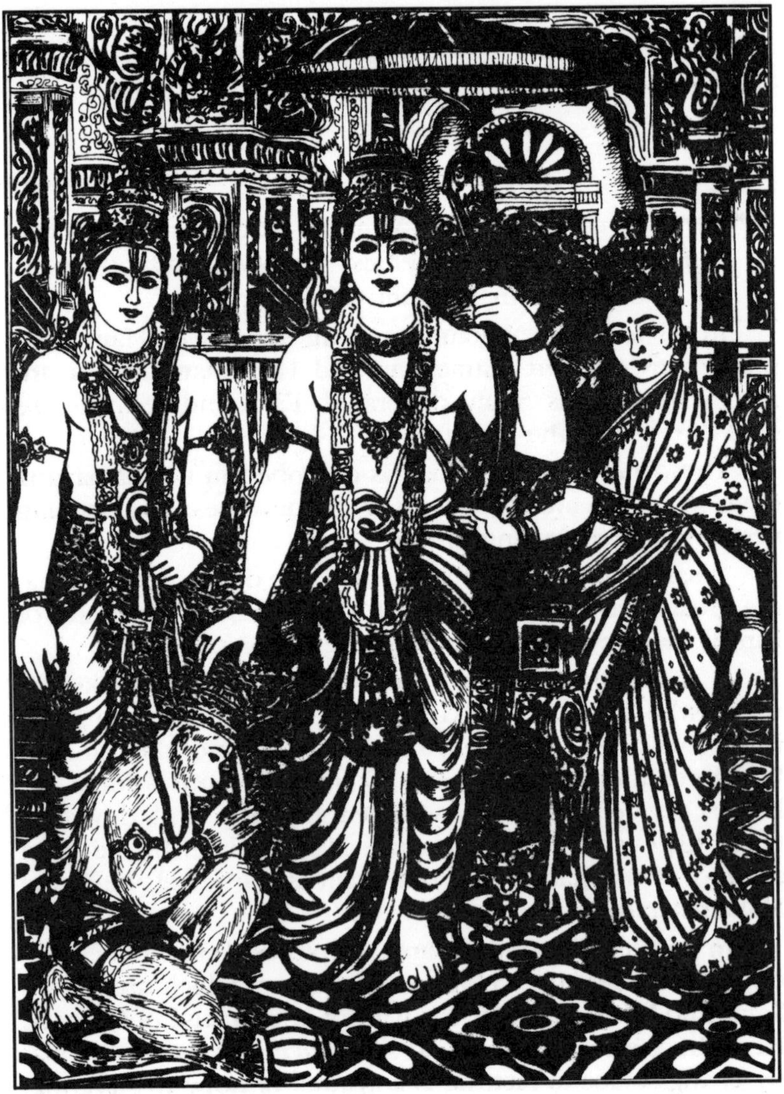

Chapter 5

VARALAKSHMI PUJA

The puja to Varalakshmi, the beautiful goddess of wealth, is done on the full-moon day of the month of Adi (July-August). The festival signals the end of the hot summer season. Cool winds are scented with the fragrance of flowers. Fruits are ripening and nature gives the hope of plentiful crops and produce. The annual festival is specially important for a happy married life and women, especially new brides pray for the good health and prosperity of husbands and families and seek the protection of the goddess. This puja is done by the people of Tamil Nadu, Karnataka and Andhra Pradesh.

THE LEGEND

The concept of Mahalakshmi or Varalakshmi as described in the Sri Devimahatmayam is one of immense grandeur and power. She is the Goddess of Ichhashakti (will and volition). She has the composite powers of creation, preservation and dissolution. In her eighteen hands she holds the rosary, axe, mace, arrow, thunderbolt, lotus, bow, pitcher, rod, shakti, sword, shield, conch bell, wine cup, trident, noose and discus. Her colour is red (raktavarna), the colour of union of night and day.

In the legend, Lakshmi emerged from the ocean of milk during the churning of the ocean (Samudramanthana) and became the consort of Vishnu. She protects and preserves life. In her other form of Rajyalakshmi (Royal Lakshmi) she enters people's homes briefly, brings riches and often deserts them suddenly. Her vehicle is a white swan or an elephant, and she is depicted as being seated on a red or pink lotus.

DESCRIPTION

The puja begins with the formal welcome of Lakshmi into the home. A wooden tray or stand is placed outside the threshold. A rangoli is drawn in the puja room inside the house. A kalash (brass or silver pot) is placed on the tray outside the house. The pot is decorated with mango leaves and flowers. A number of auspicious items such as rice, betel leaves, turmeric sticks, bananas and coins are placed within the pot. Thread dipped in turmeric is tied around the neck of the pot. A coconut scrubbed with turmeric is placed on the top. The face of the goddess may be drawn on the coconut, or a brass or silver face may be kept on the pot and decorated with kumkum and turmeric and sandalwood powder.

At the selected time, ladies sing a welcome song to Lakshmi and carry the tray and kalash into the puja room. After lighting the lamp and doing arati, slokas and songs of the goddess are recited and sung. Then the yellow thread is untied and a piece is given to each girl or lady to tie around her right wrist. This is symbolic of the conclusion of the auspicious puja receiving the blessings of the Goddess. It is a day to prepare four varieties of kozhakattai, payasam and vadai for naivedyam or offering.

The next day, Lakshmi puja is performed. Cooked rice, sundal, fruit and betel leaves are offered to all ladies. Then the face of the Goddess is turned towards the west and the kalash with its contents is placed inside a drum of rice, keeping, as it were, the Goddess safely inside the house until the next year.

Chapter 6

MANGALA GOURI VRATA

In the auspicious month of Adi (July-August) the vrata or fast to goddess Gouri is observed by girls and married women. The fast observed on every Tuesday of the month brings great solace, courage and inner strength. The Mangalvar vrata to Gouri is significant for young girls who want a suitable groom, and for married women whose prayers invoke the Goddess to bless the family with her radiance.

DESCRIPTION

When the vrata is performed by married women, the first vrata is observed in the parents' home, and four subsequent vratas in the husband's home. In many households the vrata is invariably performed for the first five years after marriage, thereafter the annual Mangalvar vrata is observed as convenient.

In some families Gouri vrata is observed by the bride-to-be before the marriage for an auspicious start in her new life.

The puja place facing east is decorated with kolam. A photo or a drawing of the Goddess is kept in the puja. Offerings of flowers, fruit, betel leaves, arecanut, comb, mirror and kumkum are made. The Goddess is invoked through mantras and meditation. Relatives and friends (especially married women and girls) are invited and given prasad, betel leaves, flowers, fruit and coconut. A gift of blouse piece, comb, mirror, kumkum, turmeric is given to each guest, after the puja.

Chapter 7

NAG PANCHAMI

The festival of the serpent king Ananta or Adisesha occurs on the fifth day of the bright half of Adi (July-August). Women observe a strict fast, and go in groups to the nests of serpents. They offer milk and flowers. In many homes, the serpent deity made of silver, stone or wood, or painted on walls is bathed in milk and worshipped. By piety and prayers, on this day, the protection of the family against snake bite is assured. Real cobras and snakes are worshipped at big fairs arranged on the day. On this day, digging the earth is avoided because snakes live under the ground.

THE LEGEND

Ancient puranas like Agni Purana, Skanda Purana and Narada Purana give details of the practice of snake worship. Nagas or snakes are semidivine beings born of Kadru, the wife of Sage Kasyapa. They reign in great splendour in Patala, the underworld, and wear priceless gems. The most powerful of all is Seshnag, the thousand-hooded cobra, also called Ananta who bears the earth on his crown. When he nods or yawns, oceans and mountains tremble.

Snakes were considered semi-human. The serpent princess Ulupi married Arjuna in the Mahabharata. Snake deities are also worshipped as custodians of the treasures of lord of sea. Ananta, the serpent king has six heads. Vishnu reclines on him between the dissolution of one universe and creation of another.

DESCRIPTION

Nag Panchami is an important festival in Karnataka. The preparations start five days earlier, on the new moon day, known as Bhima amavasya. Girls offer prayers for a good husband. They prepare clay images and decorate them with white dots. These are placed in the puja. After vrata and puja, a thread dipped in turmeric is tied on the right wrist. Then the figure of the snake god is drawn on the doorway and worshipped with offerings of milk. Women do puja for the welfare of brothers. On the day before Panchami, a salt-less diet is kept or strict fast is observed. After Nag Panchami puja, a traditional feast is served.

Chapter 8

SRAVAN PURNIMA
(Avani Avittam)

The full-moon day of Avani (July-August) marks the auspicious start of Chaturmas, a four month period of penance and austerity. In ancient India, it was a period of heavy rains; students who lived in gurukuls (ashramas) could not move about freely. Hence this was the time to learn by heart all the earlier lessons, and start further studies. This was done after changing the sacred thread (Yagyopavit), and chanting the Gayatri Mantra.

Menfolk of many communities, including brahmins, kshatriyas and vaishyas of South India, observe the festival of Sravan full moon, or Avani Avittam when the star Avittam is in ascent. After doing japas, the new yagyopavit is worn. Gayatri Mantra (named after poetic metre in which the mantra is composed) is recited before sunrise and after sunset. It is believed to develop spiritual and mental energy and give protection from harmful negative forces. Invoking the sun god, the mantra repeatedly prays for protection from the sins of the mind, of the lips and of the body.

THE LEGEND

The demon Medhas worshipped Brahma, and became powerful. He attacked the sun, and tried to capture his thunderbolt. It was then that Surya, the sun god, recited the

Gayatri Mantra, invoking Varuna with a handful of water. Reciting the mantra before sunrise, at noon and after sunset, he was saved from the demon by mantras of great power and spiritual energy.

DESCRIPTION

Menfolk gather at rivers, ponds, or beside wells, for a bath, then the new yagyopavit is dipped in turmeric and saffron. Japa is done, Gayatri Mantra is recited by the group, Vedas are recited and the old sacred thread is replaced by the new one. Tarpan or prayer is done for the gods and seven great rishis.

The Gayatri Mantra consists of three lines from Rig-Veda (II.62.X), namely:

Om bhur-bhuvah-svah
tat savitur-varenyam
bhargo-devasya dhimahi
dhiyo yo nah prachodayat
(Om).

This has been variously translated, but its general meaning given by Max Muller is as follows: "Let us obtain (or according to Hindu tradition, let us meditate on) the adorable splendour of Savitri (Sun), may he arouse our minds." All Hindu sacred books of later times proclaim these to be the most holy lines of the Vedas. For example, the Manu Samhita the most authoritative of books on sacred law (Dharma Sastra) says:

"Prajapati also milked out of the three Vedas the letters a, u, and ma, together with the words bhuh, bhuvah, svah. Prajapati also milked from each of the three Vedas one of the portions of the text called Savitri, beginning with the word tat...."

The three great imperishable particles preceded by Om and the Gayatri out of over one thousand hymns and 10,500 verses of the Rig-Veda are selected as the supreme credo and prayer for a Hindu. The Gayatri Mantra japa is done during the sacred thread ceremony. It is a part of everyday prayer and japa. It is chanted together at mass prayers and all major events and ceremonies.

Chapter 9

TIRU ONAM

(Kerala)

Tiru onam the splendid annual festival of Kerala is celebrated in the Malayalam month of Chingam, corresponding to August-September. The festival starts with the advent of the moon in the star Hastham and continues for 10 days, until it enters the star Tiruonam, which has given its name to the festival.

THE LEGEND

Onam takes one back to the distant past. Mahabali, a great emperor of the Asuras (demons), ruled over the land. There were golden harvests and rivers of milk. Peace and joy filled all living beings.

The story of Mahabali is narrated in the Puranas. Mahabali was the powerful and noble son of the Demon Virochana, and grandson of the great devotee Prahlad. Bali did severe penance, by which his powers grew. He defeated Indra, Lord of the Heavens, and came to rule over the three worlds. Harassed and homeless the gods appealed to Vishnu to stop Bali from doing the 100th Aswamedha Yagya which would make him invincible. Vishnu in his fifth avatar was born to rishi Kasyapa and Aditi, mother earth. Sage Kasyapa did the yagyopavit (sacred thread ceremony) of his son the short statured Vamana, in which priceless gifts were presented by the gods. Brahma gave a perennially filled water jug or kamandal, Surya, the sun god, presented an umbrella. Setting forth to gather alms in the tradition of brahmacharis, the boy came to the court of Bali, just when the 100th yagya was to commence. Though warned by his Guru Shukracharya, Mahabali came out to welcome the young brahmin. Vamana asked for only three steps of land as alms from the king.

Mahabali promised the gift. At once Vamana grew to an enormous size. In two paces he covered the earth and the heavens, restoring their home to the gods. When there was

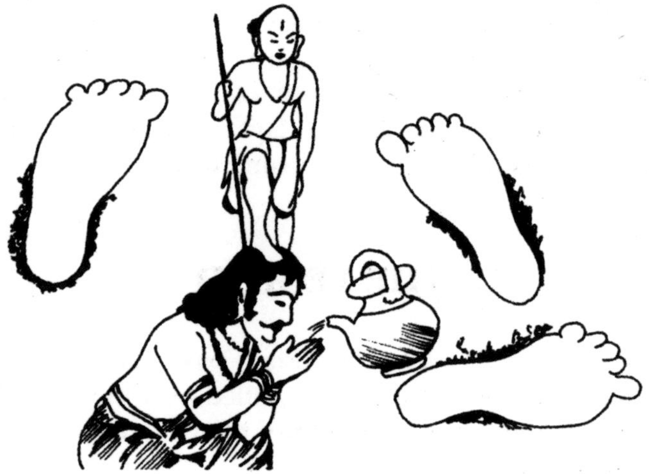

Legend of Onam

no place for the third step, Bali bowed before Vamana and offered his head. Vamana spared Bali, and banished him to the Patala Lok the nether world, with a promise that every year Bali would visit his kingdom and see his loving subjects. Hence the joyous celebration of Onam to mark the annual visit of the noble and generous king Bali. A popular folk song sung on the occasion describes the golden age of Kerala under emperor Mahabali.

Onam is also a festival of thanksgiving and rejoicing in a fine harvest. This is the season when paddy and many other foodgrains are harvested. Fruits, vegetables and flowers abound.

DESCRIPTION

Before start of the Onam festivities, houses and localities are cleaned and decorated. Flowers are collected and multi-colour flower decorations and flower-carpets are prepared with great artistic skill. Kolam (floor-decoration of rice flour) is drawn in all temples, courtyards and entrances. Gift sets of mundu (sarong) and upper cloth are bought for the family members. A number of conical figures about 2 feet high are made of clay and put up outside houses. One of these symbolises Thirukkarappan or Mahabali. The figures are decorated with kumkum paste and sandal paste. Gifts of clothes, fruits and sweets are sent to married daughters before Onam. After the morning bath, new clothes are worn. Puja is done on the three days preceding Onam day. On Tiruonam day, new clothes are worn and a grand feast is prepared. A number of traditional games including ball games, ball and stick games, boxing, wrestling, and the world-famous snake-boat races are organized. Competitions of music and dance help to discover young talent.

Chapter 10

SRI KRISHNA JAYANTI (JANMASHTAMI)

The birth of Krishna, the eighth incarnation of Vishnu, is celebrated at midnight on the eighth day of Avani (August-September). The auspicious and holy night is celebrated throughout the country. In the song celestial, the Bhagawat Gita, Krishna declares "The Universe was created by me, and all things exist in me." Arjuna in the Mahabharata describes Krishna as "The supreme universal spirit, the supreme dwelling, the eternal entity, with divinity earlier than that of the Gods, unborn, omnipresent." Destruction of evil and establishment of Dharma was the reason for the birth of Krishna.

Observation of Janmashtami (Krishna Jayanti) brings the blessings of good children, salvation and prosperity.

THE LEGEND

King Kamsa the demon king of Mathura was a tyrant, but loved his sister Devaki. He celebrated her marriage with Prince Vasudeva and became the charioteer for the couple. Suddenly an oracle announced that the eighth son of Devaki would cause his doom and death. Vasudeva stopped him from killing Devaki by promising to hand over each infant born to them. Kamsa imprisoned Vasudeva and Devaki. Thus seven infants were born and killed by Kamsa. The star Rohini

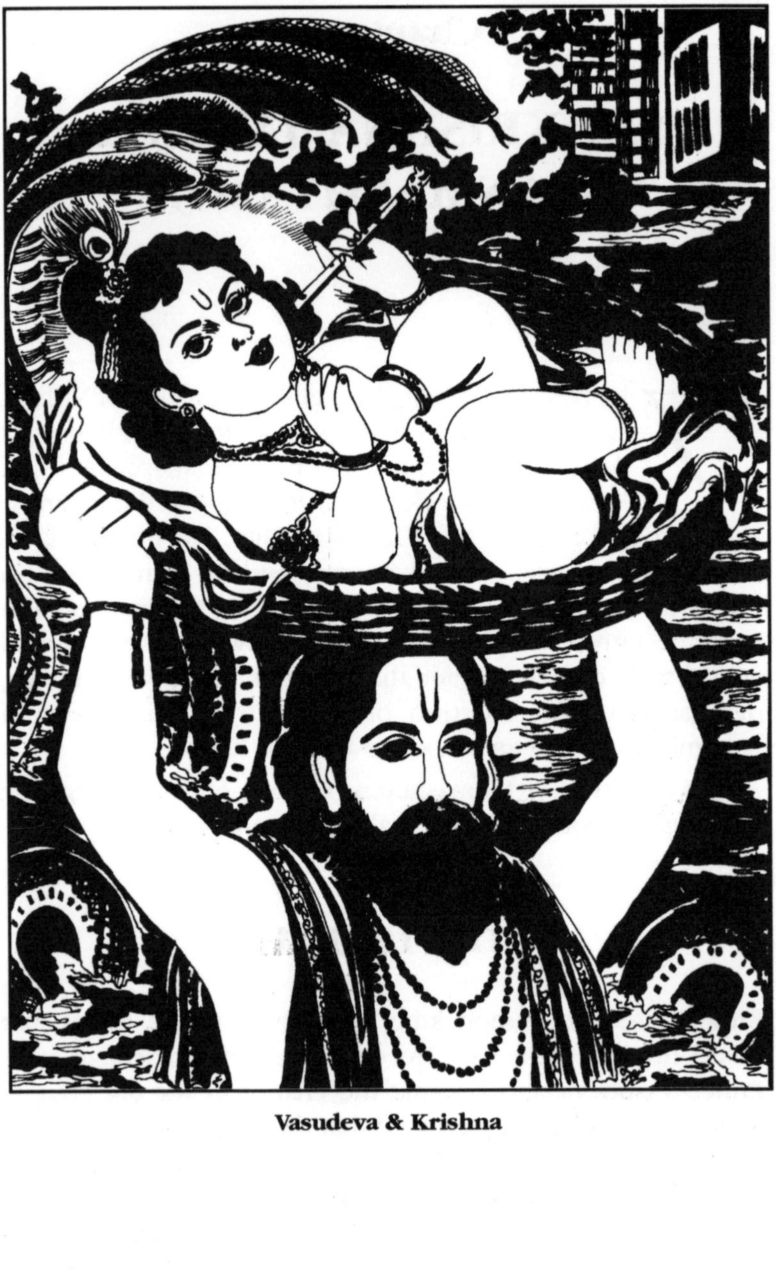

Vasudeva & Krishna

was in ascendant when Krishna was born at midnight and an oracle told Vasudeva to carry the baby out of prison. And behold the fetters broke, the guards fell asleep and the gates of the prison opened. When Vasudeva came to the Yamuna river, the water parted beneath his feet. He crossed over to the house of Nanda in Gokul village. There he placed his son beside Yasoda, the wife of Nanda and brought back their new born baby girl to the prison in Mathura. Kamsa heard of the birth of a baby girl. He rushed to the prison and was about to fling the baby on a rock when it slipped out of his reach with the words "Wretched one, your destroyer lives in Gokul".

The story of Krishna, his childhood with the cowherds of Gokul, his killing of Kamsa and rule in Mathura and his many miraculous deeds are told in the Bhagavatam. In the Mahabharata he appears as a wise counsellor and guide of the Pandavas, who helped them to win the great battle of Kurukshetra.

The legend of Krishna has long inspired writers, poets and artists in all parts of the country. To this day the legend is depicted in many art forms and handicrafts.

DESCRIPTION

The celebrations start with an early morning bath, prayer and fasting upto midnight. Houses are decorated with a special kolam (rangoli), and small steps are drawn to symbolize Krishna entering the home to bless the household. On this day all kinds of savouries, sweets and fruits loved by children are kept in the prayer room. Butter, milk, curd, sweets and seasonal fruits, loved by Krishna are arranged in the puja. Panchamrita in which fruits, honey, sugar, curds and nuts are mixed is prepared.

Temples are gaily lit, and decorated with scenes from the childhood of Krishna and scenes from Gokul. A small decorated swing, with a baby Krishna in it, is rocked throughout the day by devotees in temples and homes.

Singing of religious songs, chanting of verses from the Bhagavata and the Gita create a mystic fervour. Just before midnight, arati is done, the prasad is distributed and the day-long fast is broken.

Chapter 11

GOURI-GANESH PUJA

In Karnataka, Goddess Gouri is worshipped the day before Ganesh puja in the month of Avani. Houses are thoroughly cleaned. The rich and poor assemble near a pond or river, early in the morning; clay images are made of Gouri and Ganesh and are brought to the house, with much fanfare and music. The images are arranged in the puja room, mantras are chanted to invoke the deities' presence in the household.

Women decorate the face of the Goddess with kumkum, sandal paste and turmeric powder. Garlands made of cotton are gaily decorated and placed on the deities. These are called "Gajja Vastras", and are a special feature of the puja.

Women observe a strict fast and meditate on the Goddess, prasad is offered after arati. A thread dipped in turmeric (sharadu) is tied on the right wrist as a token of the puja. A fast is kept throughout the day, and a traditional feast is served on breaking the fast. Gouri puja in Karnataka precedes many important festivals and occasions, because the Goddess is the patron of married happiness and family prosperity. The blessings of the Goddess bring worthy husbands to girls.

For the bride-to-be, Gouri puja is a must. Before start of the marriage function the groom departs on a symbolic "Kasi Yatra". The bride completes Gouri Puja, and enters the wedding pandal with the blessings of the Goddess.

Chapter 12

GANESH CHATURTHI

The birthday of the popular elephant god is celebrated with joy on the fourth day (Chaturthi) of the bright fortnight of Avani (August-September). Ganesh or Vinayaka is the patron god of learning, prudence, success and power. He has the power to remove obstacles in any venture. Hence his names are repeatedly invoked at the start of a journey, a function, birthday, marriages, writing letters, starting a book or a business, or any other activity. Ganesh controls the mind and energy through the Muladhara Chakra, the psychic centre of the body. He is also a great scribe, scholar of the scriptures and is believed to have written the epic dictated by Rishi Vyasa.

THE LEGEND

There are two interesting legends about Ganesh. One legend is that annoyed by Siva's surprise visits when she bathed, Parvati took some dirt from her body, made it into a human shape and gave it life.

She placed the human being outside her bath-house to guard it. When Siva found his way barred, he cut off the guard's head. Parvati was upset, so Siva sent for another head. The first to be found was an elephant head, which was planted on Ganesh's shoulders.

In another version, all the gods had assembled to bless the lovely son of Siva and Parvati, only Sani (Saturn) did not look at the boy because he was cursed to have a fatal gaze. But Parvati insisted, so Sani gazed at the infant which was burnt to ashes. Parvati wept and cursed Sani. Brahma intervened. He told Parvati that if the first available head was placed on his shoulders, her son would live. Vishnu's eagle Garuda found a sleeping elephant. Its head was placed on the infant's shoulders giving it life.

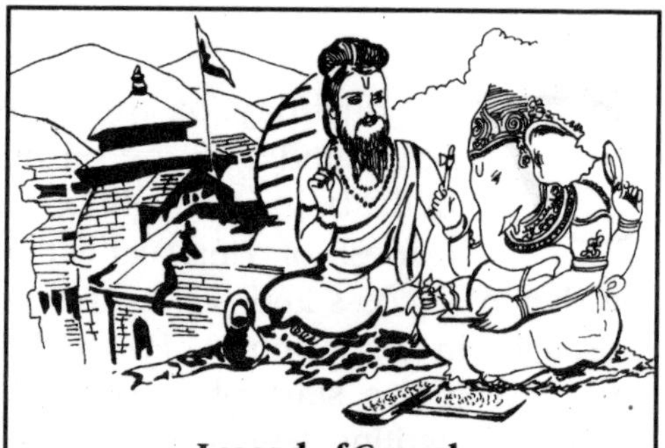

Legend of Ganesh

The legend of the single tusk goes back to the ancient times. When Vyasa was dictating the Mahabharata he made two conditions to Ganesh. The first was that he should never be stopped in his composition, the second was that Ganesh should write down the composition only after he understood it. Vyasa composed 8 main verses, each of which was followed by 1000 verses. The time taken by Ganesh to understand the main verse was used by Vyasa to go ahead in composing the subsequent 1000 verses. However the quill broke during the dictation. Ganesh had promised not to stop Vyasa, so he broke off a tusk and continued the epic work.

DESCRIPTION

Three days before Chaturthi, clay idols of Ganesh are placed in a decorated pandal, or in the Puja room. On twenty-one banana leaves, or leaf-plates, sweets are arranged, along with idli, four types of kozhakattai and puffed rice-jaggery ladoos are offered. Oil lamps are lit, incense is offered and the story of Ganesh and his names are repeated. After meditation and prayers, arati is offered and the various food-offerings (naivedyas) are distributed. After three days, on Chaturthi day, the idol is taken in a procession and immersed in the sea, river, tank or well. Great religious fervour, pomp and colour are characteristic of Ganesh Chaturthi celebrations throughout South India.

Chapter 13

NAVARATRI

Nine sacred nights are observed twice in the year. Once in the month of Panguni preceding Ramanavami and again after Mahalaya Amavasya in the month of Purattasi (September-October). From the new moon of Ashvin to Mahanavami, the ninth lunar day, there is meditation, prayer and fasting, devotees worship different forms of Shakti the Divine Mother. The prayers during Navaratri are meant to awaken our subconscious strength and energy and bring enlightenment. Shakti, the dynamic principle of the universe, removes the veil of delusion and ignorance, leading to the liberation of the soul.

THE LEGEND

The legend of Navaratri shows how invincible strength comes from unity. Demon Mahishasura, through meditation to God Siva, received many boons. He could not be killed by any man and became almost indestructible. The demon waged war in the heavens and imprisoned the Gods. He created havoc on earth. Brahma, Vishnu and Siva held council. Then Lakshmi, Saraswati and Parvati did rigorous meditation, balanced on the point of a needle. From their combined strength came forth Adi Shakti full of terrible strength and power, riding a lion with her trident in her hand. To escape the fury of the Goddess, Mahisha changed his form into a lion, then a man, an elephant and returned to his buffalo form. On the tenth day of the battle, at midnight, the Goddess pierced a trident into his chest and beheaded him.

Through nine days of fasting and prayer, devotees add to the powers of Adi Shakti and on the tenth day, celebrate Vijaya Dashami, the day of victory.

DESCRIPTION

The nine days are divided into three parts. The first three days are for Durga, the manifestation of Shakti, the primal energy, the next three days for Lakshmi, goddess of prosperity, the final three days for Saraswati, patron goddess of all learning and skills.

On pratipada, the first day of the festival, a kalash, an earthen or brass or silver pitcher is filled with water, its mouth is covered with leaves, topped with a coconut. The pitcher is garlanded, and installed in the house with an invocation to Ganesh. Then invoking Goddess Durga, puja is offered with druva grass (kusa grass), flowers, oil lamps, and incense. Barley is sprouted in a small earthen pot. There is a daily recitation of Durga saptasthi, Devi Bhagawat Purana and Devi Mahatmya from the Markandeya Purana.

'Kolu' or arrangement of clay, wooden, ivory or stone idols and toys is done generally on wooden steps or benches and boxes arranged in steps, covered with a sheet. The first item kept in the kolu is an earthen idol, a wooden figure of a man or a woman. Next come the Gods and Goddesses, scenes from the epics, scenes from Krishna's childhood and topical scenes from everyday life.

During the eight days of kolu, ladies visit each other to receive betel leaves, turmeric, betel nut and fruits or coconut, along with small presents of a mirror, a comb and kumkum box. Young girls are invited and given sweets and money. During the festive days they represent the Goddess. Sundal and/or other sweets and savouries are given to all children and elders who are invited to the house.

On each day of Navaratri special songs to the Goddesses are sung. It is a festival for girls and women who are invited to every home, offered sweets, savouries and pan/supari and coconut or fruit, sundal, and presents. Vada and payasam are made every day and offered to the Goddess. Each day different sweets or sundals are made and distributed.

On the tenth day, the dolls are removed from the kolu, only one doll that is of a man is left lying down to symbolize the end of kolu. On the tenth day, Vijaya Dashami, the Goddess is taken in a procession in a decorated car and immersed in a tank, river or ocean. In South India, the dolls are removed from the steps, wrapped in paper or cloth, and stored in boxes.

Saraswati puja day is celebrated on the ninth day in South India. The books used by children for their studies, religious books, music books are all arranged before the kolu or in front of the puja, after drawing a kolam on the floor or on a plank. If oil bath is taken in the morning, then books are arranged on the plank. Even pencils, pens, notebooks, scales and geometry boxes are kept by children. The lady of the house prepares sundal, vada and payasam and offers it to Saraswati, Lakshmi and Hayagriva. All the musical instruments are kept in the puja. On Vijayalakshmi day puja is done as on the previous day, and betel leaves, nuts and plantain fruit are offered as naivedyam, then the books are removed from puja and read. Music students learn new songs from their teachers and offer him or her Dakshina in cash or gifts. They practise or sing the songs they have already learnt. Cars, motor cycles and other vehicles are washed and chandan and kumkum is applied on them. Then lemons are kept under the wheels and the vehicles are driven over them symbolizing destruction of negative forces. Sundal is prepared for naivedya and prasad as for Navaratri puja.

Navaratri, Saraswati Puja and Dussehra in Karnataka

Navaratri the festival of nine nights is celebrated with great fervour in honour of Goddess Chamundeswari, who killed the demon Mahishasura after nine days of battle. Kolu or arrangement of dolls is done in every house. Raja and Rani two dolls made of sandalwood, gods, goddesses and fancy dolls and scenes can be seen in the kolu. Wooden and clay dolls are an essential feature. On every day of navaratri, sweets are made and offered in puja. By way of welcoming the Goddess Chamundeswari, the threshold of the house is worshipped with flowers and incense and kolam is drawn every morning.

Women and children go visiting, sing songs to the Goddess at the kolu, and receive betel leaves, arecanut, fruits, flowers, coconut, small presents and sundal. Children have a great time as they are welcomed with sweets and snacks in every home.

Saraswati Puja and Ayudha Puja in Mysore

Saraswati puja is done on the Saptami (7th day of navaratri). Books, tools, musical instruments are kept in puja. Appam made of rice flour and jaggery is offered to Saraswati and distributed as prasad. On the 9th day (Navami) Ayudha puja is done in all homes, factories, workshops, and business houses. A mixture of puffed rice, groundnuts, copra pieces and jaggery is distributed as prasad. The tenth day is Vijaya Dashami, the day of victory. The festival is celebrated with royal grandeur in Mysore, with ceremonial processions, music and pageantry. Hundreds of thousands of people gather for the competitions, feasting and merry-making. Earlier, people thronged to the Royal Durbar and received gifts. At the Durbar, you can see men wearing the traditional ceremonial costume of a long black coat and dhoti, "angavastra", a gold-bordered cloth draped over one shoulder of the coat, and turban with gold lace. It was customary to offer a flower or a coin to the king, and receive his greetings.

An interesting custom in the royal household is that on Vijaya Dashami day the king goes in procession on elephant's back to the "Banni mandapam", a tree with a golden canopy. This symbolizes the Banni or bilva tree of the epic Mahabharata where the Pandavas hid their weapons, which were retrieved by Arjuna on the Vijaya Dashami day. In remembrance of that ancient incident, the king offers puja to the tree, and brings back its leaves which are distributed to all.

In all households the festival is celebrated with gaiety. It is a day for start of studies or lessons in any art or skill, because the blessings of the Goddess are believed to bring good luck and achievement in any venture.

Ayudha Puja

The puja is started on the ninth day of the Navaratri festival and concluded on the tenth (Vijaya Dashami) day. The festival is observed in the Indian month of September-October in the English calendar.

Ayudha means a weapon. This ancient puja was important to warriors, craftsmen, scholars, artists, labourers, indeed to all who used tool and implements for livelihood or trade. In fact it is a day of thanksgiving to Saraswati, the goddess of wisdom and knowledge, for all the skills and knowledge gifted to man, and to all teachers, craftsmen, and gurus, who have given skills to others and contributed to social well-being.

THE LEGEND

The importance of Ayudha puja is described in the epic Mahabharata. Before going into a year's exile, Arjuna gathered the weapons of all the Pandavas, and buried them deep in an old bilva tree in a forest. For about a year, the Pandavas lived in secrecy in different disguises. Before the Ayudha puja, Arjuna went to the hiding place, performed the puja, drew out his mighty bow the Gandiva, and as was the custom shot an arrow from the bow. The roar of the Gandiva was quite distinctive. The Kauravas in their camps quite far away recognised the sound. They came rushing out to trace and capture their cousins. Fortunately, it was also the last day of the exile of the Pandavas. They threw away their disguises, and once again became a band of warrior princes.

DESCRIPTION

During Navaratri, select a place in the house or community centre for arranging books, instruments, tools, machines etc. along with a statuette or photo of the goddess Saraswati. On the ninth day of Navaratri, after the morning bath, draw a rangoli or kolam, then place photo and a tray of incense, flowers, oil lamps, camphor, and akshada inside the rangoli. Arrange all the items to be placed in the puja, apply kumkum, chandan, and akshada to the photos. Then light the lamps and incense and do puja, reciting Saraswati stotra, offer prasad to the goddess, and conclude with arati.

After the puja do not disturb the items until the next morning. On Vijaya Dashami morning, prepare the special prasad of milk payasam and vada, and do the Ayudha puja. After arati, you can remove the items and use them by reading the books, playing on musical instruments or working on the machines. It is believed that after the puja the objects kept in the puja become imbued with the grace of the goddess and gain power in performing tasks. On Ayudha puja day, you must visit your teachers and gurus, giving gifts as a token of your affection and respect. It is also the day on which you can start learning a trade or skill with the blessing of the goddess Saraswati. In some houses akshara abhyasa of children who have completed four years of age is done. Music students learn a new song that day and give their teachers gifts or a token amount of money and receive their blessings.

Chapter 14

TALA KAVERI FESTIVAL

The river Kaveri arises in the hills of Coorg in Karnataka, and flows down to the Bay of Bengal in Tamil Nadu. The river brings bountiful harvests of paddy and many other crops. The patron deity of the river, Kaveri amma, is worshipped as a goddess of prosperity. Tala Kaveri festival is celebrated at the source of the Kaveri in the dense green forests of Coorg. In this festival Goddess Kaveri, the daughter of Rishi Kaveri, is worshipped along with Lord Iguthappa, an incarnation of Lord Subramania.

Thula Sankaramana festival is celebrated around 17th November at Tala Kaveri, the source of the river, at Bhagamandala, and the annual festival at Padi. Every house is purified by sprinkling the waters of the river. Thousands throng to the temples at Padi, Mercara, and Iguthappa's temple at Kakkabe in Mercara Taluka. Prayers are offered, community feasts and fairs are held. At Bhagamandala, where the Kaveri meets the stream Kannike, "shraddha" is done and rice balls are offered to departed ancestors.

Goddess Kaveri is also worshipped in the Adi festival in Tanjore, and at Kodamukham, near Mayavaram, where the river meets the ocean. The festival is held on the last day of the Tamil month of Masi, around mid-April. Farewell offerings are made to the Kaveri at the place where she parts from her land and people.

Chapter 15

DEEPAWALI

The festival of lights, Deepawali, is a major festival celebrated in one form or another throughout India. In South India it occurs on the Chaturdasi, a day before amavasya, the last day of the dark half of Kartikai (November-December).

THE LEGEND

The popular legend associated with Deepawali in South India is the killing of demon Narakasura by Krishna. Narakasura was the son of Demon King Hiranyakashyap and Bhumi devi, or mother earth. To protect him from demonic traits and teach him godly virtues, his mother sheltered him in the depths of the earth.

The demon world was in need of a commander. The demon generals traced Naraka in the secret hiding place. They met him secretly and taught him the wonderful skills and powers of the demon world.

Bhumi devi was surprised to see her son change from a pious, compassionate being into an arrogant, powerful young warrior. Soon he left her and became the commander of the demonic army. His mother had persuaded Vishnu her husband to give him the invincible weapon the Narayanastra.

Naraka had also received another boon that he could not be killed by anyone except his mother.

The powerful demon laid the heavens waste. The heavenly hosts retreated before his fierce onslaught. He took away Indra's royal umbrella and Indra's mother Aditi's nectar-dropping earrings.

The Gods appealed to Vishnu for help. Naraka was planning to capture Indra's white elephant Irawatam, when Vishnu as Krishna flew in a winged chariot driven by Queen Satyabhama, who was in reality another form of Bhumi devi. The demon kingdom in east Pragjyotisha (Assam) was a place of mighty rivers and oceans. Naraka and his brother Mura hid under water, but Krishna broke all the barriers one by one. He killed the sea-elephants and powerful demons guarding Naraka and then the killed five-headed demon Mura. Naraka attacked with his winged weapons, and the Narayanastra, until killed by Satyabhama's arrow and Krishna's discus. Naraka died realizing that she was his mother and the prediction of his death had come true. He prayed that the day of his death should forever be a day of great rejoicing. Bhumi devi prayed that Krishna who had killed her son should protect all his descendants and his kingdom forever, and Vishnu granted the boon.

DESCRIPTION

Deepawali is celebrated in southern India when the north-west monsoon brings rain and storms. The festival gives the signal for cleaning and decorating the house, and the place of worship. A toran of mango leaves is hung over the front entrance. Special shops and bazaars are set up for sale of new clothes, sweets and utensils and crackers.

Deepawali is an occasion for a get-together of the family, for greeting friends with sweets and presents. Diwali marks the start of a new agricultural season. It is believed that Vikramaditya, a great king of ancient India, was crowned on this day. Hence it is the first day of the year in the calendar of the Vikram Era.

If the amavasya coincides with dawn on Deepawali day, the bath is had before 5.00 a.m. because the celebrations must precede amavasya, the day for remembering dead parents and grandparents by Tarpanam or oblations.

Sweets and savouries are prepared before Deepawali. The night before Deepawali, turmeric and pepper are added to gingelly oil and boiled for the early morning oil bath. Sikakai powder for washing the hair and turmeric, sandalwood paste is kept ready for applying on the body. The ritual bath is had at about 3 a.m. before start of the amavasya. Oil and turmeric sandalwood paste is scrubbed on the body. Just before applying oil on the heads of children by older ladies of the house the names of great epic heroes are invoked for the boys and men of the family, Aswatthama, Bali, Vyasa, Hanuman, Vibhishana, Kripa, and Parasurama. In the case of girls, great pativratas or chaste women are invoked, Ahalya, Sita, Tara, Arundhati, Anasuya and Mandodari. After the bath, new clothes are worn, and crackers are burst. Vada and payasam are offered in worship and a grand feast is enjoyed by all. Special items on the menu are ukkarai and idli. After crackers are burst sweets are given to all. Then families visit relatives to exchange greetings.

After the bath, it is customary to greet one another with the words, "Have you had a bath in the Ganges?" The reference is to the purifying bath after the death of Narakasura. It is said that the holy river Ganga flows in all wells at dawn on Deepawali.

For newly weds the first Deepawali is very important and diamond rings or gold jewellery may be presented to the bride and groom along with new clothes for the couple.

On the evening of Deepawali, Lakshmi, goddess of prosperity, is worshipped. Lamps are lit to welcome the goddess. In business houses, new account books are opened.

Deepawali bath in Karnataka

It is called the "neer thumba habba" in Karnataka (Oil bath festival). The ceremonial Deepawali bath takes place in a freshly whitewashed bathroom. Kolam is drawn in the bathroom, where water is heated and oils and shikakai powder are kept ready. One by one, children enter the bathroom, and are anointed with oil and turmeric on the arms, feet, face and forehead, to the chanting of the names of the great pativratas (pious women) of mythology, and chiranjeevis (immortal ones) of the epics, in the case of boys.

Chapter 16

SABARIMALA YATRA (PILGRIMAGE TO THE SHRINE OF LORD AYYAPPA)

Every year hundreds of thousands of people of all faiths and communities undertake the hazardous and arduous trek into the dense forests of the Western Ghats. They cross slippery mountain streams, climb boulders, and brave wild animals. The pilgrims wear black or ochre clothes, wear garlands round their necks, and carry wooden staffs. Their foreheads are smeared with holy ash (vibhuti), kumkum and sandalwood paste. Each pilgrim balances on his head a small holy bundle called "Irumudi" in which he carries the requirements for puja, and the symbolic three-eyed coconut. A continuous chant of "Swamiye, Saranam Ayyappa" ("Lord Ayyappa, I take refuge in Thee"), comes from their lips.

The Mandala yatra to the shrine of Lord Ayyappa is undertaken with great piety and reverence from the first day of the month of Vrischika (around 17th November). It concludes at Makara Sankranti in mid-January when pilgrims see the wonderful, radiant Makara Jyoti star rising above the hill shrine of Sabarimala.

THE LEGEND

The story of the bachelor god is told in the Puranas. At the primeval churning of the ocean, a pitcher of amrit—the nectar giving immortality, emerged. Devas and Asuras fought for its possession. When the Asuras snatched away the pitcher, the gods appealed to Vishnu. He came in the form of Mohini, an enchanting dancer who enticed the Asuras, and got back the amrit, giving it to the Devas. Siva was enchanted by Mohini, and of their union a child was born.

At that time, King Rajasekhara of the Pandya dynasty ruled the country of Pandalam, now in Kerala. The righteous and devout king prayed to Lord Siva for a child. One day while hunting in the forest, he heard an infant crying, and found a baby wearing a gold chain with a tiny bell, a gift given at birth by Siva to the infant. Just then a holy man appeared in the forest, he asked the king to rear the infant, who he said belonged to the kshatriya or warrior caste. He said that the divine nature of the child would be known when he was twelve years old, and by his spiritual powers he would mitigate sorrow, and bless people with peace and prosperity. Because of the gold chain with a bell around the infant's neck, he named him Manikantan.

The divine child filled the king's household with joy. He grew up to excel in the scriptures and the martial arts. Soon, the king was blessed with a son who was named Rajarajan. Just before the coronation of Manikantan as the Crown Prince, a jealous minister persuaded the queen to make a pretence of being ill, and demand the milk of a tigress for curing her illness.

The king was perplexed by the strange request, but Manikantan understood the pretence made by the queen, yet he offered to fetch the milk. For his protection, the king gave him a three-eyed coconut, Trinetra—which symbolised Lord Siva, the family deity. The boy also carried some rice in small bundle of cloth which he carried on his head. The "Irumudi" or holy bundle which pilgrims carry to this day represents the cloth bundle carried by Manikantan. The young prince succeeded in his mission. When he returned with a pack of tigresses at his heels, the king and the entire royal

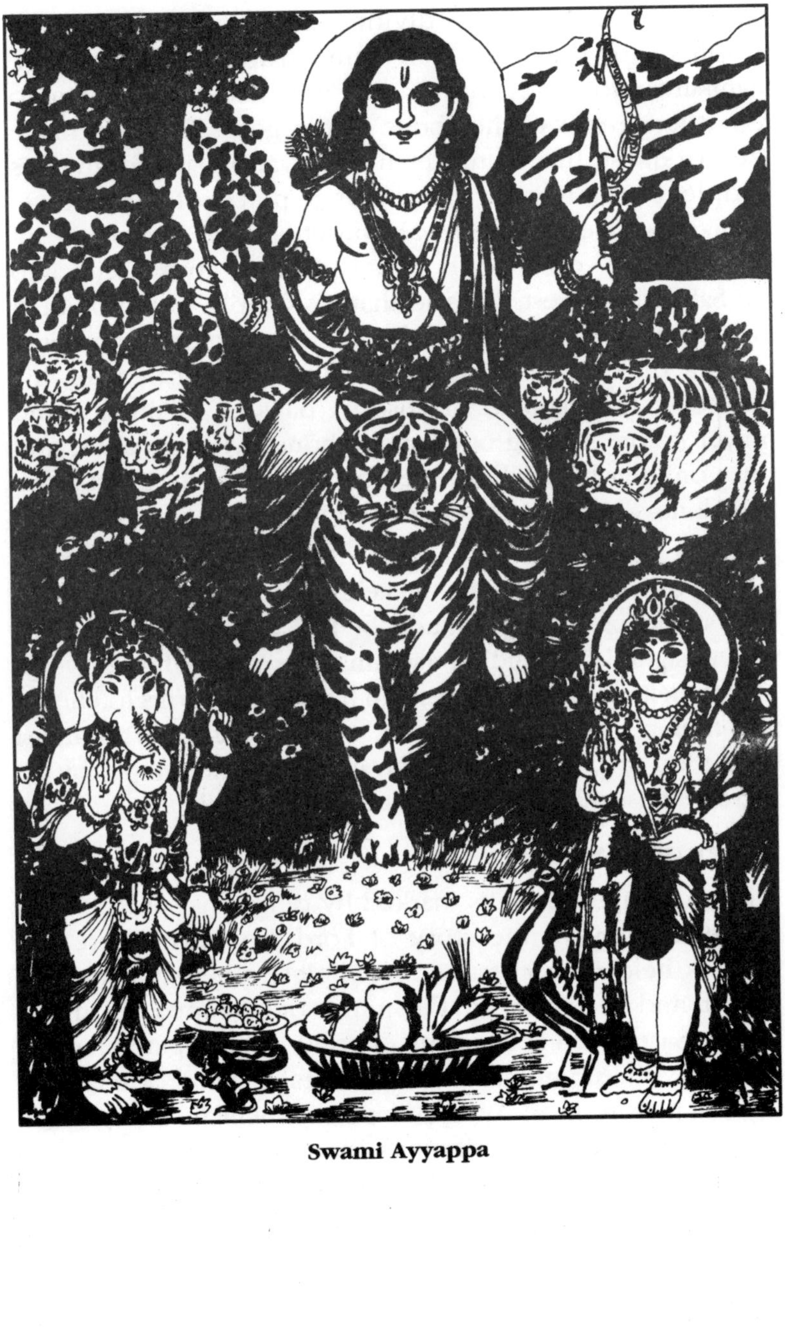

Swami Ayyappa

household realized the divine nature of the boy. The prophecy of the holy man came true at this moment. Manikantan told his father that the time had come for him to return to devaloka—the abode of the gods. The king made a last request, that Manikantan or Ayyappa should give his people darshan in a temple in a place of his choice. Manikantan blessed the royal household and the people of Pandalam. He drew his bow and shot an arrow deep into the Sabarimala crest. He said that his temple would be built on the spot, and prescribed the auspicious months and time for his darshan. He also prescribed austerities for his devotees. They should practise 41 days of abstinence and prayer before starting out for his shrine, wear garlands, and carry on their heads three-eyed coconuts and food just as he had done when he set out for the forest.

Folk songs and plays of the region describe how the temple came to be built by the celestial architect Viswakarma. The statue of Ayyappa made of five metals (panchaloha) was designed by Sage Parasurama, the seated figure wears a cloth belt around the knees and holds together his forefinger and thumb in the chinhamudra, symbolising the Tatwamasi (that thou art). A feature is the ascent to the temple by 18 sacred steps, made of panchaloha or 5 metals.

DESCRIPTION

The pilgrimage season is marked by devotional plays, songs and enactment of the story of Lord Ayyappa. There are prayers held in homes or in temples, where the devout gather and meditate on the name of Ayyappa. In many places, Sastapreeti is done, by offering puja, singing bhajans, and a lavish community feast. In Kerala, before leaving for the yatra, there is an Ayyappan pattu in which the legend is symbolically depicted, offerings are made, there is dancing and singing, and enactment of Ayyappa's brave deeds.

The next important stage is the wearing of the garland or maladharan. This is performed before the deity in a temple or in the home after prayers. The garland is received from a guru, or a priest or an elder in the family, amid loud chanting of Saranam Ayyappa. After wearing the garland, the pilgrim becomes an Ayyappa, he withdraws from social life, wears blue, black or ochre clothes, grows a beard, bathes twice a day, eats plain (satvic) food, attends religious lectures, and lives the life of an ascetic. Women pilgrims of over 50 years age join the pilgrimage and practise the austerities. The reasons for the austerities are the rejuvenation and revival of the inner consciousness, and gathering physical and mental strength for the strenuous and long pilgrimage.

The pilgrim prepares for the journey by packing the three-eyed coconuts, puja materials and some rice in a cloth bundle. A hole is drilled in a coconut, clarified butter (ghee) is poured in and the coconut is sealed. On reaching the shrine, the ghee is poured before the deity. Once packed and tied, the Irumudi or holy bundle is treated with reverence, offered puja, and morning and evening arati.

Two coconuts are added one for breaking before ascent of the I8 steps and another for breaking after descent from the steps. A token amount of rice is kept in the bundle. The pilgrim carries a sling bag for his clothes or personal requirements.

Once the bundle is ready, the pilgrim has a meal, he receives the blessings of elders, and without bidding farewell, taking leave of anyone, or giving a backward glance, he sets forth barefoot with the words Swamiye, to which others respond Saranam Ayyappa.

The concept behind the chanting of Saranam in the worship of Ayyappa is the total surrender to the Lord, for attaining self-realisation.

The pilgrimage itself is symbolic of the long and hard struggle of the individual soul, the jivatma, to attain the supreme paramatma.

The trekking route

There are three routes to the 3000 foot high Sabarimalai. The most difficult but most popular one is the 70 odd kilometre trek from Erumeli, which goes over hill tracts over 6000 feet high, forests and hill streams. This route is considered the most sacred. Crossing the mountains of Azhutha, Karimala and Neelimala requires an escort of seasoned guides.

Pilgrims from different centres, ashrams and temple towns of the South, and devotees of different faiths gather in batches at Erumeli, in the base camp for the trek to Sabarimala.

They first pay their respects at the shrine of Pir Vavar said to be a traveller from Arabia, who was a faithful lieutenant of Lord Ayyappa. They receive prasad and blessings from the Moulvi and proceed on the journey. En route they visit shrines and temples, resting at night, and resuming the trek at dawn. Generally, an advance party of pilgrims goes ahead to prepare the evening meal at the resting place. As the devotees walk in procession through the towns and villages wearing their garlands of rudraksha or tulsi beads, they are greeted with reverence, and escorted with music on the nadaswaram, and singing of devotional songs and are welcomed in the name of Lord Ayyappa.

A strenuous ascent of Mount Karimala brings pilgrims to the holy river Pampa, evoking memories of the Pampa river described in the Ramayana, and Sabari, a woman of the forest tribe who offered berries to Lord Rama, after whom Mount Sabari is named.

Thousands of weary pilgrims take a dip in the chill waters of the river, and partake of a feast, pooling together all their provisions. On Makara Sankranti, it is believed that Lord Ayyappa is present in Pampa, hence myriad of lights are lit in all the camps, huts, and in front of bonfires and on small boats on the river, creating an unforgettable sight. At

Pampa, pilgrims offer their thanks and give presents to their gurus. Shraddha or prayers to departed ancestors are offered at the river banks.

From Pampa, the pilgrims climb for about 6 kilometres up Mount Neeli (Neelimala) on a steep and slippery trail. As they go nearer the goal, the shouts of Saranam Ayyappa gain intensity. After a short rest they walk to Sabari peetham, the place where Sabari is said to have offered fruit to Lord Rama. Finally they reach the sacred eighteen steps, and have their first sight of the temple on top of the steps.

The steps are climbed only by those pilgrims who carry the Irumudi, and have done the vrata of 41 days. For others, there is another route on the side of the hill. A coconut is broken by the first timer at the first step, the second at the second step and so on.

After climbing the eighteen sacred steps, the pilgrim enters the temple, has darshan of the deity, and pours the ghee into a vessel for the priest to do abhisheka, another abhisheka is that performed with the sacred ash or vibhuti brought by the pilgrims. Afterwards, each pilgrim is given some ghee packed in a container, and other prasad. Pilgrims later visit the shrine of goddess Mallikapurathamma.

The biggest festival at Sabarimala is the Makara Sankranti festival of seven days, which starts with the sighting of the brilliant star Makara Jyoti, all other important festivals are observed at the temple.

On returning home, the pilgrim breaks a coconut before entering the home, he prays to family gods, and removes his garland thus completing his vrata.

Chapter 17

KARTIK PURNIMA

The south Indian festival of lights is celebrated in honour of God Kartikeya, the handsome warrior God. The festival occurs on the full-moon night of the month of Kartikai (November-December) when the moon enters the star Kartikai or Pleiades. It is a very important festival for married women. Vaishnavas celebrate it as the day Mahabali attained moksha. Earthen lamps (ahal) are filled with oil, lighted and kept outside the house. Different kinds of oil lamps are lit inside the house in the evenings of the sacred month of Kartikai.

THE LEGEND

In ancient writings Kartikeya, the God of War, is depicted as living mainly in hills and forest. His colour is like that of the rising sun. He has six faces, twelve eyes and twelve arms. Peacocks accompany him. The "vel" or spear is his emblem, and red flowers are offered to him in prayer.

The purpose of the birth of Kartikeya is linked with the story of a powerful demon Tarakasura. At his birth, evil signs rocked the three worlds. Comets flashed across the heavens, thunderbolts struck the earth. Brahma who was his forefather, blessed him with strength, courage, and the will to bear all austerities of prayer. When Tarakasura grew up, he did penance, but with the single objective of conquering

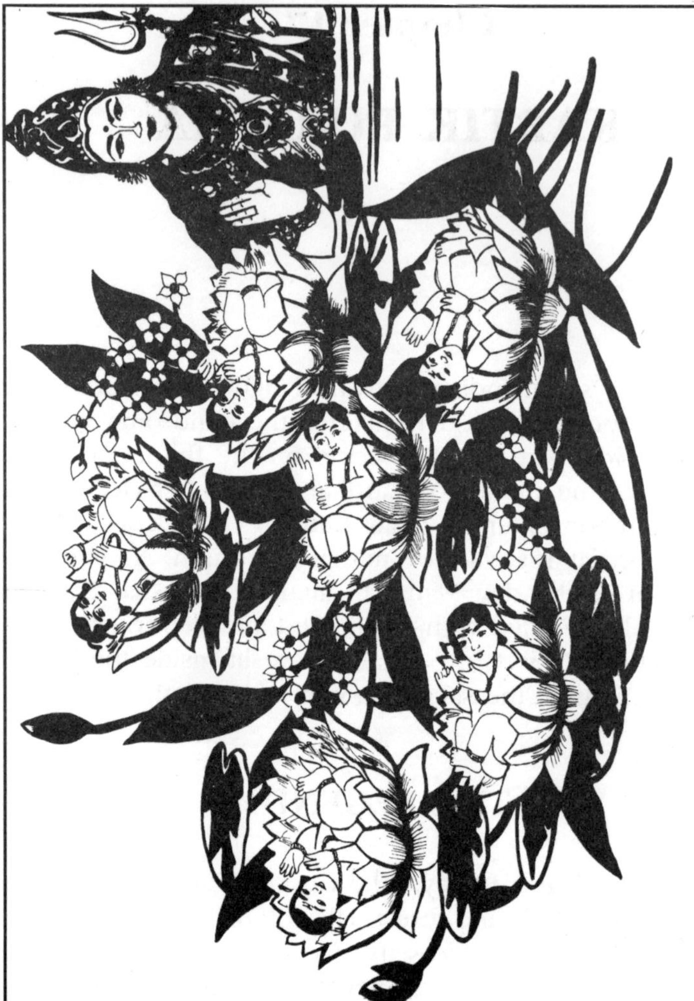

Birth of Kartikeya

the gods and becoming the supreme king. His rigorous penance frightened the gods and rishis. It drew the attention of Brahma who asked him the reason for his penance. Tarakasura first asked for the boon of immortality, when it was refused he asked for death only at the hands of the son of Siva, the supreme yogi. The gods appealed to Vishnu who found the way to break the rigorous penance of Siva by the re-birth of Sati, Siva's consort as Parvati, to win the heart of Siva.

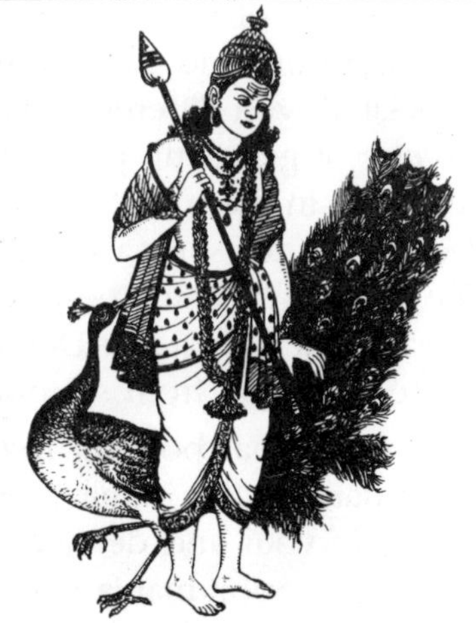

Kartikeya

The popular legend is that the gods had prayed for a son to be born to Siva to contain the forces of evil. Agni the god of fire secretly carried away six sparks from the eyes of a meditating Siva and buried them in the reeds and water of the lake Sharavani. On the sixth day the sashti, Kartikeya was born. He was nursed by the Pleiades (the Constellation of six stars, or Krittikas) for whom he assumed 6 forms. Parvati came to bathe in the lake and saw the 6 forms of a child in the water; she held them tight, so that they became one child with 6 faces.

The news reached Siva's followers. The search for Siva's son, born in the lake, brought the commander of Siva's army to the lake, where he found the child with six faces. The handsome child was taken to Siva and Parvati in procession with the blowing of trumpets and conches and dancing and singing in praise of the young hero. Later he went to battle the demon.

The fierce battle with Tarakasura took place at the confluence of the river Mahi and the Arabian Sea. The demon fought bravely but when struck with the spear of Kartikeya, he died knowing that Brahma's boon had been fulfilled, and that Siva's son was his destroyer. Each of the six faces of Shanmukha or Kartikeya has a special significance. The first face removes darkness and ignorance, the second grants boons, the third protects yagnas or sacrifices, the fourth discourses on knowledge of the self, the fifth is the destroyer of demons and the sixth showers love and affection on devotees.

Festivals of Skanda or Subramania, in Palani, Swamimalai, Tiruchendur, and Tiruparankundran, and other temples associated with different lilas or legends of Murugan, present a scene of grandeur, pageantry and devotion. Skanda sashti, occurring in the month of Kartikai, is celebrated to mark the death of Tarakasura, also called Surapadman by Subramania. The celebrated battle between the demon in four forms and Subramania is enacted. Devotees fast for six days, and listen to the recitation from six puranas of Skanda.

In the Thai poosam festival occurring in the last week of January in the Tamil month of Thai, you can witness a tide of fervour and devotion, as millions of people carrying prasad for Subramania on their shoulders on cane frames called kavadis walk all along the pilgrim route to the temple. Different ways of offering thanks or doing penance include piercing of the lips, cheeks or the body for worshipping and offering prasad to the deity.

Chapter 18

ARDRA DARSHAN

The ascent of the star Ardra in the month of Masi (February-March) is the occasion for Ardra Darshan when devotees can have a vision of the magnificent dance of Nataraja and worship the akashaya linga the formless manifestation of Siva.

THE LEGEND

An argument between Siva and Parvati (Siva and Shakti) about their skills in dance led to their descent into the world for a competition in dance. The entire assembly of 33 crore gods and the entire world witnessed that wonderful, awe-inspiring primeval dance. In the last movement of his dance Siva using his right foot wore his earring. Parvati was defeated as she could not repeat the movement.

The legend is remembered on the Tiruvadurai day. It is especially significant for young girls who pray for a loving husband and a happy marriage like that of Siva and Parvati.

DESCRIPTION

The festival is splendidly celebrated in the temple at Chidambaram where Siva is said to have danced his cosmic dance. It is a ten day festival. Thousands of devotees chant the sacred songs of Siva (Tiruvempavai). At 3 a.m., the

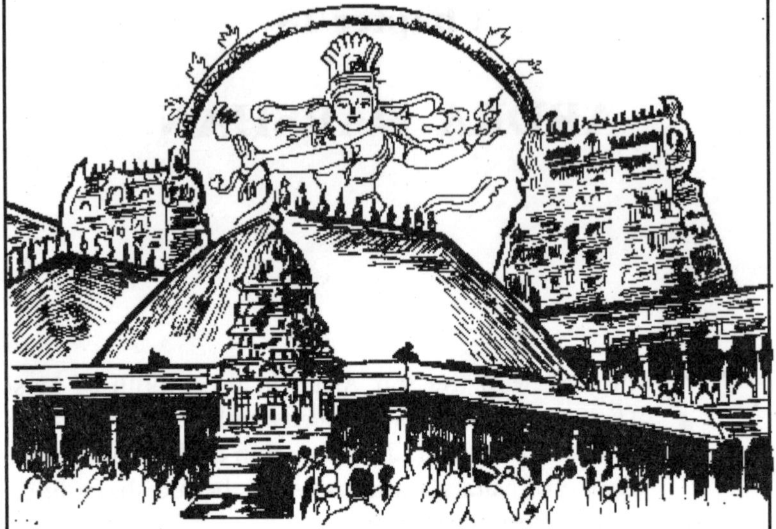

Ardra Darshan

ritual bath (abhisheka) is done of the linga, and thousands of pots of milk, honey and curd are poured on the linga. Around midday the curtain is removed, and devotees have a darshan of the linga. On the auspicious day, it is believed that all the gods are awake to witness the dance in the early hours before dawn. By prayer and meditation, devotees can have their darshan and blessings.

Chapter 19

VAIKUNTHA EKADASHI

The Vaikuntha Ekadashi occurs in the Tamil month Margazhi soon after the start of the northern journey of the sun (uttarayana). This is the time when heavenly beings (devas) are closer to human beings. In all Vishnu temples, pre-dawn prayers are held, prabandhas, slokas of great saints invoking Vishnu are recited for 20 days. On the day of Vaikuntha Ekadashi a small door in the temple sanctorum is opened. Chanting slokas devotees throng through the doorway to heaven or "Bhooloka Vaikuntha" as it is known, believing that they have achieved the goal, and will no longer go through the cycle of re-births. The Vaikuntha Ekadashi fast is believed to have the power of 12 ekadashis kept round the year. Hence it has a special sanctity for the devotee.

Ekadashis specially sacred to Vishnu occur on the 11th day of the bright fortnight of June-July or August and on the 11th day of the bright fortnight of October-November or Kartik. In the intervening period the Lord is said to be in slumber. This coincides with the rainy season, which was a time for meditation and solitude. The ekadashi fast fulfils the need for the digestive system to take rest and helps periodically clear the digestive tract of food, oils and spices.

THE LEGEND

The story of King Ambaresa illustrates the power of the Ekadashi fast observed by a sincere devotee. The king had invited the short-tempered sage Durvasha to break the fast with him on Dwadashi (the day after Ekadashi) with a meal before dawn, but was delayed while bathing. On return he saw that the auspicious time for offering food to the Lord, and breaking the fast, would soon be over, so he took a sip of sacred tulsi (basil) water kept in the puja.

Durvasha entering the puja room was shocked to see the king sipping "tulsi water". He threw down a hair from his head which turned into a destructive fire (Kalagni) which would have burnt Ambaresa into ashes, but for the piety of his Ekadashi fast in the name of Vishnu, Ambaresa was saved by his prayer. Now the Kalagni turned towards Durvasha. The sage fled across the three worlds and was refused help by Brahma and Siva. But Vishnu, who had intervened for his devotee, asked the sage to beg forgiveness of Ambaresa, because he was pure of heart and had not intended to cause offence. Humbled, repentant, and realizing the power of Ambaresa's Ekadashi fast, the sage came to him and was released from Kalagni.

Chapter 20

MAKARA SANKRANTI, PONGAL

Depiction of the sun in prehistoric paintings and seals of the Indus Valley civilization shows the great importance of sun-worship in India. Of all sacred mantras the Gayatri mantra, called the soul of the Vedas, invoking the sun-god is said to be the most powerful mantra. The sun was represented as born of Maharishi Kasyapa and Aditi, the earth. The Mahabharata describes sun as the supreme deity. The sun was worshipped as the creator, nourisher, protector, and destroyer, who travelled across the heavens in a chariot drawn by seven horses.

Makara Sankranti is an ancient festival celebrating the return of the sun across the equator in a northern direction after 6 months of moving in a southern direction. The auspicious journey towards the north occurs in the month of Magh, around the middle of January when the sun enters Makara (Capricorn).

THE LEGEND

It is the sacred day when the Ganga descended from God Siva's matted locks, and flowed over the sixty thousand sons of King Sagara of Ayodhya. They had been burnt to ashes by the rishi Kapil, to avenge an insult. The princes were revived and purified by the Ganga and ascended to heaven. The epic Mahabharata describes how the mighty warrior Bhishma lay wounded on a bed of arrows for fifty-eight days. He awaited death at the auspicious moment when the sun started its northern journey and his soul could ascend to heaven. On the auspicious day of Sankranti, he had the fatal arrows pulled out from his body, and died at the time of his choice.

Pongal

Pongal is a three day festival celebrated in the south on the occasion of sankranti, and is the biggest festival for all farmers, and all people living on the land.

DESCRIPTION

The first day is the bogi festival. It is an occasion for cleaning up the house and the surroundings, old furniture, brooms, pots, and household waste are thrown out, and at night a bonfire is made. Traditionally, along with whitewashing and repainting of the house, all clothes were washed in water and then dried as a symbolic way of throwing out the old and ushering in the new season with prayer and thanksgiving to the sun.

Traditionally, villagers brought home their harvest of sugarcane and paddy before the festival. Before every house, a symbolic picture of the sun is drawn. Big new earthen pots are placed on a wooden hearth in the courtyard outside the house. The bogi feast includes poli, amavada, kadapu, vada. Coconuts are broken after the puja. Cash packets are tied to the horns of young bullocks, and the daring youth who captures bullock, has the hand of the prettiest village belle.

Then comes the big day of Pongal. After an early morning oil bath, new clothes are worn, houses are decorated with festoons of mango leaves and flowers. The courtyard and rooms are decorated with rangoli. After praying to Suryanarayana, the sun, and seeking his blessings, the wood-fire in the courtyard is lit. The neck of the Pongal pot is tied with fresh turmeric leaves and sugarcane pieces. Pongal is made with rice and green gram, to which milk is added. When the pongal boils there are cries of "Pongal-O-Pongal". Pongal is a simple dish, with deep significance for the community. The boiling over of the milk to the right side of the pot is believed to be a happy omen. Pongal is a time for forgetting old enmities, for giving gifts and for family and community get-together in a spirit of goodwill and happiness. It is an auspicious day on which the bride comes to her husband's home decked in all her finery, bringing with her pongal gifts and all the ingredients for the feast.

The next day is the feast for cows and cattle, called "mattu pongal". Cattle are bathed, their horns are painted and decorated. They are worshipped and fed. An offering of sugarcane and fresh turmeric is made on this day. A variety of rice preparations is made. It is a day when sisters pray for their brother's good health and prosperity, by symbolically offering small portions of different rice-dishes to crows and other birds calling out to them with the words "Kakai Ku Pidi, Kuruvi Ku Pidi".

Bullock cart races, wrestling competitions and village fairs mark the Pongal festival.

The Pongal celebrations link us with our past, and our roots in village communities. Cleaning, decorating the house, wearing new clothes, offering prayers to the sun, cooking and eating sweet and savoury pongal and giving gifts are all symbolic of our identity. Recitations from the sacred books, singing devotional songs, and making offerings to God, revive our spiritual vitality at the start of the sun's journey northwards.

Sankranti

Sankranti in Karnataka is a grand festival in honour of the Sun God and the auspicious period of Uttarayana, the sun's northern journey when the gods are believed to be closer to mortal beings.

A special feature is the preparation of laddus or sweet balls of sesame, jaggery, and copra pieces. Pongal is prepared by cooking together newly harvested rice, fresh jaggery and sugarcane juice.

In many households, new clothes are worn and sesame is roasted and offered to God before distribution. If there is a new born infant in the house, the first Sankranti of the infant is an important occasion when silver coins are distributed to all. Traditionally, a scraped half of a coconut gaily painted and decorated is given to all visitors. Giving of betel leaves, nuts, flowers, fruit and home-made sugar dolls on Sankranti day is customary.

An interesting feature of traditional Sankranti is that cows are beautifully decorated. They are taken to temples and fed prasad. Then they are brought back at sunset (go-dhuli lagna as it is known) and jump over a long line of straw bundles set on fire. After the ritual, all are given Sankranti prasad.

Chapter 21

SIVARATRI

The festival is observed on the fourteenth day of the dark half of Masi (February-March) with meditation, prayer, fasting, reading and recitation of the Siva Mahima and Siva tandava slokas. The Sivalinga is worshipped with Ganga water, milk, curds, honey and ghee. Offerings of belpatra (Aegle marmelos), berries of dhatura (Dhatura metel), aak (calstropis) leaves, and jabakusum (hibiscus) all dear to Siva are offered.

THE LEGEND

The night-long vigil, fasting and prayer of Sivaratri are in remembrance of Siva's drinking the poison churned out of the earth, which saved the inhabitants of earth and heaven. To illustrate the power of prayer to Siva on Sivaratri, the story is told of a hunter named Suswar who made a living by selling birds and beasts. Once he was lost at night in a forest and climbed a bel tree for safety. Hungry and afraid, he stayed up all night in the tree, throwing down bel leaves at the prowling beasts below. He did not know that the leaves fell on a Sivalinga below the tree. Siva was pleased by the night-long offering. The hunter returned home safely. When he died in due fullness of time he reached the abode of Siva.

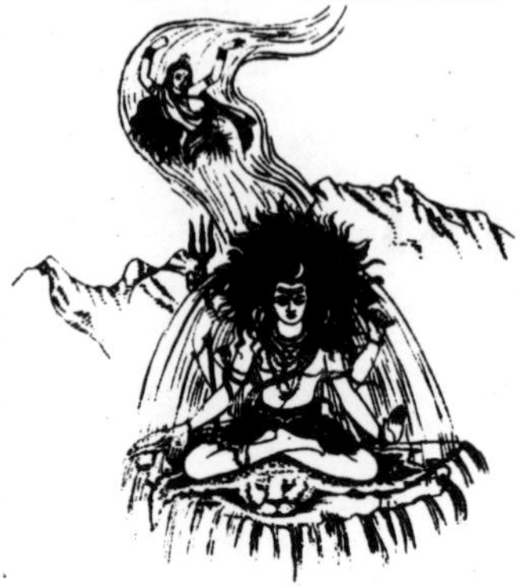

Siva & Ganga

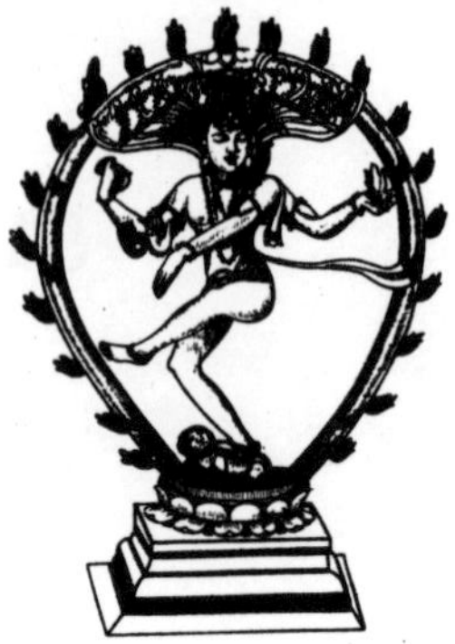

Siva: Nataraja

DESCRIPTION

On the sacred night of Sivaratri not a morsel of food nor a drop of water is taken. The night is spent in prayers and offerings to Siva. The next day after bath, prayers are again offered and the fast is broken.

Chapter 22

KARADIYAR NOMBU

A puja for the welfare of husbands and a happy married life is performed on the first day of the Tamil month of Panguni.

THE LEGEND

The tradition is that when at the appointed time and date Prince Satyavan died in the forest his chaste wife Savitri observed the puja and because of her devotion she could see Yama the God of Death coming to fetch her husband. Savitri fell at his feet and begged him to spare her husband's life, and succeeded after following Yama almost to the end of the world.

DESCRIPTION

After an early morning bath and prayers, a thread dipped in turmeric, dried and placed in the puja is cut into small pieces. All the women and girls in the family are given a piece of the thread to tie around their wrist, with the words "May I never be parted from my husband". Salt and sweet adai is made as prasad.

SECTION III

Traditional Recipes

TAMIL NEW YEAR'S DAY MENU

On the first day of the month of Chitrai (around 13th April) the new year is welcomed with a traditional feast. This includes plain rice, red gram, buttermilk, sambar, vadai, curd pachadi, payasam, vegetable curry, kootu made of vegetables and green gram, fried appalam, rasam, and curds. A special neem flower mango sweet pachadi is a must. Panakam, a cooling drink and Kosumbari, a kind of salad add variety.

SAVOURY RED GRAM

Ingredients

1. Red gram—200 gms
2. Salt—to taste
3. Turmeric powder—1/2 tsp
4. Fresh coriander—2 tsp
5. Oil (preferably gingelly oil)—1 tsp
6. Water—for pressure cooking

Method

Wash the gram, add 3 times water and 1/2 tsp turmeric powder and a tsp of oil. Pressure cook, when gram is cooked, remove and strain out about 2 cups of gram water for making rasam. Remove remaining red gram to a small container, add salt and coriander leaves.

BUTTERMILK SAMBAR (MOR KUZHAMBU)

Ingredients

1. Sour buttermilk—1/2 litre
2. Turmeric powder—1 tsp
3. Red gram (soaked for half an hour)—3 tsp

4. Boiled diced potatoes/carrots—1-1/2 cups
5. Curry leaves, salt, green chillies—according to taste
6. Cumin seeds—1 tsp
7. Bengal gram powder—2 tsp
8. Mustard seeds—1 tsp
9. Fresh grated coconut—4 tsp
10. Spices to be fried and ground to paste:
    i) Fenugreek seeds—1/2 tsp
    ii) Red chillies—2
    iii) Asafoetida—1/4 small spoon

Method

First grind the soaked gram with cumin seed, green chillies and coriander leaves to a thick paste. Add and mix well 2 tsp of bengal gram powder with a little water. Add to sour buttermilk and stir well. Now add cooked vegetables, ground spices and curry leaves, keep on a low fire and bring to boil. Take off from the fire. Now fry 1 tsp of mustard seeds in a little ghee, when mustard seeds splutter, add to the sambar, add salt and curry leaves.

Another method is to grind together 4 tsp grated coconut, 3 tsp cumin seed, and 2 green chillies, then add bengal gram powder to the sour buttermilk, season with mustard seeds, fenugreek seeds, red chillies and asafoetida.

KOSUMBARI

Ingredients

1. Green gram—200 gms
2. Salt—3/4 tsp or to taste
3. Lemon—one, squeeze out juice
4. Scraped coconut—half a coconut
5. Green chillies—2

6. Cucumber—1 small grated
7. Mustard—1/2 tsp
8. Ghee—2 tsp
9. Coriander leaves

Method

Soak the gram for 2 hours till soft. After washing the gram, drain well and place it in a vessel, grate the cucumber, mix a little salt and after some time squeeze out the water, and add to the gram the chillies cut into pieces and coriander. Put mustard in the ghee and after it splutters add to the Kosumbari.

MANGO-MARGOSA LEAVES SWEET PACHADI

Ingredients

1. Mango medium size—1
2. Jaggery—100 gms
3. Salt—1/2 tsp
4. Turmeric powder—a pinch
5. Mustard—1 tsp
6. Rice flour—2 tsp
7. Ghee—2 tsp
8. Red chilli—1
9. Fresh Neem flowers—a few
10. Asafoetida powder—1 pinch

Method

Cut the mangoes into big pieces, boil in 250 gms of water with salt, or pressure cook mango bits on the lid of a pan of rice or lentils. Then remove and put them in a thick bottomed vessel, add jaggery and 125 gms (½ a tumbler) of water. When the jaggery has melted, mix well with rice flour, and a little water. Take down from fire. Fry the mustard in ghee in a small kadai. After it splutters add broken chillies, asafoetida powder and fresh neem flowers. When the neem flowers become brown remove from fire and add to Pachadi. This has all the six flavours, sweet (jaggery), salt, astringent and sour (mango), pungent (chillies) and bitter (neem flower). The pachadi with the six flavours is taken on New Year day to symbolize acceptance of all joys and sorrows in the coming year.

AMAVADAI

Ingredients

1. Red gram—200 gms
2. Black gram—100 gms
3. Bengal gram—100 gms
4. Salt—2 tsp
5. Green chillies—4
6. Red chillies—2
7. Asafoetida—a small piece
8. Curry leaves—4 sprigs
9. Cut coriander leaves—4 tsp

Method

Soak the red gram and black gram together, add bengal gram after one hour. Grind the grams (after draining them) together into a rough paste with a little water, along with red and green chillies, salt, asafoetida and curry leaves. Add the coriander leaves. Mix well. Boil oil in a kadai and when it smokes reduce the heat to medium. Take a little bit of batter, flatten it on a plantain leaf or plastic sheet into a small round shape, gently lower into the oil. You can put 5 or 6 vadais together if the oil is sufficient. Fry the vadais till a reddish brown colour. Strain and take out with a perforated ladle. The vadai should be crisp and should be eaten hot.

PAYASAM

Vermicelli, beaten rice, bengal gram, sago, green gram, and milk payasams are made for special occasions. You can try variations using other ingredients such as cooked grated carrots or pumpkin.

Ingredients

1. Vermicelli—1 cup crushed
2. Sugar—1 cup
3. Boiled milk—2 cups
4. Ghee—2 tablespoons
5. Cashew nut pieces—4 tsp
6. Golden raisins—2 tsp
7. Water—2 cups
8. Saffron—2 pinches soaked in a tsp of warm milk
9. Cardamom powder—1 tsp
10. Camphor—1/4 tsp
11. Nutmeg—1

Method

First heat the ghee in a kadai or flat bottomed saucepan with a low rim. Fry the cashew nuts and raisins to a golden brown, remove from the pan. Fry the nutmeg piece in the same way, remove and powder it. Now fry the vermicelli pieces to a golden brown colour and remove from the fire. Boil water in a vessel, add the fried vermicelli along with ghee. When it becomes soft add the sugar. When sugar becomes of 1 thread consistency add milk and boil for 5 to 10 minutes till it becomes a little thick. Add cardamom powder, camphor, soaked saffron, and fried nuts and raisins. Remove from fire and offer the payasam as naivedyam to the deity before distributing it.

If saffron is not available use a pinch of golden yellow Kesari powder.

BEATEN RICE PAYASAM

Ingredients

Beaten rice—25 gms, other ingredients as for vermicelli payasam

Method

The same as vermicelli payasam.

SAGO PAYASAM

Ingredients

70 gms of sago, rest the same as vermicelli payasam.

Method

Fry the sago to a reddish brown colour in ghee. Boil the water, add sago and cook till grains swell and become transparent, stirring often to prevent lumps. Add sugar, let it mix well, add milk. When payasam boils add saffron, nuts, colour and flavours, take down from fire.

SEMOLINA PAYASAM (Rawa or Suji Payasam)

Ingredients

1. Rawa—1/2 cup
2. Sugar—1 cup
3. Milk—2 cups (boiled)
4. 2 cups (hot water)

5. Ghee—2 tablespoons
6. Fried cashewnut pieces—2 tablespoons
7. Golden raisins—2 tablespoons
8. Cardamom—1 tsp
9. Camphor—1/4 tsp (soaked in 2 tsp of warm milk)

Method

Fry the cashewnuts and raisin in ghee to a golden brown colour. Remove from ghee and keep aside in a bowl after draining. Fry the rawa to a golden colour. If you fry all these in a stainless steel frying pan, you can add the boiled water to the rawa in the same frying pan. When rawa is cooked well add sugar. When sugar dissolves boil for 5 minutes. Add milk and boil for 10 minutes stirring with ladle, and take down from fire. Add the ground saffron, cashewnuts and camphor. This payasam will be thick and tasty.

RICE AND BENGAL GRAM PAYASAM

Ingredients

1. Raw rice—1 cup
2. Bengal gram (Chana Dal)—1 cup
3. Jaggery powder or brown sugar (as available)
4. Water—4 cups
5. Milk—1 cup
6. Ghee—1 tsp
7. Coconut grated fresh—1 cup
8. Cashewnuts sliced—2 tsp
9. Cardamom powder—1 tsp
10. Raw camphor—a pinch

Method

Fry the rice and gram separately in ghee until golden brown, add bengal gram and water, cook for 20 minutes. Then add rice, continue boiling till the gram becomes soft and rice is cooked. Alternately pressure cook rice and gram. Then remove them to another vessel. Add jaggery powder, boil till it dissolves. Then add coconut and boil for 5 minutes. Add boiled milk and stir the payasam for a few minutes. Remove from fire, and add cardamom powder.

GREEN GRAM PAYASAM

Same method as rice and bengal gram payasam, using green gram in place of rice and bengal gram.

MILK PAYASAM

Ingredients

1. Raw rice—1/4 cup
2. Sugar—1-1/4 cup
3. Milk—4 cups
4. Ghee—1 tsp and cardamom—1 tsp
5. Saffron—2 tsp
6. Water—1 cup

Method

Boil the water in a wide mouthed vessel or saucepan. Add the washed rice and boil on a medium heat for 30 minutes. When the rice becomes soft mash it well. Add milk and boil for 40 more minutes. Then add sugar and stir and boil for 10 minutes. Then take down from fire. Add the cardamom powder, saffron and fried cashew nuts. Offer as prasadam or naivedyam to the deity on festival days before serving. I have mentioned varieties of payasam because you can prepare different varieties for different festivals.

OTHER NEW YEAR RECIPES

AVAL UPPUMA (Uppuma of Beaten Rice)

Salty and Sweet

Ingredients (for two cups of uppuma)

1. Beaten rice—3/4 cup
2. Mustard, green chillies—for seasoning
3. Red chillies, green coriander—for seasoning
4. Curry leaves—a few
5. Cashewnut pieces—2 tsp
6. Salt, chilli powder—to taste
7. Asafoetida—a pinch

Ingredients for Sweet Beaten Rice

1. Beaten rice—3/4 cup
2. Raisins—20 gms
3. Water—1/2 cup
4. Cashewnut—a few pieces
5. Sugar—4 large tablespoons
6. Saffron—a pinch

Method

For making uppuma, wash beaten rice in running water and drain off the water quickly. Lightly fry cashewnut pieces and remove. Put frying pan on the gas. Put in 3 tablespoon oil, fry the mustard seeds, add chopped green and red chillies, and fry a little to release the flavour, add a pinch of asafoetida. Now toss in the beaten rice and green coriander, curry leaves, salt and coconut, mix well and remove from fire. Add fried cashew pieces.

Sweet beaten rice is also prepared and distributed. This is prepared by roasting the beaten rice and adding a little water to cook. After it is cooked, add sugar and flavour (elaichi or small green cardamom) and mix thoroughly.

PANAKAM

This is a refreshing drink which is distributed to all especially during the summer. It has a cooling effect on the system and helps digestion.

Ingredients (for making 8 cups)

1. Dried ginger—a few pieces
2. Jaggery—1/4 kg, broken into pieces
3. Cardamom—5 pods, peel and crush grains

Method

Crush the ginger. Put a pan on the gas, with 10 cups of water. Put in the crushed ginger and boil for 5 minutes. Then add the jaggery and crushed cardamom. Boil for another 5 minutes. Remove from fire and cool. Serve in cups or glasses.

CHUNDAL (Savoury Gram or Peas)

Chundal of bengal gram, dried peas, kabuli chana or any other dried grams, peas etc. is prepared for prasad.

Method

Soak bengal gram or dried chick peas the previous night. Next day cook them in pressure cooker with a pinch of soda and salt. Drain the water. In a kadai put in oil and add 1/2 tsp of mustard and 2 red chillies broken up and a pinch of asafoetida powder, when mustard splutters, add the cooked gram or chick peas, add grated coconut; mix well and take off the stove.

NEW YEAR RECIPES—ANDHRA PRADESH AND KARNATAKA

The New Year's day must start with a few spoonfuls of the special pachadi which prepares you for the changing flavours, moods and fortunes of the year ahead.

TRADITIONAL NEW YEAR'S BEWU BELLA PACHADI

Ingredients

1. Neem (margosa) flowers—1 cup
2. Jaggery powdered—1 cup
3. Grated dried coconut or copra—1 cup
4. Broken, roasted groundnut—2 tsp

Method

Pound together all ingredients till blended, make into small round shapes. The neem flowers symbolize the painful or sad events of the old year which are to be forgotten, the other ingredients give a pleasant beginning to the New Year and are a token of good times to come.

UGADI PACHADI

Ingredients

1. Neem (margosa) flowers—1 cup
2. Tender mangoes cut into cubes—½ cup
3. Juice of lemon sized tamarind—½ cup
4. Powdered fresh jaggery—1½ cups
5. Water to mix

Method

Mix all the ingredients with a little water until blended. In a well made pachadi you should not be able to make out any separate individual flavour.

UGADI POLI

Sweet poli is prepared on New Year's Day. The recipe is given later in this section.

RECIPES FOR VISHU, KERALA

PUTTU

A light and easily digested dish it can be eaten for breakfast or as a snack.

Ingredients

1. Raw rice—1 cup
2. Coconut—one grated
3. Salt—to taste, soaked in 4 tsp water
4. Water—1 cup

Method

Soak the rice for 3 hours. Drain. Roast in a kadai till light brown. Then grind to coarse powder. Now spread the powder in a flat dish. Sprinkle salt water and keep kneading the powder with the fingers, so that the water is absorbed.

If you have a traditional puttu pipe, place 2 teaspoons of rice powder, and 2 teaspoons of coconut alternately till the pipe is filled. Cover with lid. Place on a bowl of boiling water, and steam for five minutes. Repeat with remaining powder till all the rice powder and coconut are used up. Hot steaming puttu can be eaten with groundnut cooked in gravy or with small papadam or seasonal fruits.

SWEET PUTTU

For making sweet puttu, take the rice powder mix, sprinkling water in place of salt water. Then knead sugar powder or sugar into the flour, till both water and sugar are absorbed. Cook as for salty puttu.

OLAN

This is a traditional side dish in a feast. It can be eaten mixed with rice or separately as a vegetable dish.

Ingredients

1. White pumpkin—1 kg peeled and cut in 4 cm long pieces
2. Coconut—1 grated
3. Coconut milk—1 cup of first milk, one cup of second milk (to get the milk, drain 2 cups warm water through 1 cup grated coconut. The milk of each cup to be strained and kept separately. These are the first milk extract and the second milk extract.)
4. Green chillies—4 cut in strips
5. Salt—to taste
6. Coconut oil—3 tsp
7. Dried string beans soaked and cooked—2 tsp
8. Soaked and boiled string beans (karamani or lobia)

Method

Boil or steam the cut pieces of pumpkin. Add second cup of coconut milk extract and boil; add cooked beans, salt and slit green chillies. Remove from fire and add coconut oil.

PRATHAMAN

The pride of place in a feast is given to the prathaman. It is also a test of the housewife's cooking talent. A successful prathaman made by the young bride gives her a wonderful start in her new home.

Ingredients

1. Green gram (whole)—1/2 cup
2. Coconut—1 grated 1 cup first milk extract and 1 cup second milk extracted and kept separately in cups
3. Water—3 cups
4. Cashewnut, raisins, copra pieces—a few
5. Ghee—2 tsp for frying cashewnut and seasoning
6. Jackfruit—2 cups of small cut pieces

Method

Roast the gram till reddish, then remove skin and powder coarsely. Boil the gram in water to which a second cup of coconut milk is added. The proportion is 2 cups of coconut milk to one cup gram powder. When cooked add the cup of first milk. Cook stirring briskly to prevent the prathaman from sticking to the pan. Now add cashew, raisin, copra pieces fried in ghee to the mixture, finally add jackfruit pieces and stir well.

As an alternative to gram you can roast and powder raw rice for making prathaman. Nendran variety of banana can be used in place of jackfruit.

TAMARIND GINGER CHATNI

The spicy chatni is an additional item in the traditional feast. It is also useful as a digestive.

Ingredients

1. Tamarind—the size of a large marble
2. Fresh ginger—50 gms
3. Green chillies—4
4. Jaggery—3 tsp
5. Mustard—1/2 tsp
6. Curry leaves—a few leaves

Method

Soak the tamarind in 1/4 cup of water, drain out the water. Grind ginger to a paste and add to the tamarind pulp. Mix in jaggery powder and place in a vessel, add seasoning of mustard seeds and karipatta, place vessel on the stove and stir chatni for about 3 minutes.

KALAN

This popular dish adds flavour to the feast. It can be prepared from any suitable seasonal vegetables.

Ingredients

1. Jimmikand (a yam variety)—1/2 kg
2. Cocolasia—or peeled raw banana—1/2 kg
3. Pepper powder—1/2 tsp
4. Salt—to taste
5. Turmeric powder—1/2 tsp
6. Cumin seed—1 tsp
7. Coconut—1 grated
8. Red chilli—2
9. Mustard seeds—1/2 tsp
10. Kari leaves—8 or 10
11. Sour buttermilk—1/2 cup
12. Water—1/2 cup

Method

Boil and peel the vegetables, cut in 2 cm long pieces. Place in a vessel, and add salt, pepper powder and turmeric powder. Add half a cup of water, and bring to a boil. Now grind 1/2 cup grated coconut and cumin seed to a fine paste; add chilli powder and put the paste into the three quarter cooked vegetables. For seasoning the Kalan, fry mustard seeds till seeds splutter, add 2 whole red chillies and kari leaves, pour this over the vegetables. Finally add 1/2 cup of buttermilk and cook till blended without over-cooking.

RICE DISHES FOR CHITRA PURNIMA

Different rice dishes are prepared jointly, and families have a picnic by the riverside, or on a moonlit terrace on festivals like Chitra Purnima, Adi festival, or Kanu festival.

PULIYODARAI (Tamarind Rice)

Ingredients

1. Plain boiled rice—3 cups
2. Tamarind—a small lump
3. Water—1/2 cup
4. Mustard—2 tsp
5. Bengal gram—1/4 cup
6. Juice of big lemon—3 tsp
7. Red chillies—1 or 2
8. Asafoetida
9. Fenugreek (Methi seeds)—1 tsp
10. Gingelly oil—1/2 cup
11. Salt—to taste
12. Curry leaves

Method:

Soak the tamarind (after washing it) in warm water for 5 minutes. Then squeeze well the tamarind in water till you get a thick dark coloured liquid. Residue should not have any juice. Strain the juice and keep aside. Pressure cook the rice adding 2-1/2 times or 2 times water depending on the rice. Cooked grains should be separated and spread on a plate. Mix 2 or 3 tsp of til oil and turmeric powder.

Put a frying pan on the stove and pour the rest of oil into it. Fry the asafoetida and mustard, add the bengal gram, broken chillies, and curry leaves. When gram becomes golden brown and chillies become crisp add the tamarind water and boil in reduced heat (sim). The sauce will thicken. When all the water has evaporated and oil floats on top and leaves the sides, take it down from stove and pour it in a bowl. Mix this sauce (when it is cool) with rice, and remove to a vessel and cover. You can add fried groundnuts or cashew-nuts and decorate with curry leaves.

MYSORE PULIYODARAI

In this variation you do not fry bengal gram in oil but add powder made with the ingredients given below: Fenugreek seeds—2 tsp; Coriander seeds—3 tsp; Cumin seeds—2 tsp; Pepper corns—2 tsp; Red chillies—3 or 4; curry leaves—a few. Fry all these in oil and when cool make into powder. Add a little jaggery powder and mix. Add as much as powder as per your taste to the puliyodorai. This is called Mysore Puliyodarai.

COCONUT RICE

Ingredients

1. Plain boiled rice—3 cups
2. Bengal gram—3 tsp
3. Dry chillies—a few
4. Asafoetida—1 pinch
5. For garnish, mustard—1-1/2 tsp
6. Broken cashewnuts—20 gms
7. Coconut grated—3 cups (fresh)
8. Black gram—3 tsp
9. Salt—1/2 tsp

Method

Boil enough rice to make 3 cups of cooked rice. The grains should be separate. Spread it on a plate and mix 4 tsp of ghee. Fry the grams and chillies. Let dals cool on a plate, then grind them into a fine powder, add this mixture to rice and stir well. Fry the mustard, asafoetida powder in 2 tbsp of ghee. When mustard splutters, add black gram and cashewnuts till they are golden brown. Add the grated coconut and fry for 5 minutes. Add rice to mixture in a skillet. Keep covered for 5 mts or on reduced heat; remove from heat. Serve hot or cold with fried papads and sago or rice wafers.

LEMON RICE

Ingredients

1. 3 cups of cooked rice, cooled
2. 2 big lemons
3. Bengal gram—2 tsp
4. Red chillies—3
5. Green chillies—4 or 5
6. Til oil—7 or 8 tsp
7. Salt—1-1/2 tsp
8. Curry and coriander leaves
9. Asafoetida—to taste

Method

Fry gram and mustard seeds, the gram should become golden brown, add asafoetida. Add to the rice previously spread on a plate mixed with oil, salt and turmeric powder. Squeeze the lemons, strain the juice, add to rice, mix well, and serve.

MASALA LEMON RICE

Ingredients

1. Cooked cooled rice—3 cups
2. Cardamom—4
3. Cloves—4
4. Poppy seeds—1/2 tsp
5. Cinnamon—1/2 inch

Method

Fry spices in a tsp of oil and grind into powder. Mix this powder into the lemon rice. It will have a different flavour. You can also prepare carrot rice, tomato rice etc. similarly, using cooked grated carrot or tomato puree.

BRINJAL RICE (VANGI BHATH)

Ingredients

1. Plain boiled rice—3 cups
2. Diced brinjal—1-1/2 cups
3. Mustard seeds—1-1/2 tsp
4. Salt—1-1/2 tsp
5. Turmeric powder—1-1/2 tsp

Masala Powder for Rice Dishes

1. Bengal gram—1 cup
2. Gingelly oil—3 tsp
3. Black gram—1/2 cup
4. Coriander seeds—2 tsp
5. Red chillies—10
6. Cinnamon—4 pieces

Method

Fry these in 1 tsp oil and cool, add curry leaves and grind into powder, keep aside. Put rest of the oil in a kadai and add mustard and asafoetida powder. When mustard splutters, add the washed brinjal pieces and fry well. Add curry leaves, salt and turmeric powder and keep stirring occasionally. Cover till brinjal is cooked. Add the masala powder and fry for 5 minutes more, take down from stove. Add to the previously cooked rice and mix well, vangi bhath is ready.

For all these mixed rices you can add salt or chillies as per your taste.

SWEET SAFFRON RICE (KESARI BHATH)

Ingredients

1. Boiled rice—3 cups
2. Sugar—1 cup
3. Water—1/4 cup
4. Ghee—1 tsp
5. Sliced, fried cashewnuts—3 tsp
6. Fried golden raisins—3 tsp
7. Cardamom powder—1 tsp
8. Saffron—a pinch

Method

Fry cashewnuts in ghee, then fry raisins. Keep both in a bowl. Now boil 1/4 cup of water, add sugar and make a thick syrup (you should be able to make a soft ball from it). Then add boiled (cooked) rice, cashewnuts and raisins, stir well till the syrup mixes well with rice, and is absorbed in it. Add cardamom powder and saffron.

CURD RICE (DADHYODANAM)

Ingredients

1. Boiled rice—3 cups
2. Curds—3 cups
3. Unsalted butter—1 tsp
4. Cut green chillies—3 tsp
5. Ginger—1 tsp or dry ginger powder 1/4 tsp
6. Mustard seeds and asafoetida powder—1/4 tsp

Method

Add unsalted butter to the cooked rice and cool. Add ghee, salt, fried mustard, chillies and ginger, add curds and curry leaves, and mix well. Cucumber and raw mango cubes can be added, if you like, for variety.

RECIPES FOR AVANI AVITTAM

Appam and vadai, payasam and idli are prepared on this occasion to mark the start of the month of Avani.

SWEET APPAM

Ingredients

1. Raw rice—2 cups
2. Jaggery—2 cups
3. White sesame—15 gms or 1/8 of a cup
4. Cardamom—7 or 8 powdered
5. Ghee for deep frying—2 cups

Method

First soak the rice after washing 2 or 3 times, for half an hour. Drain well and spread it on a cloth to dry in shade.

After it dries completely grind into a fine powder, remove the powder to a plate. In a kadai put 1/8 cup of water, place on a stove, on medium heat. Keep stirring constantly till the jaggery water ("paahu" in Tamil) thickens; drop a spoon of it in water kept in a bowl, and test whether it can be rolled into a ball. This is the correct time to remove from fire. Pour it on the rice flour with a deft hand, stirring the rice flour with your right hand. Mix the syrup thoroughly and add cardamom powder and white sesame seed and mix again. Then add enough water to make a thick batter as for idli or pancake batter. Heat the ghee or oil in a deep frying pan or kadai, reduce the heat to medium, pour the batter with a ladle which has a deep cup at one end either with a circular motion or directly. Let one side become dark brown and well puffed, pouring ghee or oil over the appam, then turn it and let the other side also become dark brown. Drain and keep aside.

Make appams like this with the rest of the batter. If jaggery is in excess or the "paahu" thickens more the appam will crumble. Try out one appam. If it crumbles add a little water to the batter. If there is more water the appam will not puff up, so be careful and by practice you will get the correct consistency. An easy and alternate way is to add powdered jaggery 2 cups dissolved in 1/8 cup of water, wheat flour 2 cups and rice flour 1/2 cup. Add enough water to make the consistency as described above. You can add 1/2 coconut grated, and a plantain fruit mashed for taste. This appam will also be tasty.

Appam is made for many festivals including Krishna Jayanti and Kartikai.

RECIPES FOR VARALAKSHMI PUJA AND GANESH CHATURTHI

KOZHAKATTAI, SWEET AND SAVOURY FESTIVE SNACK

Ingredients

For the casing:

1. Rice flour—1 cup
2. Water—1/4 cup
3. Ghee—2 tbsp
4. Pinch of salt

Method

Mix well and knead to soft dough.

For traditional casing:

1. Rice—1 cup
2. Pinch of salt
3. Water—3/4 cup
4. Oil—1 tsp

Method

Soak rice for half-an-hour, drain, spread and air dry for ten minutes. Grind to a fine powder, dry for another fifteen minutes. Now boil water in a heavy-bottomed pan, reduce heat, add salt and oil, stir in flour slowly. Cook until the dough leaves the sides of the pan, remove, cool, divide into small portions and roll into the size of large marbles.

For the filling of savoury Kozhakattai:

1. Black gram—1/4 cup
2. Mustard seed—1/2 tsp
3. Green chillies chopped—4

4. Oil—4 tsp
5. Red chillies chopped—4
6. Salt—1/2 tsp
7. Asafoetida powder—1/4 tsp
8. Fresh grated coconut—1/2 cup

Method

Rinse grams well, soak for 1-1/2 hours, drain. Add a little water, grind coarsely with chillies and salt. Fry mustard seeds in oil till they splutter, add asafoetida powder, pour it over the paste, put oil in a kadai, add mustard seeds and when it splutters add the ground paste; reduce heat and stir continuously till the coconut paste leaves the sides and is well cooked.

For the filling of sweet Kozhakattai:

1. Brown sugar or jaggery—1 cup
2. Fresh grated coconut—1 cup
3. Ghee—1 tsp
4. Cardamom powder—1/2 tsp

Method

Put a wide flat frying pan on the fire. Put in ghee, add sugar/jaggery, continue mixing till sugar/jaggery melts. Then quickly add coconut gratings, put on low fire and mix until the paste leaves the sides of the pan, adding a little ghee if necessary. Now cool, and mix in cardamom powder.

Preparation of Kozhakattai

The method is the same for both sweet and savoury kozhakattais, the difference is in the filling.

Method

Divide the rice flour dough and roll into medium sized balls. Roll out each ball in about 4 inch diameter circles on a flour board. Place a small ball of filling off-centre. Moisten edges of the circle with water, fold into half moon shape, with filling in the centre. Press edges together to close the kozhakattai. Complete all the kozhakattais, using up the rice flour dough and fillings. Place in Idli mould or steamer and steam for ten minutes. When cooked the kozhakattai will not stick to the moulds.

To differentiate between sweet and savoury kozhakattai you can place a small ball of dough on the sweet ones or shape sweet kozhakattai thus: Make small bowls of dough in the size of a lemon. Put in the sweet filling. Close with hand and shape like a small coconut (i.e. pointed on the top).

Til Kozhakattai

Casing is the same as described earlier.

Filling

White til (Gingelly seeds): 100 gms

Fry the til in a dry frying pan till it becomes golden and seeds begin to pop; cool and powder it in mixie, measure the powder. Add equal amount of powdered jaggery and powdered cardamom, mix well.

Bengal gram sweet Pooran (filling): Cook 250 gms of bengal gram in a pressure cooker, drain the gram. Mash well and add 450 gms jaggery, add cardamom powder, grated coconut (half a coconut). Place in thick-bottomed vessel and stir well till water evaporates. Fill inside the casings and steam as for other kozhakattai.

Method

Clean the til, fry it in a vessel until light brown (the til will splutter), then set aside in a basin. In the same vessel put in the ghee and powdered jaggery until the jaggery dissolves and becomes thick (of 2 thread consistency), take down from the fire. Add the til powder, cardamom and pour into a greased pan, then apply ghee to the hands and make lemon sized balls and place on a dish to cool—offer to God as naivedya after prayer.

PUFFED RICE LADDOO

Ingredients

1. Puffed rice—250 gm
2. Jaggery—200 gm
3. Cardamom powder—1/2 tsp
4. Roasted til (gingelly) seeds—1/2 tsp
5. Water—1/4 cup
6. Oil—1/4 cup

Method

Take a heavy-bottomed pan, put in water and crushed jaggery. When it melts to two thread consistency, quickly add roasted til seeds and puffed rice, pour out on a flat metal plate. Apply oil to both hands and taking up the paste, roll into lemon sized balls, place on tray to cool. Til, jaggery and cardamom laddoos are usually prepared and offered as naivedyam as it appeases the Sanigraha.

TIL LADDOO

Ingredients

1. Roasted white til (gingelly seeds)—200 gms
2. Jaggery—200 gms
3. Ghee—1 tsp
4. Cardamom—1/2 tsp
5. Bengal gram—1 tablespoon
6. Jaggery (or Sugar)—2-3/4 cups
7. Fresh coconut grated—one
8. Ghee—1 cup

9. Cashewnut—15 gm
10. Cardamom—6 pods

Method

Roast til and grind roughly to resemble rava, add 2-1/2 times water, jaggery, coconut gratings, close lid and cook. When cooked, place on slow fire, add ghee, cashewnut, cardamom powder. Mix well till the mixture leaves the sides of the pan. Roll into balls.

SANKRANTI, BOGI RECIPES

Poli is prepared on Bogi festival on the day previous to Sankranti (Pongal), on Telugu and Kannada New Year day and other occasions.

POLI

Ingredients

1. Flour—450 gms
2. Bengal gram—250 gms
3. Jaggery—450 gms
4. Sugar—500 gms
5. Cardamom—8, peel and powder the cardamom
6. Grated coconut—half cup or 6 tsp
7. White sesame—1 tsp
8. Poppy seeds (khaskhas)—1 tsp

The last two items are optional.

Method

Jaggery Poli

Pressure cook the gram after washing and soaking for 15 to 20 minutes till cooked. Drain the water, and dry. After it is cooled add jaggery and grind it in a mixie adding cardamom powder till there are no lumps and the paste becomes soft. As the gram is being cooked you can prepare the dough. Knead the flour well, add 1/2 tsp of salt, adding enough water. Add a ladle of oil and knead the dough into a soft and flexible consistency.

The jaggery gram paste is called the pooran or filling. Take a little of the dough and flatten it into a round on a piece of plastic with your hand. Put the pooran in the middle, gather the edges over the pooran well, and close. Flatten out the round as far as possible. Heat a flat pan on a medium fire, smear a little ghee on it and invert the poli on the tawa, remove the plastic paper leaving the poli on the pan to cook. Pour 1/2 tsp of ghee around it and 1/2 tsp on the poli. When one side is cooked turn the other side, cook that also adding 1/2 tsp ghee around the poli and over the poli. Fold the poli into half and remove to a flat dish and cover. You can prepare savoury polis. The fillings can be boiled potatoes mashed, with fresh coriander leaves, chilly powder, turmeric powder, salt and asafoetida powder mixed with spice powder if you like the taste. For Bogi, along with poli it is customary to make black gram vadai, curd vadai (vadai soaked in curds), salty pongal, payasam and deep fried appalam or papad, buttermilk, sambar, a curry and kosumbari.

BLACK GRAM VADAI

Ingredients

1. Black gram—2 cups
2. Green chillies
3. 4 or 5 curry leaves, a few coriander leaves cut into small pieces

4. Asafoetida powder—a pinch
5. Salt—2 tsp
6. Oil for deep frying

Method

Soak the gram for 1/2 hour. Drain the water completely. Add cut green chillies, mix well and grind to a stiff paste with as little water as possible. Then remove the dough in a vessel. Remove the blade and put in the blade which is used to beat out butter from curds or blade used for egg beating. Grind into a fluffy paste for 1 minute and remove, add ginger pieces. Heat oil in a deep frying pan (kadai). Reduce the fire to medium heat. Take a little dough and pat into a shape like doughnut (with a hole in the centre) on a washed bit of plantain leaf or on a washed plastic sheet. This is the vadai. Put 4 or 5 vadais in the hot oil and fry to golden colour or reddish brown. Drain with perforated flat ladle in the kadai itself. Remove the vadais on to a plate. Offer to the deity after the puja.

CURD VADAI (DAHI VADAI)

Ingredients

1. Black gram—2 cups
2. 5 or 6 green chillies
3. Salt—to taste
4. Curry leaves—some
5. Scraped (grated) coconut—1/2 coconut
6. Green chillies—4
7. Coriander leaves—a few, grind these all together
8. Curd—2 cups

TRADITIONAL RECIPES FOR SPECIAL PUJAS

SRI KRISHNA JAYANTI/ JANMASHTAMI SPECIALITIES

Prasadam offered to Sri Krishna on Krishna Jayanti includes milk and milk products which were the favourite of the cowherd boy Krishna. Along with milk, curd and butter, a payasam made of beaten rice and milk, sweet rice—rice cooked and mixed with jaggery and saffron flavour—are offered. Fruits and basil (tulsi) leaves are kept in the puja. Some customary rice and semolina snacks are prepared to mark the birth of Sri Krishna, and are distributed after puja.

SAVOURY RICE RINGS OR MURUKKU

Ingredients

1. Soaked rice—3 cups
2. Dry roasted black gram—1 cup
3. Butter—1 tsp
4. Cumin seed—1 tsp
5. Asafoetida—a pinch
6. Salt—to taste
7. Oil—for deep frying
8. A piece of clean cloth for making and drying murukku

Method

Soak rice for two to three hours, drain water fully, and grind to fine paste. Powder roasted black gram and add. Dissolve asafoetida in a little water, add salt. Then add butter and the dissolved salt and asafoetida to the powders, mix with a little water to make a stiff dough. Take small balls of dough, make into long rounded strips with your fingers. Make small twisted, rope-like rings with the dough on a clean cloth.

Each murukku can have 4 to 5 twisted coils. Use up all the dough in making the coiled rings. Let the rings dry for about five minutes so that the excess moisture is absorbed by the cloth. Now heat oil in a kadai. When oil is hot, gently put in the rings one by one, fry till golden brown, strain and keep in airtight tin when cool.

SALT SEEDAI

Ingredients

Same as for murukku, but add grated coconut.

Method

Mix dough with ingredients as for murukku, add coconut. Make small marble sized balls with your fingers, place on cloth to dry for five minutes. Heat oil in kadai, deep fry the balls 10 or 15 at a time, strain and store.

SWEET SEEDAI

Ingredients

Rice and roasted gram flours prepared as for murukku.

1. Jaggery—2½ cups dissolved in ½ a cup of water
2. Grated coconut—½ cup
3. Cardamom powder—a pinch
4. Sesame (til) seeds—¼ tsp

Method

Heat jaggery water mixture till jaggery dissolves. Cool. Mix flours with butter. Add grated coconut, sesame seeds and powdered cardamom. Mix into jaggery syrup and form medium stiff dough. Make small balls about half the size of a small lemon, leave on cloth to dry for five minutes. Heat oil in a kadai. Deep fry 6 to 7 balls at a time till brown and crisp. Drain and store.

For a better flavour, you can roast the ground rice flour before adding other ingredients.

SEMOLINA CRISP PAKORA (KUNNUKKU)

Ingredients

1. Semolina or rawa—1 cup
2. Sour curd—1 cup
3. Cut green chillies, ginger
4. Curry leaves—2 tsp
5. Asafoetida—a pinch
6. Salt—to taste

Method

Soak semolina for five minutes, strain well, then add all ingredients, form into stiff dough. Heat oil in a kadai. When oil is hot, break off the dough in small pieces and deep fry till crisp and brown. Drain and store.

DEEPAWALI DIGESTIVE HALWA

The digestive halwa is taken after the early morning Deepawali bath. It has medicinal properties and helps in digesting the Deepawali feast and sweets.

Ingredients

1. Dried ginger—2 inch piece
2. Jaggery—1 cup
3. Ghee—4 tsp

Method

Powder the dried ginger, mix with grated jaggery, stir in a heavy pan on the stove adding ghee till the flavour rises. When the halwa is ready, it will leave the sides of the pan. The digestive halwa can be stored for a long time and a small amount taken daily for improving digestion. The traditional Deepawali halwa contained a great many medicinal herbs, which are now difficult to obtain. The Deepawali digestive powder available in the market contains many of these herbs. The powder is added to a thin syrup of jaggery, and stirred on the stove with ghee added to the mixture till the flavour rises.

ARDRA DARSHAN PRASADAM

TIRUVADURAI KALI

Ingredients

1. Roasted and coarsely ground rice—3 cups
2. Roasted and ground green gram—1 cup
3. Jaggery—¾ cup
4. Coconut, grated or cut in pieces—½ cup
5. Cardamom powder—¼ tsp
6. Ghee—¼ cup
7. Water for cooking—¾ cup

Method

In a heavy-bottomed pan, heat jaggery with a little water till it dissolves. Now add powdered rice, green gram and other ingredients. Stir well till mixture leaves the sides of the pan. A little water can be added while stirring so that the kali has a soft, halwa-like consistency when cooked.

SAMBAR WITH SEVEN VEGETABLES

The Kali is eaten with a special sambar made of 7 vegetables. You can select seasonal vegetables. The commonly used vegetables are pumpkin (white or red), sweet potato, raw banana, brinjal, broad beans. You can add dry beans, drumstick or any other vegetable.

Ingredients for making 8 cups of Sambar

1. Mixed vegetables, peeled and cut in medium sized cubes
2. Lentils—3/4 cup
3. Black pepper corns—10
4. Tamarind-size of a small lemon, soaked in 1/2 cup water
5. Coriander—1/4 tsp
6. Coconut grated—1
7. Bengal gram—1/8 cup

Method

Fry all the spices, then grind into powder. Now cook lentils. When half done, add tamarind water, spice powder, and asafoetida. Separately fry mustard seeds, add red chillies and karipatta for seasoning the sambar. Add the boiled cut vegetables, add salt to taste, cook for 5 minutes and remove.

On Arudra darshan day, the special Kali and sambar are offered as naivedya and later given to devotees.

KARADIYAR NOMBU RECIPES

SALT ADA

Ingredients for 12 adas

1. Rice flour—2 cups
2. Water—4 cups
3. Dry string beans (karamani) cooked—¼ cup
4. Ginger—2 inch piece
5. Green chillies—4
6. Coconut, cut in small pieces—½ cup
7. Curry leaves—a few
8. Asafoetida—a pinch

9. Salt—to taste
10. Oil—¼ cup

Method

Take a heavy-bottomed pan, add 2 tsp oil, add seasoning and spices and fry. Then add all the other ingredients, stir till mixture leaves the sides of the pan. Cool. Then shape into small flat rounds with your hands. Put in a steamer and steam for 10 minutes. Prick with fork to check if adas are cooked. Adas can be eaten with chatni, or with fresh butter and grated jaggery.

SWEET ADA

Ingredients for 12 pieces

1. Rice flour—4 cups
2. Water—6 cups
3. Dried string beans—½ cup
4. Jaggery—4 cups
5. Coconut—1, cut in small pieces
6. Cardamom—6 pods, peeled and crushed
7. Bengal gram—1 tablespoon
8. Jaggery (or Sugar)—2-3/4 cups
9. Fresh coconut grated—one
10. Ghee—1 cup
11. Cashewnut—15 gm
12. Cardamom—6 pods

Method

Roast rice and grind roughly to resemble rava. Add 2-1/2 times water, jaggery, cooked string beans, coconut gratings, close lid and cook. When cooked, place on slow fire add ghee, cashewnut, cardamom powder and bengal gram powder. Mix till the mixture leaves the sides of the pan. Form into flat round shapes. Steam till cooked.